UN Rapid Reaction Capabilities:

Requirements and Prospects

Les capacités de réaction de l'ONU:

exigences et perspectives

EDITED BY DAVID COX AND ALBERT LEGAULT

The Canadian Peacekeeping Press

1995

Modern international stability operations frequently involve several warring factions, an unstable or non-existent truce, and a national theatre of operations. To deal with these operations there is a *New Peacekeeping Partnership:* The **New Peacekeeping Partnership** is the term applied to those organizations and individuals that work together to improve the effectiveness of modern peacekeeping operations. It includes the military; civil police; government and non-government agencies dealing with human rights and humanitarian assistance; diplomats; the media; and organizations sponsoring development and democratization programmes. The Pearson Peacekeeping Centre serves the *New Peacekeeping Partnership* by providing national and international participants with the opportunity to examine specific peacekeeping issues, and to update their knowledge of the latest peacekeeping practices.

Canadian Cataloguing in Publication Data

Main entry under title:

UN rapid reaction capabilities: requirements and prospects

Includes some text in French.

ISBN 1-896551-01-7

1. United Nations - Armed Forces. 2. Operational readiness (Military Science). I. Cox, David, 1937- . II. Legault, Albert, 1938- .

JX1981.P&U5 1995   341.5'84   C95-932555-7

This publication was made possible through the
Department of Foreign Affairs and International Trade

UN RAPID REACTION CAPABILITIES:
REQUIREMENTS AND PROSPECTS

LES CAPACITÉS DE RÉACTION RAPIDE DE L'ONU:
EXIGENCES ET PERSPECTIVES

The Lester B. Pearson Canadian
International Peacekeeping Training Centre
President, Alex Morrison, MSC, CD, MA

The Pearson Peacekeeping Centre supports and enhances the Canadian contribution to international peace, security, and stability. The Centre conducts research and provides advanced training and educational programmes, and is a division of the Canadian Institute of Strategic Studies. The Canadian Peacekeeping Press is the publishing division of the Pearson Peacekeeping Centre.

The Centre (a division of the Canadian Institute of Strategic Studies), established by the Government of Canada in 1994, is funded, in part, by the Department of Foreign Affairs and International Trade and the Department of National Defence of Canada.

Le centre (une division de l'Institut canadien d'études stratégiques) à été établi par le Gouvernement du Canada en 1994. Le soutien financier de Centre provient, en partie, des ministères des Affaires étrangères et du commerce international et de la Défense nationale.

Canadian Peacekeeping Press publications include:

The Persian Excursion: The Canadian Navy in the Gulf War

UN Peace Operations and the Role of Japan (forthcoming)

Peacekeeping and International Relations (bi-monthly)

The Canadian and International Peacekeeping Review (forthcoming)

The Peacekeeping Profile (bi-monthly)

The Pearson Papers (forthcoming)

For publications or course information, please contact:

The Pearson Peacekeeping Centre
Cornwallis Park, PO Box 100
Clementsport, NS B0S 1E0

Tel: (902) 638-8808 / 8611 Fax: (902) 638-8888

TABLE OF CONTENTS

ABSTRACTS

Brian Urquhart

L'auteur signale que, jusqu'ici, l'ONU a participé à deux types d'opérations de paix, à savoir les opérations d'imposition de la paix (rares, elles sont exécutées pour l'ONU par les États membres) et les opérations de maintien de la paix, accomplies avec le consentement des parties et prévoyant le recours à la force uniquement en cas de légitime défense. L'ONU n'était pas préparée pour les conflits forts différents, survenus après la guerre froide, et auxquels ni l'une ni l'autre des approches traditionnelles ne convient. L'ONU a ainsi été amenée à effectuer plusieurs opérations infructueuses; ayant perdu confiance dans l'Organisation, les États membres hésitent de plus en plus à fournir des troupes pour appuyer les opérations de paix. Maintenant, lorsque survient une crise, l'ONU doit dans tous les cas déployer ses troupes rapidement, alors qu'elle a parfois besoin de plusieurs mois, contrairement aux opérations passées. Pour répondre à ces nouveaux impératifs, l'ONU devrait disposer d'une force de réaction rapide, pour laquelle deux modèles ont été proposés: des forces de réserve sur un pied d'alerte permanent dans certains États membres et une force permanente sous l'autorité directe de l'ONU. Cette dernière aurait l'avantage de ne pas dépendre pour son déploiement des décisions d'États individuels, comme dans le cas de la force de réserve. Ces deux modèles devront cependant être soigneusement examinés et mis à l'essai. Malgré le coût élevé d'une réaction rapide, il faut l'envisager comme un investissement susceptible d'éviter le coût, encore plus élevé, des efforts internationaux éventuellement nécessaires à la remise sur pied de sociétés déchirées par les conflits.

The author notes that historically the UN engaged in two kinds of peace operations: enforcement actions—rarely used and conducted by member states on behalf of the UN—and peacekeeping operations based on consent and the use of force only in self-defence. The UN was not prepared for the very different conflicts of the post-Cold War, for which neither of the traditional approaches is appropriate. As a consequence, the UN has stumbled into several unsuccessful operations, with a consequent loss of confidence in the Organization and a greater reluctance on the part of Member States to commit troops to peace support operations. A common characteristic of the new crisis situations is the need to deploy UN forces promptly, but, in contrast to earlier operations, the UN may now require several months to complete a deployment. This suggests that a rapid response force is needed. Two models have been suggested: stand-by forces held at the ready by some Member States, and a standing force under the direct authority of the UN. The latter has the advantage that it would not be dependent for its deployment on the decisions of individual states, as the stand-by force would be. However, both models need careful examination and testing. Although rapid response is costly, it should be seen as an investment which has the potential to avert the even greater costs associated with international efforts to repair societies torn by conflict.

Jane Boulden and W. Andy Knight

Les auteurs font valoir que les procédures de maintien de la paix de l'ONU ont deux points faibles, qu'une force de réaction rapide permettrait d'éliminer. La première est le temps qui s'écoule entre le moment où le Conseil de sécurité prend la décision et celui où les troupes de maintien de la paix sont déployées sur le terrain. La seconde est l'écart qui sépare les fonctions traditionnelles de maintien de la paix et une action coercitive. Un certain nombre de facteurs retardent le déploiement: planification, disponibilité des troupes, l'échec du Comité d'état-major et l'onéreux processus d'approbation des budgets. Par ailleurs, les nouvelles dimensions de la paix et de la sécurité internationales soulignent «l'importance d'agir tôt et le coût associé à une action tardive». En particulier, il faut réagir rapidement pour empêcher qu'un conflit larvé ne se transforme en une crise d'envergure, et pour qu'une force d'avant-garde soit déployée dans les meilleurs délais aussitôt que l'accord de paix est intervenu, afin de consolider les cessez-le-feu et inspirer confiance dans le rôle de l'ONU.

□□□

The writers argue that there are two weaknesses in UN peacekeeping procedures which would be overcome with a rapid reaction force. The first is the time gap between a Security Council resolution and the actual deployment of the peacekeeping operation in the field. The second is the gap in function between traditional peacekeeping and full-scale enforcement. There are a number of factors—planning, troop availability, the failure of the Military Staff Committee, and the laborious method of approving budget—which account for the delays in the deployment of peace missions. On the other hand, the new dimensions of international peace and security underline "the value of acting early and the costs of acting late". In particular, rapid response is needed to help prevent emerging conflicts from escalating to crises of major proportions, and to ensure that, once a peace agreement is reached, a UN vanguard force is deployed rapidly in order to consolidate cease-fires and create confidence in the UN role.

Adam Roberts

L'auteur examine le pour et le contre de la création d'une force permanente, mais dans l'ensemble fait preuve de scepticisme. Ce genre de proposition, dont l'origine remonte au début des années 50, refait surface en réaction à des crises internationales à la suite desquelles il a semblé évident que l'ONU aurait pu agir beaucoup plus efficacement si elle avait disposé d'une force permanente. Cependant, on n'y a jamais donné suite, surtout parce que les États membres ne veulent pas conférer une telle autorité à l'ONU et hésitent à s'engager à fournir des troupes pour une opération avant un examen approfondi des dangers et des facteurs d'incertitude. En outre, il n'est pas certain qu'une force permanente, si elle avait existé, aurait permis de prévenir le génocide au Rwanda, comme le maintiennent la plupart des défenseurs d'une force permanente, et l'analyse de situations laisse entrevoir que toute une série d'imprévus peuvent restreindre l'utilité d'une telle force. Néanmoins, les forces onusiennes font face à de graves problèmes, et la communauté internationale doit mieux y réagir. Dans le contexte politique actuel, on obtiendrait probablement de meilleurs résultats en améliorant la capacité onusienne de fournir des services de maintien de l'ordre et des services administratifs et la gestion des opérations de maintien de la paix et en renforçant les organisations régionales, qu'en cherchant à créer une force permanente.

The author reviews the arguments for and against the establishment of UN standing forces, but is generally sceptical. Such proposals date back to the early 1950s. They have re-surfaced in response to international crises where it seemed evident that the UN's capacity to act effectively would have been greatly enhanced by a standing force, but have never been acted upon. The basic reasons for this are the unwillingness of Member States to cede such authority to the UN, and their reluctance to commit troops to a UN operation before the dangers and uncertainties have been fully assessed. Moreover, it is not clear that a standing force, had one been available, would have been effective in preventing the genocide in Rwanda, as most proponents of a standing force argue, and an analysis of actual situations suggests that a wide range of contingent factors may limit the utility of such a force. Nevertheless, the seriousness of the problems faced by UN forces is real, and requires an improvement in the response of the international community. Developing the UN's capacity to provide police and administrative services, improving the current management of peacekeeping operations, and strengthening regional organizations may be measures more likely to succeed in the present political context than the quest for a UN standing force.

J.K. Dangerfield

L'auteur examine l'organisation de l'état-major de l'OTAN, lequel pourrait servir de modèle pratique pour l'ONU. Ayant évolué au fil des ans, l'OTAN se compose maintenant de plusieurs niveaux hiérarchiques, en commençant par celui de l'orientation politiquegénérale, confiée au Conseil de l'Atlantique Nord et au Comité de planification de défense. Vient ensuite le Comité militaire, autorité suprême sur le plan militaire strictement, qui dicte les fonctions de l'État-major international, lequel se compose de personnel détaché auprès de l'OTAN par les États membres et de personnel nommé par les États membres mais approuvé par le Comité (le premier groupe seulement fait l'objet de contingents). Bien que les membres puissent affirmer leur préférences nationales, les principaux commandants sur le terrain possèdent l'autorité voulue pour diriger les opérations militaires et commander les unités nationales mises à leur disposition par entente préalable. Partout, le principe de l'unité de commandement prévaut. L'ONU ne dispose pas d'un système comparable, ni en principe (Charte), ni en pratique. L'auteur décrit les besoins auxquels devrait répondre l'état-major de l'ONU et conclut que l'expérience de l'OTAN est pertinente et pourrait servir à en améliorer la capacité.

□□□

The writer examines the organization of NATO's headquarters with a view to exploring a feasible model for the UN. Over time, NATO has developed a tiered system, beginning with the overall political direction, which is vested in the North Atlantic Council and the Defence Planning Committee. Responding to this overall political direction, the Military Committee is the highest, strictly military authority. It tasks the International Military Staff, which is composed of personnel seconded from Member States on a quota basis, and non-quota staff who are nominated by the Member States but approved by the Military Committee. Although there are opportunities for members to assert their national preferences, at the field level the major NATO commanders have the authority to conduct military operations and command the national units placed at their disposal by prior agreement. Throughout the NATO structure, the principle of unity of command is accepted. Neither in principle (the Charter) nor in practice does the UN have a comparable system. The author discusses the headquarters requirements of the UN and concludes that the NATO experience is relevant and valuable to proposals for an improved UN capability.

A.G. Christie

L'auteur examine l'organisation et les procédures de la force mobile (Terre) du CAE de l'OTAN, en commençant par la planification et le développement de la force. La force mobile (Terre) est une force de base composée de 12 à 13 000 militaires sur un pied d'alerte et pouvant déployer à 7 jours d'avis de 6 à 8 000 soldats dans une zone de contingence désignée. Force multinationale, elle est organisée comme une brigade légère aéroportée. Elle a par conséquent été contrainte, comme toute force multinationale, de répondre à des questions fondamentales, portant par exemple sur les procédures communes, la formation intégrée, la langue, la normalisation et la spécialisation. Pouvant aussi faire appel à l'infrastructure de l'OTAN, la force mobile (Terre) a été conçue pour fonctionner dans un contexte géographique plus précis qu'une force onusienne de réaction rapide, mais dans l'ensemble les leçons tirées de son expérience pourraient profiter à l'ONU. L'auteur suggère que pour améliorer la capacité de l'ONU, il conviendrait de prendre à court terme une mesure d'ordre pratique, à savoir créer un état-major opérationnel pouvant planifier, mettre en route et diriger des opérations d'urgence.

□□□

The writer examines the organization and procedures of NATO's ACE Mobile force [Land], beginning with force planning and development. AMF[L] is a base force of 12-13,000 personnel held at seven days notice with a capacity to deploy 6-8,000 personnel to an assigned contingency area. Organized as a light, air-transportable brigade, AMF[L] is a multinational force. Therefore, it has been forced to address basic issues endemic to all multinational forces such as developing common procedures, integrated training, language, standardization and specialization. The AMF[L] can call upon the infrastructure of NATO and was designed to operate in a more specific geographical context than would be the case with a UN rapid response force, but many of the learning experiences in AMF[L] are germane. The writer suggests that, to improve the UN's reactive capability, a practical, near-term initiative would be the establishment of a UN operational headquarters able to plan, initially implement and command contingency operations.

J.A. MacInnis

S'inspirant en partie de son expérience en ex-Yougoslavie, l'auteur soutient que l'ONU devrait distinguer clairement entrele maintien et l'imposition de la paix. Bien qu'il faille adapter les opérations de maintien de la paix aux besoins et à la situation, un aspect n'a pas changé, à savoir l'impartialité du soldat de la paix, fondement de la crédibilité des opérations onusiennes. Néanmoins, au fur et à mesure que l'ONU participe à des opérations humanitaires, il va de soi que le représentant spécial du secrétaire général sur le terrain et le commandant sur le terrain sont aux prises avec d'importants défis et des décisions complexes. Les solutions consistent notamment à prendre des mesures préventives dès que possible pour maîtriser ou atténuer le conflit, intégrer les organismes de secours à la mission de maintien de la paix et se concentrer sur l'appui à fournir aux victimes du conflit. Pour réagir efficacement aux crises actuelles, les forces chargées du maintien de la paix doivent être mieux équipées et les soldats de la paix doivent adhérer à un code de conduite fondé sur l'impartialité et mettant l'accent sur la discipline, la retenue, la conscience des différences culturelles et la primauté du droit.

Basing his comments primarily but not exclusively on his experience in the former Yugoslavia, the writer argues that the UN should maintain a clear distinction between peacekeeping and peace enforcement. While peacekeeping must be adapted to current needs and situations, there is one indispensable requirement that has not changed: the impartiality of the peacekeeper, on which the credibility of the UN operation rests. Nevertheless, as the UN becomes more involved in humanitarian operations it is evident that the Secretary-General's Special Representative in the field and the Field Commander are faced with great challenges and complex decisions. The solutions include taking preventive measures at the earliest possible point to control or moderate conflict, integrating relief agencies into the peacekeeping mission, and focusing on support of the victims of conflict. To deal effectively with current crises, peacekeeping forces must have better capabilities and peacekeepers must develop a code of conduct based on impartiality and emphasizing discipline, restraint, cultural sensitivity and the rule of law.

M.K. Jeffery

S'inspirant de son expérience avec le GANUPT (Groupe d'assistance des Nations unies pour la période de transition [en Namibie]), l'auteur décrit les circonstances qui ont entouré le déploiement du GANUPT, y compris l'accord de paix et les particularités démographiques et géographiques de la Namibie, qui ont posé des difficultés particulières au Groupe. Au tout début de la mission, le Groupe a été confronté à la frontière nord à un grave incident qui risquait de compromettre tout le processus de transition. Parce que le déploiement, mal préparé, se faisait à pas de tortue, le Groupe n'a pas pu réagir à cet incident comme il aurait dû. À un niveau plus fondamental, cependant, le volet militaire du Groupe était mal commandé et mal contrôlé et ne possédait pas la mobilité nécessaire pour accomplir son mandat. Bien qu'à terme la mission ait été couronnée de succès, une force mobile moins nombreuse et rapidement déployée aurait coûté moins cher et accompli davantage.

❑❑❑

Drawing upon his experience in UNTAG, the writer describes the background to UNTAG's deployment, including the peace agreement and the demographic and geographic characteristics of Namibia which posed particular challenges to UNTAG. At the very beginning of the mission, UNTAG was challenged by a serious incident on the northern border which threatened the entire transition process. Because deployment was slow and poorly prepared, UNTAG was not in a position to respond adequately to this incident. More fundamentally, however, the military side of UNTAG suffered from poor command and control and lacked the mobility necessary in the light of the tasks to be performed. Although the mission was ultimately successful, a smaller, mobile force deployed rapidly would have accomplished more at lower cost.

Alex Morrison

L'auteur examine des points de vue et des discussions antérieures au sujet du déploiement de forces militaires sous la direction du Comité d'état-major, et conclut que, dès le début, deux modèles étaient envisagés. Le premier était celui de la force permanente, au sein de laquelle l'ONU aurait sa propre force militaire pour maintenir la paix et la sécurité internationales. Le second était celui de la force de réserve, formée d'unités désignées fournies par les États membres et prête à exécuter les opérations de l'ONU. Au fil des ans, alors que les propositions concernant la formation d'une force de réaction rapide se sont succédé, ces deux modèles ont façonné le débat. Cependant, les faits permettent d'affirmer que le modèle de la force permanente est voué à l'échec, car les États ne veulent pas céder le contrôle de leurs forces à un organe international. Il serait par conséquent préférable de s'attacher à améliorer les arrangements ad hoc et de reconnaître que, en raison de leur caractère multidimensionnel, les opérations de maintien de la paix exigeront une étroite collaboration de la part des organismes militaires et civils, et que le nouveau partenariat pour la paix serait mieux servi par une souplesse accrue et une meilleure planification.

The writer reviews some early views and discussions about the deployment of military forces under the direction of the Military Staff Committee, and concludes that, from the beginning, two models were considered. The first was the standing force, in which the United Nations would have its own military force available to maintain international peace and security. The second was the stand-by force, in which Member States would hold designated units in readiness for UN operations. As proposals for UN rapid deployment forces have surfaced and re-surfaced over the years, these two models have shaped the debate. However, the historical record suggests that the standing force model will always fail in the end because states are unwilling to cede control of their forces to an international body. It may be better, therefore, to concentrate on improving existing *ad hoc* arrangements and to recognize that, as peacekeeping operations become multidimensional, requiring military and civilian agencies to work in close cooperation, the new peacekeeping partnership may benefit most from a combination of flexibility and improved planning.

Romeo Dallaire

Le major général Roméo Dallaire propose l'établissement d'une force de réaction rapide de l'ONU qui pourrait être rapidement déployée dans les zones de conflit. À l'origine, cette force serait composée par des contingents fournis par des États autres que par les P-5 (les cinq membres permanents du Conseil de sécurité). En effet, les forces des P-5 devraient être considérées comme une force de réserve stratégique, ne devant être déployées qu'au moment et que si les autres forces échouent dans leur mandat de rétablir l'ordre ou encore d'en prévenir sa rupture. Cette situation serait analogue à celle qui existe à l'intérieur des États, estime le général Dallaire, là où en règle générale on ne fait appel aux forces armées que si les forces de l'ordre sont débordées par les événements.

Sur le plan des réformes souhaitées, Dallaire propose l'établissement d'une équipe de gestion de crise multidisciplinaire, dont les tâches seraient de colliger l'information, de fournir une alerte anticipée des crises en gestation, et de prévoir une planification intégrée des aspects civils et militaires d'une mission quelconque. L'ONU devrait disposer d'un système administratif et logistique efficace qui pourrait être rapidement déployé avec un minimum d'obstacles bureaucratiques ou encore avec un minimum de responsabilité directe de l'ONU dans la conduite des opérations. Les «forces en attente» ainsi que de l'équipement devraient être mis à la disposition de l'ONU sur une base permanente; une organisation humanitaire devrait être principalement responsable de tous les aspects des activités des ONG sur le terrain; et l'ONU devrait avoir ses propres services d'information, ayant accès aux médias de la presse internationale tout en étant capables de diffuser ses propres messages dans la zone de conflit, dans le but de corriger les informations fausses ou encore la propagande destinée à désinformer la population.

Les faiblesses de l'ONU sont celles de toute la communauté internationale, conclut le général Dallaire. Celle-ci a le devoir juridique et moral d'intervenir dans les cas de désastres humanitaires ou dans les cas où les régimes s'affaissent et où la rupture de l'ordre mène à des génocides. Il est donc urgent de réformer l'ONU et de la doter d'une Force de déploiement rapide. De réactive qu'elle était, l'Organisation deviendrait ainsi proactive. Le major général Dallaire trouve ironique de constater qu'il a été plus facile pour Diane Fossey d'attirer l'attention de la communauté internationale sur la nécessité de protéger une espèce en voie de disparition, c'est-à-dire les gorilles, que cela ne l'a été pour coordonner les efforts de la communauté internationale pour empêcher les massacres au Rwanda.

Major-General Romeo Dallaire proposes the establishment of a UN rapid reaction force which could be promptly dispatched to areas of conflict in case of crisis. This initial force could be composed of contingents provided by states other than the P5. The P5 military forces should be considered as a strategic reserve force which could be deployed if and when the initial coalition fails in its task of restoring order or of preventing its breakdown. This situation would be akin to the one that exists within internal states, according to Dallaire, as armed forces are usually called upon only if the original police forces are overwhelmed by the events.

In terms of UN reforms, Dallaire argues in favor of the establishment of a multidisciplinary crisis management team, tasked to collect information, to provide timely early warning of impending crisis for the international community and to do contingency planning that integrates both the civilian and the military aspects of a potential mission. The UN should have an efficient administrative and logistical system that could be rapidly deployed with a minimum of bureaucratic obstacles and/or degree of UN responsibility in the actual conduct of the operation. Stand-by forces and material should be made available to the UN on a permanent basis, a lead humanitarian agency should coordinate all aspects of the NGO activities in the field and the UN should have at its disposal an information service which has access to the international media and has the capacity to deliver its own information in an area on conflict in order to counter false information or propaganda aimed at disinforming the population.

The weaknesses of the UN are the weaknesses of the international community, argues Dallaire. The international community has the legal and moral obligation to intervene in case of humanitarian disasters or in the case of "failed states" where the breakdown of order leads to genocide. It is therefore urgent to reform the UN and to empower the organization with a rapid deployment force. The UN would henceforth become a proactive rather than a reactive organization. Major-General

Dallaire finds it ironic that it was easier for Diane Fossey to attract the attention of the international community on the need of protecting an endangered species in Rwanda, the gorillas, than it was to pool the resources of the international community to prevent massacre and genocide in Rwanda.

Cathy Downes

L'auteur énumère un certain nombre d'événements récents à la suite de laquelle il est devenu plus difficile pour les nations fournissant des troupes de répondre à un appel de l'ONU en vue d'une opération de maintien de la paix. Au nombre des facteurs cités, on peut mentionner le risque accru de victimes, des exigences accrues sur le plan des ressources et de la performance militaires et un plus grand risque d'échec de la mission et de critiques de la part de la population pour avoir accepté d'y participer. Le concept de groupes d'avant-garde, permettant d'agir rapidement grâce à une force de réserve, bien que prometteur, suscite un grand nombre de questions pour les pays qui fournissent des contingents. Premièrement, aucun pays n'appuiera le concept si l'on ne modifie pas sensiblement la structure de l'ONU afin de garantir qu'il y aura, avant tout déploiement de forces, une planification et une organisation suffisantes. Deuxièmement, la force devrait être prête à fonctionner dans un milieu semi-permissif ou non permissif. On rechercherait alors surtout des unités bien équipées et bien entraînées, capables de fonctionner comme une force intégrée. Une formation et une doctrine conjointes seraient alors essentielles. Troisièmement, il faudrait prendre en compte le coût du maintien des forces en état avancé de disponibilité opérationnelle, tout comme celui du réapprovisionnement et de la nécessité de remplacer les groupes d'avant-garde après un certain temps par des troupes «régulières» de maintien de la paix. À terme, le succès d'une force d'avant-garde tiendrait à la capacité desÉtats membres de former un nouveau type de partenariat entre les pays qui fournissent des contingents et l'ONU, au sein duquel il y aurait un juste partage des responsabilités.

□□□

The writer identifies a number of recent developments in peacekeeping which have complicated the responses of troop-contributing nations to a UN request to participate in a peacekeeping operation. These include the significantly greater risk of casualties, greater demands on military resources and performance, and greater risks of mission failure and domestic public criticism of the decision to participate. The Vanguard concept of a standby, rapid response force is promising, but raises many questions for troop contributors. First, it would not likely be supported unless there were significant structural changes at the UN to ensure that there was adequate planning and organization in place before any force was deployed. Second, the force would need to be prepared to operate in a semi- or non-permissive environment. This would place a premium on well-equipped, well-trained units able to operate as an integrated force. Joint training and doctrine would be essential. Third, the costs of maintaining forces at the necessary high level of readiness would need to be considered, as would re-supply and the necessity to replace the Vanguard force after a given period with a "regular' peacekeeping operation. In the outcome, the success of a vanguard force would depend on the ability of the Member States to fashion a new kind of partnership between the troop-contributing countries and the UN in which responsibilities were appropriately shared.

Peter Langille, Maxime Faille, Carlton Hughes and James Hammond

S'inspirant de la proposition selon laquelle l'ONU devrait maintenant établir un état-major opérationnel, les auteurs suggèrent quelques idées et concepts à long terme, conçus pour favoriser le développement cumulatif des capacités onusiennes de maintien de la paix. Dans un premier temps, l'ONU établirait une base et y étendrait et renforcerait son état-major par l'élaboration d'une doctrine, de procédures opérationnelles et de normes de formation communes. Les pays assigneraient ensuite des groupes militaires et civils à la base dans le cadre de la force permanente, l'accent étant mis sur la formation en fonction de missions précises, l'interopérabilité et les capacités de transport aérien. Au cours de la troisième étape, des bénévoles professionnels seraient intégrés à la force permanente pour que le déploiement de la force dépende moins de la volonté individuelle des États participants. Ces mesures seraient cumulatives dans le sens que l'exécution réussie d'une étape inspirerait suffisamment confiance pour que l'on puisse envisager de passer à l'étape suivante.

□□□

Building on the proposal that the UN should now establish an operational headquarters, the authors suggest some longer term ideas and concepts designed to facilitate the cumulative development of UN peacekeeping capabilities. In the first stage, the UN might establish a UN base where the headquarters would be expanded and strengthened through the development of common doctrine, operating procedures and training standards. In the second stage, countries might assign military and civilian groups to the UN base as part of a standing force, emphasizing mission-specific training, inter-operability and lift capabilities. In the third stage, professional volunteers might be integrated into the standing force in the expectation that this would lessen the degree to which the deployment of the force was subject to the individual decisions of participating states. These measures are seen as cumulative in that success at any one stage would increase confidence in the feasibility of moving ahead to next stage.

Introduction and Summary

David Cox and Albert Legault

Background

In his speech to the 49th General Assembly of the United Nations on 29 September 1994, Canada's Minister of Foreign Affairs, André Ouellet, reviewed the efforts under way at the United Nations to improve the management of peacekeeping operations, and commented:

> The experience of the last few years leads us to believe that we need to explore even more innovative options than those considered to date. Recent peacekeeping missions have shown that the traditional approach no longer applies. As we have seen in Rwanda, rapid deployment of intervention forces is essential. In light of the situation, the Government of Canada has decided to conduct an in-depth review of the short-, medium- and long-term options available to us to strengthen the UN's rapid response capability in times of crisis. Among these options, we feel that the time has come to study the possibilities, over the long term, of creating a permanent UN military force.

Foreign Minister Ouellet, therefore, was careful not to specify the form that a UN rapid response capability might take, but in proposing the study he was drawing upon a number of recent proposals and discussions at the United Nations. As many commentators have noted, the idea of a standing UN Force goes back to Trygve Lie's proposal for a UN Legion. This idea was given a new lease on life when, in June 1993, Sir Brian Urquhart declared his view that, despite all of the difficulties involved, a UN volunteer standing force seemed to be the only way that the UN could ensure the availability of a rapid response force.

David Cox teaches in the Department of Political Studies, Queen's University, and is the Chair, Research and Operations, of the Canadian Center for Global Security. He was a member of the international consultative group for the rapid response study.

Professor Albert Legault is director of program, international peace and security, at the *Institut québécois des hautes études internationales*, Laval University. He also teaches in the Department of Political Science at Laval University. He was a member of the international consultative group for the rapid response study.

Since the publication of Urquhart's observations, the feasibility of a standing volunteer force has been hotly debated. The requirement for a UN rapid response capability, however, has been broadly accepted. In his 1992 report, *An Agenda for Peace,* Secretary-General Boutros Boutros-Ghali made a number of recommendations intended to improve the speed of response of UN peace operations. These included the suggestion, in Paragraph 44 of the report, that the Security Council consider the establishment of "peace enforcement units" designed to restore and maintain ceasefires:

> Such units from Member States would be available on call and would consist of troops that have volunteered for such service. They would have to be more heavily armed than peacekeeping forces and would need to undergo extensive preparatory training within their national forces."

Since 1992, the concept of peace enforcement has also been vigorously debated, but, insofar as it involves a higher state of readiness than is the case in peacekeeping operations, there has been little challenge to the claim that the United Nations needs to respond more promptly and flexibly to crisis situations. The Secretary-General returned to this theme in the *Supplement to An Agenda for Peace,* published in January 1995. Noting that there was no guarantee that troop contributions would be made available promptly for any given mission, he commented:

> In these circumstances, I have come to the conclusion that the United Nations does need to give serious thought to the idea of a rapid reaction force. Such a force would be the Security Council's strategic reserve for deployment when there was an emergency need for peacekeeping troops. It might comprise battalion-sized units from a number of countries. These units would be trained to the same standards, use the same operating procedures, be equipped with integrated communications equipment and take part in joint exercises at regular intervals. They would be stationed in their home countries but maintained at a high state of readiness. The value of this arrangement would of course depend on how far the Security Council could be sure that the force would actually be available in an emergency. This will be a complicated and expensive arrangement, but I believe that the time has come to undertake it.[1]

The Canadian Study

The study promised by Mr. Ouellet was carried out jointly by the Departments of Defence and Foreign Affairs. In December 1994, the two departments established a core working group consisting of officials from the two departments, academics and other experts with a range of backgrounds relating to the United Nations. This group acted as the core of the consultative process that took place during the first six months of 1995.

In addition to the work of the core group, the consultative process centred on three meetings. In the first two meetings, the core group met with experts who had been asked to undertake studies of specific questions, and with officials from various departments and agencies of the United Nations with experience in issues relating to rapid response. A wide range of issues were discussed at these meetings, including the nature of the UN Secretariat machinery for dealing with UN military operations, the status of efforts to improve stand-by arrangements for peacekeeping operations, the UN budgetary process, NATO's experience with the development of a rapid response force, and the experience of other UN agencies, such as UNHCR, in dealing with rapid response situations. Representatives of other agencies and non-governmental organizations also participated in these meetings.

In order to draw further on international expertise, an international consultative group was established. In a third meeting, this group brought together Canadian and international experts. Its purpose was to comment on the working papers and preliminary recommendations of the study, and to furnish the working group with further proposals and ideas. At this point, the principal elements in the consultative process were largely complete. The various written papers and records of discussions formed a basis on which the drafters of the official report to the United Nations could draw. For the most part, the papers included in this volume are those which examined the technical aspects of rapid response forces. An introductory section, however, offers different views on the political feasibility of a rapid response force, and on the political needs that such a force would meet.

The Need for Rapid Response

Sir Brian Urquhart's initial statement of the case for a standing UN force has lost neither currency nor relevance in the past two years. As co-chair of the international consultative group, Urquhart's contribution notes two key points in the UN's recent responses to conflict situations.[2] First, many of the new situations are ones for which neither traditional peacekeeping nor enforcement are appropriate. Second, even though it is evident that rapid and effective action is necessary if these crises are to be contained and prevented from developing into large and volatile mixes of humanitarian, military and environmental problems, the UN response time has lengthened. In part, this is because the increase in demand for peacekeeping units, combined with the higher risks incurred by troop contributors, has made potential contributors hesitant and cautious in making their decision to participate. In part, as well, it is because the size and complexity of these new operations has strained the resources and structures of the UN Department of Peacekeeping Operations, which has traditionally operated on a modest basis with largely *ad hoc* procedures.

An examination of UN efforts to cope with the exacting demands now placed upon it reveals a number of structural problems which militate against rapid response. These include the increased wariness of the troop contributors and the traditional *ad hoc* tendencies of the Department of Peacekeeping Operations as discussed above. In addition, there are other problems which have yet to be re-solved. Particularly, the planning and implementation of a peacekeeping operation generally tends to await the outcome of deliberations and decision-making in the Security Council, thereby creating a time lag between Security Council considera-tion of a problem and the actual arrival of the peacekeeping force in the field. It is not unusual, for example, for this time lag to be six months or more. Moreover, even where the UN has been successful in its mission, as in Namibia, tardiness in deployment has threatened to jeopardize operations and unhinge peace agreements which are almost always fragile.[3]

Comparable problems exist in the financing, where the gap between a Security Council decision and financial authorization may be three to four months, making it difficult to plan and commit resources even to approved peace operations. De-spite substantial reforms and improvements in the management of peacekeeping missions, therefore, there are two serious gaps that can be identified in UN man-agement processes: the gap between authorization and deployment, and the gap between traditional peacekeeping and full-scale enforcement. A rapid response capability might fill those gaps, but, among other conditions, only if financial resources are made available to ensure that rapid response is not obstructed by other inefficient procedures at the UN.[4]

However, it must also be noted that some observers accept that reforms are evidently required at the UN, but argue that, while a rapid response capability may be desirable, it is more practical to concentrate on low cost, near-term incremental reforms which have a higher chance of success. These could include strengthen-ing the Department of Peacekeeping Operations, focusing on improvements to the logistics system, making greater use of the option of requesting individual coun-tries to lead a peace operation under a UN mandate rather than the UN implementing the mandate itself, and placing longer-term emphasis on the role of regional or-ganizations. Placing priority on such measures, it can be argued, recognizes that there is little prospect that the major powers will approve and fund a rapid re-sponse force, and focuses instead on the kind of incremental changes which are more likely to succeed at the UN.[5]

The Vanguard Concept

Despite such doubts, there continues to be a strong sense that a qualitative change in the UN capacity to launch peace operations is required. Even in "suc-cessful" operations, such as Namibia and Cambodia, delays in deployment came near to upsetting the accords reached after protracted negotiation. In more recent cases, inadequate and tardy deployments have contributed to local tragedies and eventually demanded many more resources from the international community than would be required to develop a rapid response capability. The UN experience in Angola in 1993 was a clear signal of the problem. Faced with the possibility that the two sides would agree to a settlement, the UN was called upon to provide a buffer force to guarantee the separation of the military forces. The UN special representative, however, was obliged to advise the parties that, for practical reasons, no UN troops could be made available for at least six to nine months.

This incapacity was glaringly revealed in Rwanda. Following the Arusha peace agreement of 4 August 1993, it was three months before the first peacekeepers arrived, and when the full-scale genocide erupted in April 1994—more than six months after the Security Council decision to deploy a peacekeeping mission—the UN force was sadly under-manned and under-equipped. General Roméo Dallaire, the UN force commander, bears witness to the UN predicament:

> UNAMIR could have saved the lives of hundreds of thousands of people. As evidence, with the 450 men under my command during this interim, we saved and directly protected over 25,000 people and moved tens of thousands between the combat lines. A force of 5,000 personnel rapidly deployed could have prevented the massacres in the south and west of the country that did not commence in earnest until early May ....[6]

Events in Rwanda, therefore, offer a telling argument for the development of a vanguard force which would be organized and trained to deploy rapidly once the Security Council had approved a peace operation. However, a fundamental assumption of the Canadian approach is that a rapid response capability depends on appropriate UN command and control arrangements, raising the prospect that a commitment to rapid response might begin with improvements in the management of peace operations. These improvements would have rapid response as the goal, but would also provide an immediate impetus to the strengthening of UN operations. Cast in these terms, the development of a rapid response capability may benefit first from an appreciation of the NATO experience in developing a rapid response force.

The NATO Experience

THE CHAIN OF COMMAND [7]

Although UN efforts to develop an improved peacekeeping capability will need to be compatible with the Charter and in keeping with UN experience and traditions, the NATO experience can be instructive. NATO is an alliance, and necessarily reflects a greater community of interest and common policy than is feasible in the United Nations. Nevertheless, in certain respects NATO has faced similar problems in seeking to organize multinational forces. The member states of NATO have committed themselves to their common security, but they still wish to retain a national decision in crucial matters such as NATO policy towards Eastern Europe and the commitment of troops to implement NATO plans. The North Atlantic Council, therefore, operates on the principle of consensus, but there is a strong interest in achieving consensus, and member states are seldom willing to be the sole dissident in Council decision-making.

At the highest level, political questions in NATO are resolved in the North Atlantic Council (NAC), which might be considered as an analogue to the UN Security Council. Unlike the UN, however, the NATO structure has a mechanism—the Military Committee, on which all members are represented and which also operates on the principle of consensus—which serves as an interface between political decision-making and military implementation. At the UN, the Military Staff Committee (MSC) does not represent all members of the Security Council, and is in any case ineffective. NATO has both a civilian International Staff and a sizable International Military Staff composed primarily of officers seconded from the member states. The Military Committee can task the Staff, and the Director of the Military Staff must submit recommendations to the Military Committee before they are transmitted to the political level.

Finally, NATO has standing field headquarters—Supreme Allied Command Europe (SACEUR) and Supreme Allied Command Atlantic (SACLANT)—whose commanders are tasked to conduct operations with the forces assigned to them by prior agreement with the member states. Although the member states have various opportunities to make their views known, and may reserve the right not to commit their forces, they accept that the major NATO commanders exercise operational control over national forces in the field assigned to that command.

Although not without its complexities, therefore, NATO has been able to resolve certain key difficulties which remain to be resolved at the United Nations. First, it has a workable chain of command from political decisions to military organization to field operations. Second, it has maintained the principle of unity of command both in the sense that there is a single chain of command and in the sense that the commander in the field exercises operational control over his forces, who respond to him and not to a national operational control system. Third, NATO has created a staff headquarters which is able to conduct the normal range of military planning functions while firmly integrated in a chain of command which is designed to ensure that it responds to the Military Committee and is, through the Committee, subject to political oversight.

By comparison, the Military Staff Committee envisaged in Article 47 of the Charter of the United Nations is composed of permanent representatives only from the Permanent Five, and the MSC is exclusively at the disposal of the Security Council, and therefore excludes other key actors—especially the non-permanent Council members and the Secretary-General—from the chain of command. Since the MSC is not a functioning body, and there is little prospect that it will become one, its institutional limitations are not a serious obstacle to changes at the United Nations. More generally, however, the Charter concept of the MSC indicates that the UN has yet to achieve the unity of political decision and command and control which modern peacekeeping operations demand. This unity would require an institutional process like that in NATO which would include the Security Council as the supreme political authority in matters of international peace and security, the Secretary-General and the Secretariat as an executive body, the troop contributing countries and the commanders in the field. Also required would be a suitably constituted Military Staff Committee, or a more appropriate functional equivalent, able to provide military advice to the Security Council and the Secretary-General, and, possibly, able to task the military component in the Secretariat, or a separately constituted operational headquarters staff.

NATO RAPID REACTION FORCES[8]

NATO established multinational rapid reaction forces in the 1960s in order to respond to contingencies on its northern and southern flanks. In the late 1980s, following the changes in the security situation in Europe, it has established additional land and naval rapid response forces as the number of stationed standing forces in the NATO area has declined. Of these various forces, however, the most instructive from the UN viewpoint is the Allied Command Europe Mobile Forces [Land Component] (AMF[L]). This force draws upon a base of 12,000-13,000 personnel, and has a capacity to deploy some 6,000-8,000 on seven days notice. Unlike the UN, however, where a peacekeeping operation might be authorized in any part of the world, the AMF[L] deployment would be to one of seven pre-assigned contingency areas. Moreover, the AMF[L] can draw upon the substantial infrastructure of NATO to support its operations.

Since it is a multinational force, the contributing NATO countries can and do impose constraints on the use of their forces. Although most of these are minor in nature, some constraints are such that the AMF[L] has a system of primary and secondary troop units for each contingency area, so that there is a known replacement for a primary unit which is withdrawn for reasons of national policy. Once again, it is clearly the case that a comparable UN system would be significantly more complicated given the greater variety of political circumstances in which the UN is required to act, but the AMF[L] experience indicates that it is possible to plan for constraints on troop unit use as long as these constraints are clearly identified in advance by the troop contributors, and are not so comprehensive as to forestall all contingency arrangements.

Similarly, as a multinational force, the AMF[L] has been forced to come to grips with the various problems of interoperability which are inevitable when a number of countries with different national practices come together in one command. As it has evolved, the AMF[L] has paid particular attention to the development of standing agreements on operations, tactics, and logistics, on the basis of which it has developed standard operating procedures for the use of participating national units. AMF[L] units train together on an annual basis, exchange detachments with each other to increase familiarity with other national procedures, and seek to develop common training standards for use in national training programmes. Great emphasis is also placed on the common training of commanders and staff officers, where relatively inexpensive programmes, such as one-week study periods and logistics courses, greatly increased commonality and cohesiveness among national units.

Language and standardization are also key factors in multinational operations. The working language of the AMF[L] is English, which means that the majority of contributors must operate in a foreign language when interacting with other units, while retaining their national language for internal purposes. Training for proficiency in English is therefore essential for commanders and staff officers, but other, simpler programmes, such as handbooks with key sentences, phrases and military expressions, can help at all levels of the command. The UN would certainly benefit from this experience. On the other hand, standardization of equipment is a daunting challenge for any multinational force, and the limited success of NATO in this regard suggests that the UN would need to settle for maximizing interoperability rather than pursuing standardization of equipment in an international force.

Finally, the AMF[L] headquarters organization may be instructive in thinking about a UN rapid response capability. The headquarters is a small unit composed of 45 permanent staff. This staff can be doubled when the AMF[L] is deployed by adding staff officers from contributing countries who have already been trained in AMF[L] procedures. It can also be divided into two smaller headquarters in the event that two deployments take place at the same time. The headquarters therefore provides continuity and stability in contingency planning and training, progressively creating a body of knowledge and experience on which both NATO and the national contributors can draw as required.

The AMF[L] has highly developed procedures for logistics movement and deployment, including sophisticated air transportation arrangements and demanding standards for the deployment and support of its units. Many of these would be inappropriate for the UN, which would seldom if ever choose to deploy a strictly UN force in a high intensity conflict environment. However, many aspects of the AMF[L] experience have a bearing on the feasibility and effectiveness of a UN rapid response capability, particularly the central importance of a small but expandable headquarters, and those elements of training and procedures which are intended to overcome the inherent problems in creating a multinational force based on national contingents with diverse traditions, procedures and languages.

THE HEADQUARTERS REQUIREMENT FOR A VANGUARD FORCE[9]

While the UN has made significant improvements in its management of peacekeeping operations, there is widespread recognition that qualitative changes are needed if peace support operations are to be conducted in environments where ceasefires are fragile, or where there is a strong possibility that peacekeeping forces will be harassed, threatened, or otherwise denied the ability to implement their mandate. This is clearly the case where a Vanguard force is planned on the assumption that it must deploy quickly and be prepared to operate in a semi- or non-permissive environment. Specifically, a Vanguard force would require re-forms at the UN to recognize the following needs.

First, an Operational Headquarters should encompass the planning and control of the peacekeeping operations which would follow-on from the Vanguard force mandate. This implies some reorganization of the Department of Peacekeeping Operations. Second, the Operational Headquarters would provide advice to the Security Council and the Secretary-General, including the development of standard operating procedures, standardized rules of engagement, and training packages for national forces. Third, the Headquarters would have as its central responsibility the tasks required to manage a Vanguard force, including contingency planning, concepts of operations, and the command and control of Vanguard forces in the field.

The deployment of Vanguard forces raises many crucial questions concerning the training, preparation and integration of national units. To begin, troop contributing countries holding forces in a high state of readiness incur considerable costs. It is not likely that they would commit such units to a UN multinational force unless they were confident that other national units were trained to a high standard as an integrated force. This may be antithetical to the UN need for broadly representative multinational forces. However, imaginative solutions can be found. For example, the most sophisticated military establishments could make available advanced training systems; commanders, staff officers and small units could be routinely exchanged as in NATO; and training packages could be developed and used in national training systems.

In the outcome, however, it is evident that a well-trained, well prepared Vanguard force held at a high state of readiness would involve an intricate distribution of responsibilities and burdens within the UN system, and between the UN and the troop contributing countries. This would require all of the parties involved to engage in constructive negotiation and planning, with a recognition that the financial costs in particular would need to be dealt with in a manner which recognized the added burden assumed by the troop contributors and proposed imaginative financial arrangements to offset this added burden.

The Longer Term and First Step

Focusing on the creation of a standing Operational Headquarters as a substantive, near-term objective has the additional benefit that it provides a basic building block for the long term.[10] Although more ambitious blueprints may have limited prospects in the short run, it is valuable to identify a comprehensive and cumulative process which, in the long run, would culminate in a standing UN emergency capability. Following the establishment of an operational headquarters, the first stage in this process might be the establishment of a dedicated UN rapid response base which could be expanded at an appropriate point to include a number of regional UN bases. A dedicated base could begin with a focus on tasks such as common training manuals, the development of standard operating procedures, and encouragement of multinational exercises.

A logical second step would be the creation of a standing rapid response force based on national units assigned to the UN base and under the command and control of the UN. In a third stage, it might be possible to reconcile the competing visions of a UN volunteer standing force and a multinational stand-by force by merging suitably trained volunteers with the national units assigned to the UN base.

Of course, the purpose of such a long-term blueprint is not to prescribe a specific path but to set a goal which can be pursued in a variety of ways. The goal in this case is to create a UN capacity for timely response which has the broad support of the Member States. Competing visions of that ultimate capacity should be encouraged. In the meantime it is evident that, in the present political and financial climate at the UN, leading Member States will need to be persuaded that it is militarily and financially practical to take a modest but valuable first step. That first step appears to be the establishment of an operational headquarters, possibly located off-site from the UN headquarters in New York. An operational headquarters, perhaps financed in part by voluntary special contributions from Member States, has the merit that it would benefit all peacekeeping operations while providing the basis for further efforts to develop the rapid response capabilities of the UN.

Notes

1. *Supplement to an Agenda for Peace,* S/1995/1, paragraph 44.
2. See Urquhart, Paper 3, for comment on this point.
3. See Jeffery, Paper 9, for an account of the operation in Namibia.
4. See Boulden and Knight, Paper 4, for further analysis of these issues.
5. See Roberts, Paper 5.
6. See Paper 11 for General Dallaire's views.
7. See Dangerfield, Paper 6.
8. See Christie, Paper 7.
9. See Downes, Paper 12.
10. See Paper 13, Langille, et al., for the development of a longer-term approach based on the idea of cumulative stages.

Introduction et Résumé

David Cox et Albert Legault

Contexte

Dans son allocution devant la 49ᵉ Assemblée générale des Nations unies, prononcée le 29 septembre 1994, le ministre des Affaires étrangères du Canada, M. André Ouellet, a passé en revue les efforts déployés actuellement à l'ONU pour améliorer la gestion des opérations de maintien de la paix et les a commentés.

«L'expérience des dernières années nous porte à penser qu'il faut être prêt à envisager des approches encore plus innovatrices que celles débattues jusqu'à maintenant. Nos missions de maintien de la paix sont sorties de leur cadre traditionnel. Comme nous l'avons vu au Rwanda, le déploiement rapide de forces d'intervention est essentiel.

Dans cette perspective, le gouvernement du Canada a décidé d'entreprendre un examen approfondi des options à court, moyen et long termes qui s'offrent à nous pour renforcer la capacité d'action rapide de l'ONU en temps de crise. Parmi ces options, nous pensons que le moment est venu d'étudier la possibilité, à long terme, de créer une force militaire onusienne permanente.»

Le ministre Ouellet a donc pris soin de ne pas préciser la forme que pourrait prendre une capacité d'intervention rapide, mais en proposant l'étude, il s'est inspiré d'un certain nombre de propositions et discussions récentes aux Nations unies. Comme bien des analystes l'ont fait remarquer, l'idée d'une force onusienne permanente remonte à la proposition de Légion de l'ONU avancée par Trygve Lie. L'idée a rejailli en juin 1993 lorsque sir Brian Urquhart a déclaré qu'en dépit de toutes les difficultés qu'il faudrait surmonter, la seule façon qu'avait l'ONU de réagir rapidement était de former une force onusienne permanente et volontaire.

David Cox enseigne au département d'études politiques de l'Université Queen's et est directeur de recherches et des activités du Centre canadien pour la sécurité globale. Il a fait partie du groupe consultatif international, chargé d'étudier la capacité d'action rapide de l'ONU.

Le professeur Albert Legault est directeur du programme «paix et sécurité internationales» à l'Institut québécois des hautes études internationales, à l'Université Laval. Il est professeur titulaire au Département de science politique de l'Université Laval. Il a fait partie du groupe consultatif international, chargé d'étudier la capacité d'action rapide de l'ONU.

Depuis la publication des observations d'Urquhart, la faisabilité d'une force volontaire *permanente* a été vivement débattue. L'idée en a été toutefois largement acceptée. Dans son *Agenda pour la paix* de 1992, le secrétaire général, M. Boutros Boutros-Ghali, a fait un certain nombre de recommandations destinées à raccourcir le délai de réaction des opérations de paix de l'ONU. Il est notamment suggéré, au paragraphe 44 de l'Agenda, que le Conseil de sécurité envisage la création d'unités d'imposition de la paix pour rétablir et maintenir les cessez-le-feu.

> «Ces unités issues des États membres seraient prêtes à intervenir sur demande et seraient composées de militaires qui se seraient portés volontaires pour servir. Elles devraient être armées plus lourdement que les forces de maintien de la paix et devraient suivre une formation complète au sein de leurs forces nationales.»

Depuis 1992, le concept d'imposition de la paix a aussi été débattu vigoureusement, mais, dès lors qu'on souhaite parvenir à un état de préparation plus avancé que dans le cas des opérations de maintien de la paix, très peu de contestations sont élevées contre la nécessité pour les Nations unies de réagir avec plus de promptitude et de flexibilité aux situations de crise. Le secrétaire général a repris le même thème dans le *Supplément à l'Agenda pour la paix*, publié en janvier 1995. Faisant remarquer qu'il n'y avait pas de garanties qu'on puisse disposer rapidement de contingents pour une mission donnée, il a ajouté:

> «Dans ces conditions, je suis arrivé à la conclusion que l'ONU devait envisager sérieusement l'idée d'une force de réaction rapide. Cette force constituerait la réserve stratégique du Conseil de sécurité, qui pourrait la déployer en cas de besoin urgent de troupes de maintien de la paix. Elle pourrait se composer d'unités équivalant à des bataillons, en provenance de plusieurs pays, qui recevraient la même instruction, opéreraient selon les mêmes procédures, seraient équipées de matériel de transmissions intégré et participeraient régulièrement à des manoeuvres communes. Elles seraient stationnées dans leur pays d'origine tout en étant prêtes à intervenir à tout moment. L'intérêt de ce dispositif serait bien entendu fonction de la mesure dans laquelle le Conseil de sécurité pourrait effectivement compter sur cette force en cas d'urgence. Il s'agit là d'un dispositif complexe et onéreux, mais je crois qu'il est temps de le mettre en place.»[1]

L'étude canadienne

L'étude promise par M. Ouellet a été effectuée conjointement par les ministères de la Défense et des Affaires étrangères. En décembre 1994, les deux ministères ont formé un groupe de travail central, composé de membres des deux ministères, d'universitaires et d'autres spécialistes possédant différents bagages de connaissances ayant trait aux Nations unies. Ce groupe a été au coeur du processus de consultation qui s'est déroulé durant les six premiers mois de 1995.

En plus des travaux effectués par ce noyau, le processus consultatif a été ponctué par trois grandes réunions. Au cours des deux premières, le groupe a rencontré des experts à qui on avait demandé d'étudier certaines questions, et des membres de divers départements et organismes des Nations unies versés dans l'intervention rapide. Une multitude de sujets ont été abordés à ces réunions, dont la nature des mécanismes dont dispose le Secrétariat de l'ONU pour s'occuper des opérations militaires onusiennes, les efforts déployés afin d'améliorer les arrangements relatifs aux forces en attente pour les opérations de maintien de la paix, le processus budgétaire de l'ONU, l'expérience de l'OTAN en matière d'intervention rapide, et l'expérience d'autres organismes de l'ONU, comme le HCR, lorsqu'il s'agit de faire face aux situations d'intervention rapide. Des représentants d'autres organismes et d'organisations non gouvernementales ont également participé à ces réunions.

Afin de tirer parti encore davantage des compétences présentes à l'extérieur du pays, un groupe consultatif international a été établi. À la troisième réunion, ce groupe a mis en présence des experts canadiens et étrangers. L'objectif était de commenter les documents de travail et les recommandations préliminaires de l'étude, et de fournir au groupe de travail d'autres propositions et idées. À ce moment-là, les principaux éléments du processus de consultation étaient passablement complets. Les différents documents et les transcriptions des délibérations constituaient une base dont pouvaient s'inspirer les rédacteurs du rapport officiel destiné aux Nations unies. Pour la plupart, les documents contenus dans ce volume portaient sur les aspects techniques des forces de réaction rapide. Une section d'introduction offre toutefois différents points de vue sur la faisabilité politique d'une force d'intervention rapide et sur les besoins politiques auxquels une telle force répondrait.

La nécessité de l'intervention rapide

Le plaidoyer initial de sir Brian Urquhart en faveur d'une force onusienne *permanente* n'a perdu ni de son actualité ni de sa pertinence depuis deux ans. En tant que coprésident du groupe consultatif international, Urquhart signale dans son texte deux points importants des récentes interventions de l'ONU dans les situations de conflit.[2] Premièrement, ni le maintien de la paix traditionnel ni l'imposition de la paix ne conviennent à bon nombre des nouvelles situations. Deuxièmement, même s'il est évident qu'une action rapide et efficace est nécessaire pour contenir ces crises et les empêcher de dégénérer en un vaste et explosif imbroglio humanitaire, militaire et environnemental, le délai de réaction de l'ONU s'est allongé. Ce phénomène est en partie attribuable aux demandes accrues d'unités de maintien de la paix et aux risques plus grands courus par les fournisseurs de contingents, d'où leur hésitation à prendre la décision de participer aux opérations. La raison tient aussi en partie au fait que la taille et la complexité de ces nouvelles opérations a grevé les ressources et les structures du Département des opérations de maintien de la paix de l'ONU, qui a toujours fonctionné a partir d'une base modeste à laquelle se greffaient beaucoup de procédures ponctuelles.

Un examen des efforts de l'ONU pour répondre aux demandes exigeantes dont elle est saisie révèle certains problèmes structuraux qui militent contre l'intervention rapide, dont la plus grande prudence des fournisseurs de troupes et le penchant traditionnel du Département des opérations de maintien de la paix en faveur de procédures ponctuelles, comme nous l'avons vu plus haut. D'autres problèmes restent aussi à régler. Ainsi, la planification et la mise en oeuvre d'une opération de paix doivent généralement attendre l'issue des délibérations et la prise d'une décision au Conseil de sécurité, d'où l'intervalle entre l'examen d'un problème par le Conseil de sécurité et l'arrivée de la force de maintien de la paix sur le terrain. Il n'est pas rare que ce décalage soit de six mois ou plus. Par ailleurs, même dans le cas des missions fructueuses de l'ONU, comme en Namibie, le caractère tardif du déploiement a mis en péril la réussite des opérations et aurait pu faire dérailler les accords de paix, qui sont presque toujours fragiles.[3]

Des problèmes comparables caractérisent le financement, puisqu'il peut s'écouler de trois à quatre mois entre la décision du Conseil de sécurité et l'autorisation financière, d'où la difficulté de planifier et d'engager des ressources même à l'égard d'opérations de paix approuvées. Malgré les réformes et les améliorations importantes apportées à la gestion des opérations de maintien de la paix, il reste donc deux lacunes sérieuses dans les processus de gestion à l'ONU: l'écart entre l'autorisation et le déploiement, et celui entre le maintien de la paix traditionnel et l'imposition de la paix à grande échelle. Une capacité d'intervention rapide pourrait corriger ces lacunes, une des conditions étant cependant que les ressources financières soient disponibles afin que la réaction rapide ne soit pas entravée par d'autres procédures inefficaces à l'ONU.[4]

Il convient également de noter que certains observateurs acceptent la nécessité de réformes à l'ONU, mais estiment que si une force de réaction rapide est peut-être souhaitable, il est encore plus utile de se concentrer sur des réformes à court terme, marginales et peu coûteuses, qui ont plus de chances de succès. Celles-ci pourraient consister à renforcer le Département des opérations de maintien de la paix, à perfectionner le système logistique, à demander plus souvent à un pays donné de diriger une opération de paix avec un mandat de l'ONU au lieu que l'ONU l'exécute elle-même, et à mettre l'accent à plus long terme sur le rôle des organisations régionales. Donner priorité à de telles mesures, pourrait-on répliquer, équivaut à reconnaître qu'il y a peu de chances que les grandes puissances approuvent et financent une force de réaction rapide, et à s'appuyer plutôt sur des changements marginaux qui sont plus susceptibles de réussir à l'ONU.[5]

Le concept des groupes d'avant-garde

Malgré ces doutes, la nette impression qui persiste est qu'un changement qualitatif dans la capacité de l'ONU de lancer des opérations de paix est nécessaire. Même lors des opérations réussies, comme en Namibie et au Cambodge, les retards accusés dans le déploiement ont failli faire dérailler les accords intervenus au terme de longues négociations. Plus récemment, des déploiements insuffisants et tardifs ont contribué à des tragédies locales et exigé en fin de compte beaucoup plus de ressources de la part de la communauté internationale qu'il n'en aurait fallu pour envoyer une force de réaction rapide. L'expérience de l'ONU en Angola en 1993 a été un signe évident du problème. Devant la possibilité que les deux camps parviennent à une entente, l'ONU s'est vu demander d'envoyer une force tampon pour garantir la séparation des forces militaires. Le représentant spécial de l'ONU a cependant dû informer les parties que, pour des raisons pratiques, on ne pourrait pas disposer d'un contingent onusien avant six à neuf mois au moins.

Cette incapacité s'est révélée avec plus d'acuité encore au Rwanda. Après l'accord de paix d'Arusha du 4 août 1993, il a fallu trois mois avant que les premiers gardiens de la paix arrivent et lorsque le génocide à grande échelle a été déclenché en avril 1994 - plus de six mois après la décision du Conseil de sécurité de déployer une mission de maintien de la paix - la force de l'ONU était malheureusement trop peu nombreuse et insuffisamment équipée. Le général Roméo Dallaire, commandant de la force de l'ONU, témoigne de la situation difficile où se trouvait l'ONU:

> «La MINUAR aurait pu sauver la vie de centaines de milliers de personnes. À preuve, avec les 450 soldats placés sous mon commandement pour la durée de l'arrangement provisoire, nous avons sauvé et directement protégé 25 000 personnes et en avons déplacé des dizaines de milliers entre les lignes de combat. Une force de 5 000 personnes déployée rapidement aurait pu permettre de prévenir les massacres dans le sud et l'ouest du pays, qui n'ont pas commencé véritablement avant le début du mois de mai[6]...»
> [traduction]

Les événements au Rwanda offrent donc un argument éloquent en faveur de la mise sur pied d'une force d'avant-garde qui serait organisée et entraînée pour se déployer rapidement dès que le Conseil de sécurité aurait approuvé une opération de paix. Or, selon une hypothèse fondamentale de l'approche canadienne, la capacité de réaction rapide dépendrait d'arrangements appropriés de commandement et de contrôle à l'ONU, ce qui laisse supposer qu'il faudrait peut-être commencer par apporter des améliorations à la gestion des opérations de paix. Ces améliorations viseraient l'intervention rapide, mais auraient aussi pour effet de dynamiser immédiatement les opérations de l'ONU. Formulé en ces termes, le développement d'une capacité d'intervention rapide bénéficierait peut-être d'abord d'une évaluation de l'expérience de l'OTAN en la matière.

L'expérience de l'OTAN

LA CHAÎNE DE COMMANDEMENT[7]

Même s'il faut que les efforts faits par l'ONU pour améliorer le maintien de la paix soient compatibles avec la Charte et conformes à son expérience et à ses traditions, l'expérience de l'OTAN peut se révéler utile. L'OTAN est une alliance et reflète nécessairement une plus grande communauté d'intérêts et d'orientation qu'il n'est possible à l'ONU de le faire. Il n'empêche qu'à certains égards l'OTAN s'est heurtée à des problèmes similaires au moment d'organiser ses forces multinationales. Les États membres de l'Organisation ont pris un engagement face à leur sécurité collective, mais ils tiennent à conserver un droit de regard national sur les points cruciaux comme la politique de l'OTAN à l'égard de l'Europe de l'Est et l'engagement de troupes pour mettre en oeuvre les plans de l'Organisation. Le fonctionnement du Conseil de l'Atlantique Nord repose donc sur le consensus, mais l'incitation à réaliser le consensus est forte et les États membres hésitent généralement à être les seuls dissidents lors des décisions du Conseil.

À l'OTAN, les questions politiques sont tranchées au plus haut niveau, soit au Conseil de l'Atlantique Nord (CAN), l'équivalent en quelque sorte du Conseil de sécurité de l'ONU. Contrairement à l'ONU, toutefois, l'OTAN dispose ensuite d'un mécanisme qui sert d'interface entre la décision politique et l'exécution militaire; il s'agit du Conseil militaire, où siègent tous les membres et qui fonctionne aussi par consensus. À l'ONU, le Comité d'état-major ne représente pas tous les membres du Conseil de sécurité et est de toute façon inefficace. L'OTAN dispose à la fois d'un Secrétariat international et d'un État-major militaire international, composés principalement d'officiers prêtés par les États membres. Le Comité militaire peut confier une mission au Secrétariat et le directeur de l'État-major militaire doit faire des recommandations au Comité militaire avant qu'elles ne soient transmises au niveau politique.

Enfin, l'OTAN a des états-majors permanents sur le terrain - le Commandement suprême des Forces alliées en Europe (SACEUR) et le Commandement suprême allié de l'Atlantique (SACLANT) - dont les commandants se voient confier le soin de diriger des opérations avec les forces qui leur sont assignées par entente préalable avec les États membres. Même si les États membres ont à diverses reprises l'occasion de faire connaître leur point de vue, et peuvent se prévaloir du droit de ne pas engager leurs forces, ils acceptent que les principaux commandants de l'OTAN exercent un contrôle opérationnel sur les forces nationales sur le terrain.

Sans éliminer toute la complexité du processus, l'OTAN a tout de même réussi, contrairement à l'ONU, à régler certaines grandes difficultés. Premièrement, elle s'est dotée d'une chaîne de commandement qui relie la décision politique, l'organisation militaire et l'opération sur le terrain. Deuxièmement, elle a maintenu le principe de l'unité de commandement en ce sens qu'il y a une seule chaîne de commandement et aussi que le commandant sur le terrain exerce un contrôle opérationnel sur ses forces, qui relèvent de lui et non d'un système de contrôle opérationnel national. Troisièmement, l'OTAN a créé un état-major qui est capable de s'acquitter des fonctions normales de planification militaire tout en étant bien intégré dans une chaîne de commandement qui a été conçue de manière à répondre au Comité militaire et fait l'objet, par le biais du Comité, d'un droit de regard politique.

En comparaison, le Comité d'état-major envisagé à l'article 47 de la Charte des Nations unies est composé seulement de représentants permanents des cinq membres permanents du Conseil de sécurité, il est uniquement à la disposition de ce dernier, et il exclut par conséquent de la chaîne de commandement d'autres intervenants importants, notamment les membres non permanents du Conseil et le secrétaire général. Étant donné que le Comité d'état-major n'est pas un corps fonctionnel et a peu de chances de le devenir, ses limites institutionnelles ne sont pas un obstacle sérieux à des changements aux Nations unies. D'une manière plus générale, toutefois, le concept du Comité d'état-major dans la Charte indique que l'ONU n'a pas encore atteint l'unité de décision politique et de commandement et de contrôle que nécessitent les opération modernes de maintien de la paix. Cette unité exige un processus institutionnel apparenté à celui de l'OTAN, processus où le Conseil de sécurité serait l'autorité politique suprême pour les questions de paix et de sécurité internationales, où le secrétaire général et le secrétariat seraient un organe exécutif, et où les pays fournisseurs de contingents et les commandants sur le terrain seraient présents. De même, un Comité d'état-major bien constitué, ou un équivalent fonctionnel plus approprié, capable de fournir des conseils militaires au Conseil de sécurité et au secrétaire général, et peut-être capable de confier des missions à la composante militaire du Secrétariat, ou un état-major opérationnel constitué à part.

FORCES DE RÉACTION RAPIDE DE L'OTAN[8]

L'OTAN a établi des forces multinationales de réaction rapide dans les années 60 pour mener des opérations de contingence sur ses flancs nord et sud. Vers la fin des années 80, après que le climat de sécurité eut changé en Europe, l'Organisation s'est dotée de nouvelles forces navales et terrestres de réaction rapide à mesure que le nombre de forces permanentes stationnées dans le territoire de l'OTAN diminuait. La plus intéressante d'entre elles, du point de vue de l'ONU, est la Force mobile (terre) du Commandement allié en Europe. Cette force compte un effectif de 12 000 à 13 000 personnes et est capable d'en déployer de 6 000 à 8 000 à sept jours d'avis. Contrairement à l'ONU, cependant, dont les opérations de paix peuvent être autorisées dans n'importe quelle partie du monde, le déploiement de la force mobile allait se faire dans une des sept zones de contingence possibles. De plus, la Force mobile peut compter sur l'importante infrastructure de l'OTAN pour soutenir ses opérations.

Comme l'OTAN est une force multinationale, les pays qui y contribuent peuvent imposer des paramètres relativement à l'utilisation de leurs forces et ils le font effectivement. Ces paramètres, pour la plupart mineurs, font que la Force mobile a un système d'unités primaires et secondaires pour chaque zone de contingence, de sorte qu'il existe une unité connue de remplacement pour une unité primaire qui est retirée pour des raisons de politique nationale. Là aussi, il va sans dire qu'un tel système serait nettement plus compliqué à l'ONU, étant donné la multiplicité des circonstances politiques avec lesquelles l'ONU doit composer, mais l'expérience de la Force mobile indique qu'il est possible de tenir compte des paramètres limitant l'utilisation des troupes dans la mesure où ceux-ci sont bien définis à l'avance par les pays fournisseurs et ne sont pas exhaustifs au point de faire obstacle aux arrangements de contingence.

Par ailleurs, en sa qualité de force multinationale, la Force mobile a dû s'attaquer à divers problèmes d'interopérabilité qui sont inévitables lorsqu'un certain nombre de pays ayant des usages nationaux différents sont réunis sous un même commandement. La Force mobile en est venue à mettre au point des accords permanents concernant les opérations, la tactique et la logistique, à partir desquels elle a normalisé ses instructions permanentes à l'intention des unités nationales participantes. Les unités de la Force mobile s'entraînent ensemble tous les ans, échangent des détachements pour les familiariser aux autres procédures nationales, et cherchent à élaborer des normes communes pour les programmes d'entraînement nationaux. L'accent est beaucoup mis aussi sur la formation commune des commandants et des officiers: des programmes relativement peu coûteux, comme des cours de logistique et des périodes d'étude d'une semaine, contribuent énormément à accroître l'identité et la cohésion.

La langue et la normalisation sont aussi des facteurs clés dans les opérations multinationales. La langue de travail de la Force mobile est l'anglais, ce qui signifie que la majorité des participants doivent parler une langue étrangère avec les autres unités, tout en conservant leur langue nationale entre eux. Les commandants et officiers doivent donc apprendre à maîtriser l'anglais; d'autres programmes plus simples, comme des manuels de phrases clés et d'expressions militaires, peuvent être utiles à tous les niveaux de commandement. L'ONU profiterait certainement de cette expérience. Par contre, la normalisation de l'équipement est un défi de taille pour n'importe quelle force multinationale et le succès limité de l'OTAN à cet égard indique que l'ONU devrait favoriser au maximum l'interopérabilité au lieu de normaliser l'équipement dans une force internationale.

Enfin, la structure de l'état-major de la Force mobile peut être une source d'enseignements intéressants pour la mise sur pied d'une force d'intervention rapide à l'ONU. L'état-major est une petite unité composée de 45 permanents. Lorsque la force est déployée, cet effectif peut être doublé par l'ajout d'officiers des pays fournisseurs, déjà formés aux procédures de la Force mobile. L'effectif peut aussi être divisé en deux petits états-majors pour le cas où deux déploiements auraient lieu en même temps. L'état-major assure la continuité et la stabilité dans la planification et l'entraînement de contingence par l'acquisition progressive d'un bagage de connaissances et d'expérience dans lequel l'OTAN et les fournisseurs nationaux peuvent puiser au besoin.

La Force mobile dispose de procédures très perfectionnées pour le mouvement et le déploiement logistiques, notamment des arrangements sophistiqués de transport aérien et des normes rigoureuses pour le déploiement et le soutien de ses unités. Un grand nombre d'entre elles ne conviendraient pas à l'ONU, qui déciderait rarement ou peut-être jamais de déployer une force strictement onusienne dans un conflit très intense. L'expérience de la Force mobile peut toutefois influer à bien des égards sur la faisabilité et l'efficacité d'une capacité onusienne d'intervention rapide; citons à ce propos l'importance capitale d'un état-major de petite taille mais extensible, ou encore les éléments de l'entraînement et les procédures qui ont pour objet de surmonter les problèmes inhérents à la création d'une force multinationale à partir de contingents nationaux ayant des traditions, des procédures et des langues différentes.

LA NÉCESSITÉ D'UN ÉTAT-MAJOR POUR UNE FORCE D'AVANT-GARDE[9]

Même si l'ONU a apporté des améliorations importantes à la gestion de ses opérations de paix, on s'accorde généralement à reconnaître que des changements qualitatifs sont nécessaires si l'on veut mener des opérations de soutien de la paix là où les cessez-le-feu sont fragiles ou là où il est fort possible que les forces de maintien de la paix soient harcelées ou menacées, ou qu'on les empêche de mener à bien leur mandat.

C'est de toute évidence le cas lorsqu'on suppose qu'une force d'avant-garde devra se déployer rapidement et être prête à fonctionner dans un milieu à moitié ou nullement permissif. Plus particulièrement, une force d'avant-garde nécessiterait des réformes à l'ONU pour tenir compte des besoins suivants.

Premièrement, un état-major opérationnel devrait englober la planification et le contrôle des opérations de maintien de la paix qui feraient suite au mandat de la force d'avant-garde. Cela suppose une certaine réorganisation du Département des opérations de maintien de la paix. Deuxièmement, l'état-major opérationnel donnerait des avis au Conseil de sécurité et au secrétaire général, touchant notamment l'élaboration des instructions permanentes, l'uniformisation des règles d'engagement, et les trousses de formation pour les forces nationales. Troisièmement, l'état-major aurait pour principale responsabilité de s'acquitter des tâches requises pour gérer une force d'avant-garde, y compris la planification d'urgence, les concepts des opérations, ainsi que le commandement et le contrôle des forces d'avant-garde sur le terrain.

Le déploiement des forces d'avant-garde soulève bien des questions cruciales concernant l'entraînement, la préparation et l'intégration des unités nationales. Pour commencer, les pays fournisseurs de contingents qui maintiennent des forces à un niveau élevé de préparation engagent des dépenses considérables. Il est peu probable qu'ils promettent de telles unités à une force multinationale de l'ONU à moins d'être convaincus que les autres unités nationales suivent un entraînement rigoureux en tant que force intégrée. Cela va peut-être à l'encontre du besoin de l'ONU d'avoir des forces multinationales largement représentatives. Il est cependant possible de trouver des solutions originales. Par exemple, les établissements militaires les plus sophistiqués pourraient mettre à disposition des systèmes d'entraînement avancés; des commandants, des officiers d'état-major et de petites unités pourraient être échangés couramment comme à l'OTAN, et des trousses de formation pourraient être élaborées et utilisées aux fins de la formation nationale.

Il demeure toutefois qu'une force d'avant-garde bien entraînée et fin prête à intervenir nécessiterait une répartition complexe des responsabilités et des tâches à l'intérieur du système de l'ONU ainsi qu'entre l'ONU et les fournisseurs de troupes. Il faudrait que toutes les parties en cause entreprennent une négociation et une planification constructives, reconnaissent le fardeau financier supplémentaire des fournisseurs de contingents et proposent des arrangements financiers astucieux pour compenser ce fardeau.

Le long terme et la première étape

Se concentrer sur la création d'un état-major opérationnel permanent comme objectif de fond à court terme a en outre l'avantage de fournir un point de départ solide pour l'avenir[10]. Même si des plans plus ambitieux ont peut-être limité les perspectives à court terme, il vaut la peine de définir un processus global et cumulatif qui aboutirait, à long terme, à une force onusienne permanente d'urgence. Après la création d'un état-major opérationnel, la première étape de ce processus pourrait consister à créer une base onusienne destinée spécifiquement à l'intervention rapide, qui pourrait être élargie au moment voulu pour inclure un certain nombre de bases onusiennes régionales. Dès le début, une base spécifique pourrait se concentrer sur des tâches telles que des manuels de formation communs, l'élaboration d'instructions permanentes, et l'encouragement des exercices multinationaux.

La deuxième étape logique serait de créer une force permanente d'intervention rapide à partir des unités nationales affectées à la base de l'ONU et sous le commandement et le contrôle de l'ONU. Comme troisième étape, il serait peut-être possible de réconcilier les visions divergentes d'une force onusienne permanente et volontaire et d'une force multinationale en attente en intégrant des volontaires adéquatement entraînés aux unités nationales affectées à la base de l'ONU.

Bien sûr, le but d'un plan à long terme n'est pas de tracer une voie à suivre, mais plutôt de fixer un objectif qui pourra être atteint de bien des façons. L'objectif dans ce cas consiste à créer une force onusienne capable d'intervenir en temps opportun et qui a le vaste appui des États membres. Les visions divergentes de cette capacité devraient être encouragées. Dans l'intervalle, il est évident que, dans le climat politique et financier qui règne actuellement à l'ONU, il faudra persuader les principaux États membres qu'il est militairement et financièrement possible de franchir une première étape, modeste mais fort utile. Cette première étape semble être la création d'un état-major opérationnel, peut-être en dehors du siège de l'ONU situé à New York. Un état-major opérationnel, financé peut-être en partie par des contributions spéciales volontaires des États membres, aurait le mérite de profiter à toutes les opérations de paix tout en constituant un point de départ pour continuer l'édification de la capacité de réaction rapide de l'ONU.

Notes

1. Voir *Supplément à l'Agenda pour la paix*, S/1995/1, para.44.
2. Voir dans Urquhart, Document 3, le commentaire sur ce point.
3. Voir dans Jeffery, Document 9, le compte rendu de l'opération en Namibie.
4. Voir dans Boulden and Knight, Document 4, l'analyse plus poussée de ces questions.
5. Voir Roberts, Document 5.

Une Allocution
de l'Honorable André Ouellet, P.C., M.P.
Ministre des Affaires Étrangères
à la Conférence Internationale sur l'Amélioration
de la Capacité d'Intervention Rapide de l'ONU
Montebello, Québec
Le 8 avril 1995

M. Polanyi, distingués invités, mesdames et messieurs, chers collègues et amis,

Je tiens à vous remercier, au nom du gouvernement du Canada, d'avoir accepté avec autant d'empressement et d'enthousiasme notre invitation de participer à cette Conférence internationale sur la capacité d'intervention rapide de l'Organisation des Nations Unies [ONU].

Cette conférence, et votre participation, sont d'une importance cruciale pour le gouvernement. Par la tenue de cette conférence, nous voulons avoir la chance d'écouter vos idées et de recueillir vos avis quant à la meilleure façon de procéder sur cette question fondamentale qu'est la capacité d'intervention rapide des Nations Unies.

Le premier ministre, le très honorable Jean Chrétien, le ministre de la Défense nationale, l'honorable David Collenette, et moi-même attendons avec impatience le résultat de vos travaux. J'ai pris connaissance des ateliers que vous avez tenu depuis votre arrivée ici, et je suis sûr que les prochains seront tout aussi productifs.

L'idée d'une étude canadienne sur l'intervention rapide est née l'année dernière face à la terrible tragédie qui secouait le Rwanda. Je n'ai rien vu depuis qui puisse me faire douter de la nécessité d'une telle étude. Au contraire. Les antagonismes ethniques, religieux ou nationalistes sont à l'origine de nombreux conflits à travers le monde. Bien qu'il puisse s'agir de conflits internes, ils peuvent devenir, dans bien des cas, des menaces réelles à la paix et la sécurité internationales. Peu importe sa nature ou son envergure, nous ne pouvons pas ignorer la dimension humaine et humanitaire de la guerre.

Les situations au Rwanda, au Burundi et en Haïti nous indiquent qu'il faut considérer la diplomatie préventive, l'intervention rapide et la consolidation de la paix à l'intérieur d'une seule et même stratégie. Elles ne fonctionnent pas séparément.

Il est clair qu'il y a beaucoup à faire dans le domaine de la diplomatie préventive. C'était là une des recommandations que j'ai faites à l'Assemblée générale à New York, en septembre dernier. Nous devons nous attaquer aux causes fondamentales des conflits avant qu'ils n'éclatent. Avant de définir un mandat clair pour des forces de maintien de la paix, il faut bien comprendre la nature du conflit. L'ONU pourrait mieux s'acquitter de sa tâche si elle pouvait réagir avec plus de cohérence aux signes précurseurs en déployant avec efficacité les instruments à sa disposition.

Une capacité d'intervention rapide doit aussi exister dans le cadre d'une série de processus au sein de l'ONU et des organisations régionales. Comme je l'ai dit plus tôt, elle échouera si l'on s'en sert isolément. Il doit avant tout y avoir une capacité de rebâtir la société après le conflit si l'on veut que l'intervention rapide porte fruit. Il doit aussi y avoir des liens clairs entre ce qu'une capacité d'intervention rapide peut faire à court terme et ce que les autres parties du système onusien doivent faire lorsqu'elles prennent la relève d'un groupe d'intervention rapide ayant répondu à une crise.

Dès le début de cette étude, nous avons décidé de nous concentrer sur l'aspect opérationnel de la question. Nous ne nous sommes pas écartés, bien sûr, du cadre politique global du dossier. Nous sommes parfaitement conscients de l'importance cruciale de mobiliser la volonté politique afin de répondre aux crises. En fait, je crois que les participants ont déjà, depuis leur arrivée, tenté de cerner les grandes questions politiques auxquelles l'ONU doit faire face pour réagir aux crises, et je vous encourage à continuer ce travail.

Ceci étant dit, le Canada mène son étude en partant du principe que sa meilleure contribution au débat pour l'instant revêt un caractère opérationnel et qu'il s'agit avant tout de donner à l'ONU de nouveaux instruments à l'intérieur d'un plus vaste processus de gestion des conflits.

Depuis mon discours devant l'Assemblée générale en septembre dernier, beaucoup de travail a été accompli, au Canada et dans d'autres pays aussi, notamment aux Pays-Bas et au Danemark. Cette rencontre d'aujourd'hui est très importante en ce sens qu'elle est l'occasion de peaufiner les recommandations que je pourrai présenter à l'ONU à la prochaine Assemblée générale en septembre. Mon collègue, le ministre de la Défense nationale, vous a fait part hier de quelques idées qui ont cours actuellement. Permettez-moi d'en mentionner d'autres sur lesquelles nous nous penchons en ce moment.

Un des points qui nous tient à coeur est de fournir rapidement au Conseil de sécurité des conseils militaires. Nous insistons, et les autres aussi d'ailleurs, sur l'importance de consultations significatives avec les pays qui fournissent des troupes. Mais nous devons réfléchir à des mécanismes permettant à ces derniers de faire connaître leur point de vue au Conseil de sécurité, particulièrement du côté militaire, au fur et à mesure que la planification avance et que l'on négocie les mandats.

Au «niveau stratégique» du système de l'ONU, il nous faut aussi des structures pour gérer les crises de façon plus cohérente. Les opérations normales de maintien de la paix évoluent au même rythme que la planification, rythme qui peut être assez lent comme nous le savons. Or, en situation de crise, il faut une approche différente. À notre avis, la solution réside dans la planification par anticipation et la rapidité d'exécution. Le personnel doit recueillir continuellement de l'information et élaborer des plans d'urgence. Les pays qui ont la capacité de prêter leur aide dans ce domaine doivent être mis à contribution et assez vite. C'est la raison pour laquelle je suis séduit par l'idée de quartiers généraux opérationnels d'intervention rapide qui pourraient réunir tous ces attributs. J'ai appris qu'elle a fait l'objet de discussions ici et aimerais en savoir davantage.

Nous devons aussi travailler davantage avec les organisations régionales, aux trois paliers d'action que j'ai mentionnés, soit la diplomatie préventive, l'intervention rapide et la consolidation de la paix. À cette fin, le Royaume-Uni et la France ont lancé des initiatives en Afrique. L'Organisation des États africains [OEA] a intensifié ses efforts dans le domaine de la gestion des conflits. Le Canada est aussi d'avis qu'il est maintenant temps pour la Francophonie d'assumer un rôle dans la diplomatie préventive. La situation au Burundi est, bien entendu, le premier cas test qui vient à l'esprit. À cet égard, lors d'une réunion ministérielle extraordinaire de la Francophonie qui s'est tenue la semaine dernière à Paris, nous avons décidé d'envoyer une mission de bons offices dans ce pays. Dans notre recherche d'une plus étroite collaboration entre les organisations multilatérales et régionales, nous avons fait coïncider la présence de cette délégation ministérielle avec celle d'une délégation de l'Organisation de l'unité africaine. Les activités des deux missions seront complémentaires.

Nous devrions aussi évaluer les possibilités de créer des centres régionaux de formation au maintien de la paix, de constituer des stocks régionaux de matériel et probablement d'établir des quartiers généraux régionaux. Nous prévoyons de chercher avec les pays latino-américains un point de départ dans ces domaines en Amérique latine, probablement par le canal de l'OEA. De plus, le nouveau forum régional de l'ANASE [Association des nations de l'Asie du Sud-Est] pourrait être un interlocuteur valable pour la région de l'Asie-Pacifique.

La création d'une force permanente de l'ONU demeure un objectif primordial pour bon nombre d'entre nous. Mais, il ne s'agit pas d'une proposition à prendre ou à laisser. À mon avis, il est possible de développer le concept « du groupe d'avant-garde » du major général Dallaire. Les accords de confirmation jouent un rôle clé dans ce concept. Dans le système de l'ONU, il nous faut une meilleure évaluation du rôle que pourraient jouer ces accords dans l'amélioration de l'efficacité des Nations Unies. Je proposerai donc à brève échéance à l'ONU une réunion des pays qui ont signé des accords de confirmation ou qui sont sur le point de le faire. Nous pourrions discuter de la voie à suivre dans le cas des normes, de la formation, des exercices conjoints et du développement du concept du groupe d'avant-garde, et penser à une façon de lier ce concept à l'objectif plus lointain d'une force permanente d'intervention d'urgence de l'ONU.

Le besoin de cohérence dans la manière globale dont les Nations Unies traitent les situations de crise constitue un autre point essentiel. Pour répondre à ce besoin, il faut conclure, dans la perspective d'objectifs communs, des ententes viables entre les organisations humanitaires, les milieux non gouvernementaux et l'ONU. Il y a des innovations qui peuvent aider à unir les efforts, ce qui est fondamental pour l'efficacité de l'action. Nous avons besoin d'un élément civil fort dans toutes les missions de maintien de la paix, qui puisse assurer la coordination humanitaire. Pour cela, il faut faire appel aux gens. C'est pourquoi le Canada est disposé à fournir à l'ONU, pour des affectations à court terme, du personnel formé, ayant des compétences linguistiques et une connaissance de la région, si les missions ont besoin d'être renforcées sur le plan non militaire.

Pour l'avenir, nous devons penser à continuer sur notre lancée. La Conférence internationale sur la prorogation du Traité sur la non-prolifération des armes nucléaires, qui aura lieu à New York, la semaine prochaine, et la réunion des ministres des Affaires étrangères de l'ANASE, que je vais organiser à Vancouver le mois prochain, m'offrent toutes les deux une excellente occasion de poursuivre un dialogue constructif sur ces questions avec un certain nombre d'intervenants clés. Je me réjouis aussi de mener des discussions avec mes collègues de l'OTAN [Organisation du Traité de l'Atlantique Nord] à notre prochaine rencontre, à la fin de mai, et dans le contexte du sommet du G-7, en juin.

Il serait peut-être utile aussi de réunir les ministres ayant une optique commune, avant de déposer notre rapport à la 50ᵉ Assemblée générale, en septembre. Tous ces efforts ont pour but de garder les interventions au niveau politique.

Une capacité d'intervention rapide ne va pas résoudre tous les problèmes d'instabilité et de conflit. Ce n'est pas moins un outil important. À l'occasion du cinquantième anniversaire de l'Organisation des Nations Unies, nous devrions avoir des visées ambitieuses. Nous devons donner à l'ONU les outils dont elle a besoin pour bien faire son travail jusque dans le XXIᵉ siècle.

Je vous remercie d'être venus à Montebello cette fin de semaine.

Speech by the Honourable David Collenette, P.C., M.P. Minister of National Defence to the International Conference on UN Rapid Reaction Capability Montebello, Quebec April 7, 1995

Distinguished Guests, Ladies and Gentlemen:

Let me first take the opportunity to welcome this distinguished gathering to Montebello. I hope the beauty of the surrounding countryside has not distracted you too much from the immediate task at hand.

Cette conférence, vous le savez, s'inscrit dans le cadre d'une étude menée par le Canada. Il s'agit d'envisager diverses façons d'améliorer la capacité d'intervention rapide des Nations unies dans le but de renforcer la paix et la sécurité internationales. Pour mener cette recherche, le Canada peut faire appel à sa vaste expérience du maintien de la paix et d'autres interventions connexes. Nous ne prétendons cependant pas en avoir le monopole. En fait, à l'occasion de la réunion du Groupe consultatif international qui se tient aujourd'hui et de la conférence qui aura lieu demain, nous avons rassemblé des experts internationaux de très haut calibre. La collaboration internationale—je tiens à la souligner—sera indispensable si nous voulons mener à bien cette tâche importante.

Canada believes that this study is part of a crucial stage in the evolution of the United Nations. It is time for change and fresh ideas. We must be innovative in our efforts to enhance the UN's capability to react quickly and effectively to conflict and humanitarian crises in the short-, medium- and long-term. At the same time, our proposals must be practical. We live in an unstable and increasingly complex world, and we cannot afford to waste time on vague and unattainable goals.

This study could not come at a more opportune time. The UN, as we all know, is celebrating its 50th anniversary this year. Over that span of time, the world has been transformed.

À la fin de la Deuxième Guerre mondiale, les rédacteurs de la Charte des Nations unies envisageaient un avenir plein de promesses. Ils avaient mis en place un mécanisme qui semblait capable de promouvoir la paix et la stabilité internationales. Mais la guerre froide a vite mis fin à ce rêve. Au cours des quarante années suivantes, l'ONU a eu beau improviser de son mieux, elle a souvent eu les mains liées, alors qu'elle tentait désespérément de faire avancer la cause de la paix et de la sécurité internationales.

La guerre froide terminée, la communauté internationale a dû redéfinir comment l'ONU pourrait jouer un rôle utile dans le nouveau contexte international. Nombre d'observateurs ont supposé qu'elle assumerait facilement celui de protecteur du nouvel ordre mondial. Mais on avait sérieusement sous-estimer la difficulté de réaliser une telle transition. Cet organisme international est alors devenu une cible facile. En fait, certaines personnes le considèrent déjà comme périmé. Un reporter a même dit de l'ONU qu'elle présentait «l'attrait d'une épave abandonnée».

This kind of cynicism serves little purpose. Few would disagree that the UN has had its share of problems in adapting to the revolutionary changes of the last five or six years. However, when we remember that the UN was designed in the 1940s, and that in the intervening years it was severely restricted in its ability to function, it should come as no great suprise that the international body has at times faltered. The UN is now being asked to shift into high gear after being stuck in first for 40 years.

Aujourd'hui, le défi que doit relever la communauté internationale consiste à remodeler l'Organisation des Nations unies et à la mettre au diapason du monde tel qu'il se présente, à la veille du vingt-et-unième siècle. En fait, l'ONU a ainsi l'occasion de se renouveler et de renaître. À bien des égards, on nous offre donc l'occasion rêvée de tenir la promesse énoncée dans la Charte originale, cinquante ans après sa conception. L'ONU peut et doit jouer un rôle central dans le monde de l'après-guerre froide. Mais, pour atteindre ce but, il nous faut agir vite.

It is difficult to know where to begin. The UN, for example, faces a chronic funding crisis and is in dire need of bureaucratic overhaul. But perhaps nowhere is the need for reform more urgent than in the area of peace support operations.

Events in today's world unfold with startling speed. We have seen numerous examples in recent years of tensions, left boiling for years, suddenly exploding with terrible ferocity. The UN's attempt to respond has been slow and at times disorganized. As one UN official recently noted, before the international body can put out a fire, it must first build the fire station from scratch each time. The consequences have at times been catastrophic. Rwanda is only one example of an emerging trend.

The UN needs to react more quickly to nip crises in the bud and prevent them from escalating. Obviously, preventive action is far more effective than action after the fact to contain violent conflict. There is no reason, in the wake of the Cold War, why the UN cannot ultimately perform this role.

Malheureusement, à l'heure actuelle, au niveau politique, militaire, administratif et logistique, les Nations unies ne possèdent pas la capacité d'intervenir rapidement en cas de conflits, ni de porter secours sans délai aux populations, lorsque la sécurité est en jeu. La méthode actuelle, qui consiste à obtenir et à rassembler des unités fournies par les états membres, tout en s'efforçant d'établir un état-major opérationnel, va à l'encontre de la notion même d'intervention rapide. Il nous faut adopter de nouvelles façons de procéder. Et c'est cela même qui a motivé le Canada à mener cette étude sur la capacité d'intervention rapide des Nations unies dans les opérations de maintien de la paix.

Comme je l'ai déjà mentionné, en quelque sorte, il allait de soi que le Canada prenne l'initiative de mener une telle étude. Car nous avons toujours encouragé les efforts visant à faire des Nations unies une organisation énergique et efficace. En fait, nous estimons être parmi les plus ardents partisans et défenseurs de cette organisation. Nous détenons d'ailleurs le record de la participation aux missions de maintien de la paix et aux opérations connexes de l'ONU. Aux yeux de la communauté internationale, le Canada représente une longue tradition d'expérience et de compétence dans le domaine du maintien de la paix. Cette tradition est fondée sur le professionnalisme et la formation de notre personnel, ainsi que sur les ressources dont il dispose.

Canada has long called for other states to follow our lead and maintain forces on stand-by for possible UN duty. Indeed, as set out in our new defence policy, we are now working out the details of an enhanced Canadian contribution under the UN Stand-by Arrangements System, while at the same time seeing whether the stand-by system itself can be made more responsive. Within the limits of our resources, we are striving to respond as quickly as possible to UN requests for expertise, individual personnel and entire field units.

But we also believe that the time has come to explore other, more innovative possibilities. It is in our national interest, and the interest of the entire international community, to do everything we can to make the UN a more effective instrument in promoting international peace and security.

Our study is now well under way. This is our third conference, having already held workshops at the Peacekeeping Training Centre in Cornwallis as well as in Quebec City. It is still too early, however, to anticipate the study's recommendations. Furthermore, it would be unwise of me to make any specific commitments at this point, since I do not want to compromise the work of this conference or the outcome of later discussions.

Cela dit, je crois être en mesure de souligner plusieurs points clés déjà mis en évidence par notre analyse, et qui méritent un examen plus approfondi. Ils englobent tous les niveaux d'appui aux opérations de maintien de la paix, soit les niveaux politique, stratégique, opérationnel et tactique.

Ces points clés recouvrent certaines lacunes relevées au sein de l'ONU. Il s'agit notamment d'un dispositif d'alerte rapide. On obtiendrait ainsi, et à temps, une information précise grâce à laquelle on pourrait prendre plus rapidement, et de façon plus éclairée, des décisions cruciales. Il convient aussi d'améliorer la coopération politique et militaire entre le Conseil de sécurité et le Secrétaire général. Pour ce faire, il faut mettre en place un processus décisionnel harmonieux et des systèmes de commandement et de contrôle efficaces s'appliquant à des opérations mises en place rapidement. Enfin, il faut pouvoir disposer d'un état-major stratégique plus efficace, qui posséderait des capacités de transport et de logistique, ainsi que les ressources financières nécessaires pour soutenir les opérations.

The UN also needs to conduct more adequate planning at the operational or mission level. Today, planning at this level is *ad hoc* at best. We need to explore the possibility of setting up an operational headquarters capable of organizing, integrating and directing multinational forces. Canada is especially interested in this issue, and I have instructed my staff to examine in detail ways in which the UN might better perform this function. For example, we need to develop better stand-by arrangements in which the relationship between a permanent headquarters and the military and civilian operations that make up a rapid-reaction group is clearly defined.

There are two other areas of peace support operations in which Canada is taking an active interest. We have adopted the OSCE code of conduct which came into effect in January 1995. We would like to see *all* nations adopt this code, to help ensure that peace support operations are carried out with clearly demonstrable integrity and impartiality.

We also need to standardize training requirements to enhance the capabilities of multinational forces. Although the UN Secretariat's Department of Peacekeeping Operations has begun looking into this subject, more needs to be done. I have discussed some of the details with my colleague, the Minister of Foreign Affairs, and we will be announcing some possible approaches to this topic in the days and weeks ahead.

This conference offers an opportunity to probe a little deeper into these and other areas. As I mentioned at the outset of my remarks, Canada is eager to draw on the experience of international experts. I would like to mention the important role of the International Consultative Group in this regard.

This impressive cast of diplomats, government officials, soldiers and academics met today for the first time as a group. We are relying on you to give us critical guidance in achieving practical and achievable recommendations that address some of the UN's current shortcomings head on. And we hope that you will continue to help us down the road. After you leave Montebello later this weekend, mull over our discussions and please let us know what you think about the practicability of any of the ideas being considered.

Je tiens aussi à souligner que le Canada a l'intention de consulter le Secrétaire général de l'ONU, ainsi que des membres permanents du Conseil de sécurité et les états membres qui participent aux opérations de paix. Nous espérons que de nombreux pays approuveront nos recommandations d'ici septembre 1995, lorsque nous présenterons notre étude à la cinquantième Assemblée générale des Nations unies.

Le Canada sait que d'autres pays mènent actuellement des études sur les opérations de paix. Les Pays-Bas, par exemple, cherchent des moyens d'améliorer la capacité d'intervention rapide de l'ONU, alors que le Danemark étudie les particularités d'une «brigade d'intervention rapide». Quant à l'Académie internationale de la paix, elle vient tout juste d'entreprendre une étude. Nous sommes et nous continuerons d'être en rapport étroit avec ces groupes afin de coordonner nos efforts. Tout porte à croire que nos études seront complémentaires.

We welcome these studies and all other efforts to enhance the rapid-response capability of the UN. We must remember that the Charter pledges all UN members "to unite our strength to maintain international peace and security." In other words, we must all pull our weight if the UN is to become a more effective international body. The UN is not a sovereign state. It is an organization that reflects and acts on the will of its members. When we criticize the UN, we are in effect criticizing ourselves.

Toute période de transition est difficile à vivre. Il est vrai que l'ONU a récemment essuyé des échecs et des déboires. Mais nous ne devons pas oublier qu'elle a aussi enregistré des succès. On a pu en tirer d'importantes leçons, surtout dans le domaine des opérations de paix, et de nouveaux concepts sont en voie d'élaboration. Si nous voulons que l'ONU devienne un instrument plus efficace, nous devons persévérer dans cette voie. Et même si beaucoup a déjà été accompli, le moment de nous accorder un répit n'est pas encore venu.

Les Canadiens veulent contribuer à trouver des solutions, et cette étude forme un élément important de cette contribution. Nous souhaitons qu'elle aide à revitaliser l'ONU et à accroître sa capacité d'intervenir rapidement et efficacement en cas de crise.

I want to repeat some of the instructions I have given my staff as they proceed with this study. First of all, they are exploring in detail the possibility of establishing a standing operational headquarters to conduct operational planning for peace support missions. They are examining means of improving the existing stand-by arrangements system and of defining the potential relationship between an operational headquarters and military and civilian organizations that might, in an emergency, come under its direction; they are looking into ways of standardizing training; and finally, they are studying ways in which the OSCE code of conduct might be adapted to the needs of the United Nations.

Let me also repeat that Canada is committed to increasing its contribution under the UN Stand-by Arrangements System. We made this pledge in our 1994 Defence White Paper, and we are now studying in detail ways we can carry it out.

Louis St. Laurent, speaking as the Canadian Minister of Justice in the House of Commons in 1945, argued that the establishment of the United Nations had laid the foundation, in his words, "for a system of international cooperation in the interests of order, security and progress." He added that "to build a solid and enduring structure will be no easy task, but the risks of failure are beyond calculation." Fifty years later, these risks remain. We must continue to build on the foundation. To that end, I look forward to working with all of you in creating an effective and dynamic United Nations for the future.

Prospects for a UN
Rapid Response Capability

Brian Urquhart

The Historical Background

Since the end of the Cold War the United Nations has been repeatedly engaged in violent situations involving human security rather than the international peace and security which the organization was set up to maintain. The member states have scarcely begun to make the changes in the organization's arrangements for peacekeeping and other activities which this fundamental change in the UN's task demands. The result has been several severely flawed operations and a serious loss of credibility and public confidence.

Until 1990 the UN's two main forms of military activity were relatively rare large scale enforcement actions (Korea, Kuwait) delegated to a major military power or powers by the Security Council, and peacekeeping, which included both peacekeeping forces and military observer groups. Peacekeeping was specifically non-forceful and required the consent and cooperation of the parties in conflict, as well as the willingness of member states to provide military contingents. The scope and limitations both of enforcement action and of peacekeeping were well understood.

The mood and disorder of the post-Cold War world were not anticipated at the United Nations, nor was the enormous increase in the demand for emergency operations. Because, for the first time, its permanent members were basically in agreement, for a brief period it was fashionable to believe that the Security Council had "come into its own". This belief failed to take account of two major factors—the change in the nature of the problems the Council was dealing with, and the very limited capacity of the UN to engage in intensive emergency operations.

In the past four years, between traditional peacekeeping and enforcement operations, there has developed a large and uncertain range of problems—civil and ethnic wars, failed states, humanitarian and human rights disasters—for which neither peacekeeping nor enforcement, and certainly not a mixture of the two, is

Sir Brian Urquhart is Scholar-in-Residence at the Ford Foundation, and Former Under Secretary-General, United Nations.

appropriate. Rapid and effective deployment was always a key to the success of UN operations, and in earlier years it was usually possible to deploy peacekeeping operations in a matter of days. Rapid and effective action is particularly important in preventing the current generation of civil conflict/humanitarian problems from spiralling out of control.

Paradoxically, however, as these problems have proliferated, the delays in mounting an effective UN response have steadily increased, often amounting to several months or more. Not only are governments increasingly reluctant to commit national contingents to violent and uncertain situations which are of no concern to their national security, even when troops are eventually made available, their state of training and equipment and their suitability for the task at hand are often inadequate. Moreover, national contingents meet for the first time with commanders, staff and other contingents in the midst of the emergency and, quite naturally, take a considerable time to acclimatize themselves to each other and to the problems and conditions they are faced with.

Experience of recent UN operations shows that even a small, highly-trained group, with high morale and dedication, arriving at the scene of action immediately after a Security Council decision, would in most cases have far greater effect than a larger and less well-prepared force arriving weeks or even months later. The failure to come to grips with a situation before it gets completely out of hand usually necessitates a far larger, more expensive and less effective operation later on. Somalia, Haiti and Rwanda are only three examples of this syndrome. The lesson from these and other recent cases needs to be learned and acted on.

Options and Arguments

The solution most often proposed for the current problems of UN operations is the organization of stand-by forces by governments for UN service. It has been further suggested by the Secretary-General that governments should train and make available stand-by rapid deployment units—possibly composed of volunteers—for immediate UN service. These units would be specially trained and would train periodically with each other as well.

The response from governments to the idea of rapid deployment stand-by units has been, at best, non-committal, and at present the signs are not encouraging. Governments are increasingly reluctant to provide troops for violent civil conflicts in countries far removed from their regional and national interests, especially for immediate deployment at the outset of a crisis. There would therefore be no certainty that—even if based on volunteers—stand-by national rapid deployments units would actually be available when they were needed. (Not one of the 19 governments with peacekeeping stand-by agreements with the UN was willing to provide troops urgently for Rwanda in the summer of 1994.) Neither the tone nor the substance of the current debate on peacekeeping in Washington are encouraging in this respect, and this may well have a considerable impact on the attitude of other governments to participating in UN operations. Therefore, in the foreseeable future it seems likely that, even when a stand-by arrangement exists, governmental response cannot be taken for granted in all cases, and especially if immediate action is needed.

An alternative would be the establishment of a small standing, highly-trained volunteer rapid response group as part of the UN itself. This is not a new idea. Something of the kind was suggested during the first Arab-Israeli war in 1948 by the first Secretary-General, Trygve Lie. What is new is the increased need for a flexible rapid response capability, reliably and immediately available for UN service.

Governmental reaction to this idea, with a few exceptions, has been extremely cautious and predominantly negative. Not unnaturally, governments are reluctant to create something new which might diminish their control over, or participation in, UN operations. They fear that the ready availability of such a force might lead to indiscriminate and unwise use of it. They are also apprehensive about the cost. Many countries, already wary of UN interventionism, believe that such a standing group would only encourage the Security Council to intervene more frequently.

These arguments need to be addressed. The Security Council authorizes virtually all UN operations, and without a Security Council decision a peacekeeping, enforcement, or any other type of action cannot be launched, except in the now unlikely event that the Security Council is blocked by the veto and the decision is taken under the Uniting for Peace procedure by the General Assembly. If the rapid response group is deployed by the Security Council, where the permanent members' veto provides an additional safeguard, it is hard to see why ready availability in a specifically UN force should be anything but a great improvement over the present system, where UN involvement is decided upon but is often rendered ineffective by delays in implementation and by weaknesses in performance.

As to cost, the training and maintenance of a rapid response group, say, 10,000 strong, would indeed be considerable. However, having to put in much larger military operations when a situation has got out of hand is likely to be even more costly and certainly much less effective. The inability of the UN to respond quickly in a crisis is also devastating to public confidence in the organization, quite apart from the cost in human lives and disruption in the crisis area which often results from a delay in UN intervention.

The Nature of a Ready Response Group

To be effective and to repay the effort and expense involved, a UN ready response group must be of the highest quality both in training and morale, easily adaptable to different circumstances, and trained to deal expeditiously with unanticipated problems. The evolution of the right composition, training, rules of engagement and relation to other UN activities will require much time and thought, as well as experimentation, trial and, no doubt, some error. There is no sense in trying to force a new institution into old patterns.

A rapid response group will not take the place of traditional peacekeeping forces, and it should be relieved as soon as possible by normal peacekeeping arrangements, should that be necessary. It will certainly not take the place of enforcement actions under Chapter VII of the Charter. Its main purpose would be to allow the United Nations to make an immediate practical response to conflict or potential conflict at a point where quite a small effort might achieve disproportionately large results. The rapid response group would stay in an area of operations for the shortest practicable time—either until the acute phase of the crisis is over or until it is relieved by a regular peacekeeping operation.

The conventional approach to a rapid reaction force is to envisage a basically military establishment. The figure of 10,000 has been mentioned as a reasonable strength for such an establishment, which would in effect be a sort of rapid deployment brigade. A number of governments are studying the organization, training, and weapons and equipment requirements of such a rapid reaction force.

As stated above, the availability of national units for such a force will depend on governmental decisions. Judging by experience, a rapid reaction force based on national stand-by arrangements cannot be relied on to be available in all contingencies.

The alternative would be a volunteer rapid reaction group as part of the UN Secretariat. While a predominantly military group would be a great deal better than any arrangement currently available to the United Nations, the nature of present demands for action indicates that some new combination of skills and disciplines should be studied with a view to defining what mixture of military, police, civilian, technical and other personnel would be more likely to provide maximum flexibility and effectiveness.

The Role of a Rapid Reaction Group

The nature and training of such a group, whatever its composition or origin, will depend in large measure on the role it is to play and the tasks it is expected to perform. Here again much work needs to be done, but an outline of probable tasks might be as follows:

1. To provide a UN presence in the crisis area immediately after the Security Council has decided that the UN should be involved;

2. to prevent violence from escalating;

3. to assist, monitor and otherwise facilitate a ceasefire;

4. to provide the emergency framework (arrangements, protection, etc.) for the UN's efforts to resolve the conflict and to get negotiations going;

5. to secure a base, communications, airfield, etc. for a subsequent UN force;

6. to provide safe areas for persons and groups whose lives are threatened by the conflict;

7.   to secure essential humanitarian relief operations;

8.   to assess the situation and provide first-hand information for the Security Council, so that an informed decision can be made on the utility and feasibility of further UN involvement.

Obviously such a group must have first-rate logistical support, including airlift.

Rules of Engagement

Rules of engagement and for the use of force will be different from either peacekeeping operations or enforcement actions. The rapid reaction group will never initiate the use of force, but will be highly trained so that it can take care of its own security and mobility and have the ability and equipment to maintain its operations in the face of harassment and even opposition. It will in no circumstances have military objectives or be required to take sides in a civil war. It will be trained in peacekeeping and problem-solving techniques but will also have the training, military expertise and esprit de corps to pursue those tasks in difficult, and even violent, circumstances.

Development of a Rapid Reaction Group

Such a composite group could start relatively small and develop according to need and the results of experience. It might also prove more acceptable, and less intimidating, to governments than a purely military rapid reaction force, and may also be more acceptable to parties in conflict.

Some of the elements of a mixed-discipline rapid reaction group already exist in different parts of the UN system. The UN Field Service, which has existed since 1948, is a uniformed service trained in security and communications functions and with a long and distinguished record of operating effectively in confused and violent situations all over the world. The United Nations Secretariat routinely supplies political, legal, and administrative officers for field missions. Many of these officials have developed skill and ingenuity in dealing with unexpected, and sometimes dangerous, situations. The High Commissioner for Refugees and UNICEF have long and varied experience in dealing at very short notice with emergency humanitarian situations. Outside the UN system there is a wide range of non-governmental organizations with a long record of dealing with humanitarian emergencies. Many of these elements could be brought together as the initial core of an established rapid response group.

The present UN arrangements for rapid response are fragmentary, improvised and under-staffed. They lack the framework of security and convincing physical presence. They often do not, at the outset of a crisis, have the capacity for effective teamwork which only a standing group, training and developing together, can acquire. They do not have military and police elements, specially trained for the job, as part of a permanent establishment. They often lack the communications and other techniques which modern technology can supply. These are some of the shortcomings which need to be addressed in planning a rapid response group. Financing of virtually any UN operational activity is now a problem. A rapid response group, whatever its basis and nature, should be seen as a vital investment for the future, and one which by its nature, is designed to act at the point where action can be most effective, thus eliminating or reducing the necessity for later, larger, less effective, more costly action.

Conclusion

Whatever approach is followed, be it stand-by national rapid response contingents, or some built-in UN rapid response group, an intensive effort of study, organization and experimentation will be required. At the present early stage both basic approaches should be imaginatively explored, so that the best aspects of both can eventually become part of a more effective and reliable system of international response to violent emergencies.

Rapid Reaction: Filling the Gap

by Jane Boulden and W. Andy Knight

Introduction

This paper argues that there is a need for a rapid reaction capability at the United Nations. In making this argument the paper examines why the United Nations has difficulty responding rapidly at the moment, outlines the nature of the need for rapid reaction, and discusses how a rapid reaction capability might work.

The gap that would be filled by a rapid reaction capability is twofold: a gap in time, between the Security Council decision to take action and getting the mission on the ground; and a gap in function, between traditional peacekeeping situations and full-scale enforcement. There are, therefore, two basic roles for a rapid reaction capability:

1. Early Crisis Response - a capability to respond quickly to emerging crises and/ or conflicts before they escalate into crises of major proportions, (this includes peacekeeping missions which run into trouble). In many situations, major crises and expanding conflict can be prevented or minimized if action is taken quickly. In those situations the cost of waiting is simply too high, especially when the costs of acting early are relatively low.

2. Vanguard - a capability to deploy a United Nations mission as a precursor to a follow-on peace support operation, where speed of deployment is necessary to ensure the overall success of a mission. In many post-Cold War conflicts, an ability to respond quickly is fundamental to success. United Nations missions should be on the ground as soon as required, for example, to consolidate ceasefires and peace agreements as soon as they are achieved, thereby acting to ensure the maintenance of a stable situation and prevent its deterioration while waiting for the full follow-on peacekeeping mission.

These roles fall between "Chapter VI-and-a-Half" traditional peacekeeping and Chapter VII full-scale enforcement operations. They either do not require action under Chapter VII, or a decision has been made not to invoke Chapter VII

Ms. Jane Boulden, Queen's University, Kingston, and Professor W. Andy Knight, Bishop's University, were members of the Core Group established to analyze the various dimensions of a UN rapid response capability.

enforcement measures. They are not a substitute for "traditional" peacekeeping missions, where the standard criteria of consent and an existing ceasefire are solid enough to go through the traditional peacekeeping channels. These are cases which are too tenuous and require too rapid a response for regular peacekeeping to handle in the initial phase.

Why Is the United Nations Unable to React Quickly to Crises?

The structure and operation of the United Nations peace and security apparatus has its roots in the Charter but has been profoundly shaped by the practices of the Cold War and the peacekeeping years. These structures and practices are deeply embedded. Though the United Nations has become more proactive and involved in ongoing conflicts it must operate through the mechanisms that are the product of this legacy.

The United Nations is ill-suited to act quickly. The decision-making process involves a large number and variety of actors. The structure of the organization does not lend itself to quick action and is in large measure dependent on the generosity of Member States to ensure that adequate resources for action are available. The major factors that inhibit a fully effective, rapid UN response to emerging crises are as follows.

THE AD HOC NATURE OF UNITED NATIONS MILITARY OPERATIONS

Because of the way the United Nations system has evolved, a standard, in-place system for establishing and running United Nations military operations does not exist. Each time a new operation is authorized by the Security Council, the Secretariat begins anew, creating a plan, looking for contributions, and establishing procedures.

Planning and Implementation

In ideal situations the decision-making process and the implementation process should overlap so that preparation for implementation begins even while the decision-making process is ongoing. At the United Nations, preparation for implementation does not begin until the decision-making process is complete. This has implications for the time required to get United Nations forces on the ground. Since the process of soliciting troop contributions, getting budgetary approval and mission-specific planning only begins once a decision is made to act, the time between a mission's authorization and its arrival on the ground can be as long as six to eight months. In some cases, peacekeeping operations are able to overcome the problems posed by the time lag. However, in emerging crises or with some peace agreements, this length of time can mean the difference between stability and instability, and between small-scale friction among the parties and large-scale crises and conflicts. When deployed in such situations, peacekeeping troops find themselves in situations which have escalated well beyond their ability to control and for which they are ill-equipped in terms of resources, planning and mandate.

Availability of Troops

Efforts to get Member States to provide information on the types and numbers of troops they would be willing to make available to the United Nations date back to the Collective Measures Committee in the early 1950s. By and large these efforts have had little success. With the proliferation of UN peace support operations after the end of the Cold War, the absence of any kind of established mechanism for keeping track of what units might be available from Member States, and for soliciting troop contributions, became a pressing problem. In *An Agenda for Peace,* Secretary-General Boutros Boutros-Ghali noted that in response to a 1990 request for Member States to state "what military personnel they were in principle prepared to make available; few replied."[1]

In 1993, a task force of seven military officers began work in the Secretariat to develop a system of stand-by resources, based on an agreed response time, for use by the United Nations. During 1993 and 1994 the task force consulted with Member States and worked to develop a usable system. This includes designing a standard system of units, sub-units and elements representing standard building-blocks of operational capability. Of the Member States consulted, 90 were able to consider making a contribution to the stand-by system (about half of the current UN membership). Of those, as of February 1995, 36 had indicated an interest in establishing stand-by arrangements.

The stand-by arrangements process is continuing and represents an important step forward from the *ad hocery* of the past. However, it remains a limited step. The proliferation of UN operations has taxed the resources of traditional contributors. Some countries which would like to contribute are not able to provide properly trained or equipped troops. All of these factors mean that the process of soliciting troop contributions for a given mission can be lengthy and difficult. In some cases, sufficient troop contributions simply are not forthcoming. The solicitation of troop contributions, therefore, remains a critical contributing factor to the time lag between mission authorization and arrival of troops on the ground.

The Multinational Nature of the Operations

The *ad hoc* nature of peace support operations, in conjunction with their multinational composition, means that participating troops from different Member States work together as a unified force for the first time only after they arrive at the mission location. In some cases the lag in effectiveness that occurs as the mission becomes integrated has a minimal impact on overall effectiveness. In other cases, it takes a considerable time for the mission to gel and be effective in carrying out its mandate. In worst case scenarios the mission never properly comes together.

Depending on the length of time before the mission works together effectively, and on the context of the situation it faces, this can have minimal or disastrous effects. For the most part, peacekeeping missions have somehow found ways to make the operations work and have successfully carried out their mandates. However, as the United Nations becomes involved in situations which are more volatile and dangerous in nature, this problem becomes critical, as evidenced in operations such as UNPROFOR and UNAMIR. There is a limit to how quickly the United Nations can react and be effective when it is dealing with troops with no prior joint training and no equipment interoperability.

THE POLITICAL-MILITARY INTERFACE

One of the major gaps in the United Nations decision-making apparatus is that between the political and strategic decision-making mechanisms and the operational and tactical levels. When the Security Council passes a resolution giving a mandate to a peace support operation, the mission commander must take the Security Council resolution as his/her guide. No body or mechanism translates the mandate into operational and tactical goals. Security Council resolutions are the result of extensive negotiations among Council members and rarely do more than outline the objectives of the mission. In particularly difficult or contentious missions this outline can be deliberately vague, the product of considerable compromise in order to get approval by Council members. The problem is compounded by the fact that the Council, as a unit, receives little military advice in forming the mandate. The United Nations experience in the former Yugoslavia demonstrates the types of mission-threatening and life-threatening problems that may emerge as the result of ambiguous mandates or mandates which are extremely difficult to implement militarily.

The Military Staff Committee was intended to translate Security Council mandates into military missions, and act as a liaison between the operation on the ground and the Security Council. Although the MSC continues to meet, there is considerable resistance, from a variety of sources, to reactivating it. In its effective absence, no *ad hoc* or formal mechanism has developed. The absence of any such mechanism affects mission effectiveness and speed of deployment. Again, as the United Nations becomes involved in more dangerous and volatile situations, this gap in the decision-making apparatus becomes more and more critical.

FINANCING UNITED NATIONS OPERATIONS

It would be difficult to underemphasize the degree to which poor, inefficient and constraining financial procedures and practices contribute to the inability of the United Nations to react rapidly or even in a timely fashion. Financial procedures are matched only by the time taken to solicit troop contributions as a problem in launching effectively manned and equipped missions in a timely manner. While some improvements have been made in the budgetary approval process, it remains time consuming and frustrating.

At present, once the Security Council agrees on the mandate for a mission, the Secretariat draws up a proposed budget for the mission. This budget goes to the Advisory Committee on Administrative and Budgetary Questions (ACABQ), the Fifth Committee and the General Assembly for discussion and approval. The General Assembly thus holds the purse strings for UN operations and this mechanism effectively gives them a say in the authorization of these operations.

In UN peacekeeping or any UN activity, the UN cannot sign any agreements that incur financial costs if the money is not held by the UN. In other words, if the UN does not have the cash then peacekeeping, rapid or otherwise, just cannot occur. At any time the [Secretary-General] has standing authority to spend $3 million annually for "peace and security", ...After the Security Council has voted to establish a new mission and pending General Assembly approval and actual funds, the [Secretary-General] has financial authority to spend up to $10 million annually per mission as part of his general "unforeseen and extraordinary expenses" authority. Slightly later in the process, after ACABQ has approved the budget but pending [Fifth] Committee and [General Assembly] approval, the Secretary-General can seek ACABQ authority to commit up to $50 million to start up a mission. Invariably both the $10 million and the $50 million are far from sufficient, and anyway ... this is spending authority and not the cash itself.[2]

The tendency in recent years has been for members of the General Assembly to "micro-manage" budgets, and in so doing contribute to delays in funding approval. In addition, the Fifth Committee works on the basis of consensus so one Member State is able to hold up budgetary approval if they disagree with the budget or the mission itself.

The time between Security Council authorization of a new mission and approval of the budget may be as long as three to four months. It is only at that point that the Secretary-General is able to send a letter of assessment to Member States. This means that 30 per cent of the funds will be received within six months and 60 per cent after nine months. In other words, as long as a year after Security Council authorization of the mission only 60 per cent of the assessed contributions will be received in cash (assuming all states pay the assessment on time).

The failure of Member States to pay their assessed contributions to the United Nations is increasingly putting a strain on general operations. As of March 1995, $2.9 billion was owed to the United Nations, of which $1.8 billion was related to the peacekeeping budget. The United States is the largest contributor to the budget, with one-third of the total. Recently, the United States Congress has indicated that it will not pay this much to the UN budget. This will further strain an already tenuous financial situation. Further pressure is likely to come from states that believe that too much of the UN's budget is being spent on political and military missions at the cost of economic and social measures. This suggests that it will become more difficult to get General Assembly approval of spending on peace support missions.

Why Should the United Nations Respond Rapidly?

THE HUMANITARIAN IMPERATIVE

The Security Council has increasingly given humanitarian mandates to United Nations operations. This is especially the case when the Council finds itself unable to agree on stronger action with respect to a conflict but feels the need to ensure that humanitarian aid reaches people affected by the ongoing conflict. This is a role that tends to receive strong public support. In addition, many intra-state conflicts, by their nature, carry with them a strong requirement for humanitarian assistance.

In spite of the well publicized difficulties with the humanitarian aspects of missions, it is in this area that the pressure for rapidity is strongest. Reactions to the situations in Rwanda and Somalia suggest that the graphic depictions of mass suffering and death lead to pressure for action, regardless of a desire or capability to deal with the political crisis. Similarly, rather than strengthen the mandate of UNPROFOR, the United Nations, drawing on key Member States, significantly increased the international presence in the former Yugoslavia with the goal of protecting UNPROFOR troops in order to ensure that they could continue to deliver humanitarian aid. The nature of the current international environment suggests that future crises and conflicts will continue to have a strong humanitarian element.

INTERNATIONAL PEACE AND SECURITY BROADLY DEFINED

With the end of the Cold War the UN Security Council has authorized more operations than ever before and has done so on the basis of a definition of international peace and security that extends well beyond the limits previously considered the norm. Failed states, humanitarian emergencies, humanitarian assistance in areas of conflict, and civil wars have all been classed as matters of international peace and security. Specific examples of this trend include the mandate to assist in the delivery of humanitarian aid in the former Yugoslavia, the use of the Unified Task Force to establish a secure environment and ensure the delivery of aid in Somalia, and the mission in Haiti to oversee and enforce the transition to democracy.

The willingness to get involved in intra-state conflict, bringing an end to the legal fiction that the United Nations should only be concerned with inter-state conflict, is as much a response to the types of conflicts that have arisen after the Cold War as it is a reflection of a new activism in the Security Council. Threats to international peace and security since the late 1980s have primarily been from within rather than between states. In his *Supplement to An Agenda for Peace,* the Secretary-General noted that of the peacekeeping operations in existence in 1988, only 20 per cent, or one in five, related to intra-state conflict. Of the operations authorized since then, 62 per cent have related to intra-state conflicts and of the 11 operations established since January 1992, 82 per cent relate to intra-state conflict.[3]

Intra-state conflicts, especially those of the type that have emerged after the Cold War, have extremely complex and deep-rooted origins and generate multi-faceted conflict situations. This means that United Nations operations must deal with a variety of issue areas and face situations and actors which are not as clearly defined as is the case in inter-state conflicts. The Secretary-General describes the context as follows:

> The new breed of intra-state conflicts have certain characteristics that present United Nations peace-keepers with challenges not encountered since the Congo operation of the early 1960s. They are usually fought not only by regular armies but also by militias and armed civilians with little discipline and with ill-defined chains of command. They are often guerrilla wars without clear front lines. Civilians are the main victims and often the main targets. Humanitarian emergencies are commonplace ...[4]

These types of conflicts and situations do not lend themselves to long lead times in terms of a UN response. A response to a crisis of the order of Goma or Somalia must be immediate if it is to be effective: a lead time of upwards of six months in getting troops to Angola to verify a ceasefire is simply not going to prevent a return to fighting; a six-month wait in getting UN troops and personnel to Somalia or Rwanda is the difference between a situation of imminent conflict and crisis and one of ongoing conflict and crisis.

THE VALUE OF ACTING EARLY AND THE COSTS OF ACTING LATE

Certain recent UN operations have demonstrated that the costs of intervening in a crisis, in terms of lives lost and endangered, and resources required, escalate dramatically the longer intervention is postponed.

Once a crisis emerges, it initiates a chain reaction that becomes very difficult to control. For example, an initial conflict may spark a refugee problem. Depending on the environmental situation the combination of the conflict and the refugee problem may contribute to a famine (as in Somalia) or to a health crisis (as in Goma). These new problems feed back into the conflict, deepening the enmity and determination to fight. This new level of conflict then spawns or exacerbates other problems.

De-escalating the crisis is not simply a matter of reversing the chain reaction. Each level of escalation in the situation represents an exponential increase in the scope of the problems and requires a commensurate escalation in the proposed intervention. The earlier intervention occurs in the cycle, the easier it is to affect the chain reaction. The longer intervention waits, the more resources and determination will be required to deal with the situation.

Crisis Response During Peacekeeping—The Case of Rwanda

The events in Rwanda in 1994 have been the basis for many of the recent calls for a rapid reaction capability. The international community's reaction to the unfolding crisis in Rwanda demonstrates (1) how delays in getting peacekeeping missions going on the ground can cripple an operation, and (2) how the absence of an ability to sustain and reinforce an ongoing operation translates into ineffectiveness in the face of an emerging crisis, to the point where the UN mission becomes part of the crisis rather than the spearhead of a response.

The Arusha peace agreement, the basis for the UNAMIR operation, was signed on 4 August 1993. Two months later, on 5 October 1993, the Security Council passed Resolution 872, authorizing a peacekeeping mission for Rwanda. The Security Council made clear that it wanted the operation conducted with a minimum of expense. Of the $200 million estimated cost of the operation, only a fraction of the funding was ever received. As it was, the operation began on the basis of funds borrowed from the budget for the UN operation in Somalia.

The initial UNAMIR team included Canadian General Roméo Dallaire and three supporting officers. They arrived in Kigali on 21 October. The next day, a coup d'etat occurred in Burundi prompting a crisis that generated 300,000 refugees, 600,000 displaced persons and one million in need of food. It also brought about the stagnation of the political process and generated activities within Rwanda that were warnings and indications of imminent conflict. Already the situation had moved far beyond the context of the Security Council resolution.

The plan for the operation, developed during September 1993, called for 4,500 troops. The total number of troops involved in UNAMIR never exceeded 2,600.

Table 3
Arrivals of Contingents for UNAMIR

Country	Sep 93	Oct 93	Nov 93	Dec 93	Jan 94	Feb 94
Bangladesh			485	369		
Ghana					800	
Belgium			403			
Tunisia	60					

Of the troops that were provided, only the Belgians were fully equipped. They were withdrawn part way through the operation. The other contingents were either partially equipped or came with no equipment at all. The time needed to obtain financial approval for the equipment required to make the troops militarily useful was estimated at nine to 12 months. Many states were willing to provide troops for UNAMIR but most of them were unable to provide any equipment. Only partially manned and equipped, the UNAMIR team continued to carry out the mandate of the mission to the extent possible in the face of ever deteriorating conditions. By April 1994, the situation had deteriorated into full-scale, ethnically-based civil war.

At this point the decision was made to withdraw most of the peacekeeping forces from their locations. The troops were in the middle of a war zone with little equipment, virtually no ammunition, and only a few days supply of fuel, water and rations.

In June 1994, the United Nations Security Council approved a new mandate for the Rwandan operation. The estimated number of troops required to carry out the mandate was 5,500. By August 1994, 2,500 troops had been provided.

Pre- and Post-Crisis Financial Commitments

The lack of funding and material support for UNAMIR stands in sharp contrast to the money spent by the international community in aid and human resource support once the crisis attracted the attention of the international media.

In a single donors' pledging conference at Geneva on 2 August 1994, $137 million was pledged by Member States. By 30 November 1994, responding to the escalation of the crisis, Member States had contributed $483.5 million.[5] The United States, (which had previously refused to provide 50 APCs for UNAMIR, and eventually provided them on a rental basis for a charge to UNAMIR of $10 million) unilaterally provided $350 million in aid in the first six weeks of the Goma catastrophe.

Political and Military Commitment

UNAMIR clearly suffered from being underfunded, understaffed and under-supported in material and political terms. These deficiencies meant that UNAMIR was unable to deal with the escalation of events and unable to implement its mandate sucessfully. These problems undermined the mission's credibility with local Rwandans, making it even more difficult to deal with unfolding events. The UNAMIR Commander claims that a UN force of 5,500 promptly deployed could have prevented many of the massacres that took place several weeks after the outbreak of the civil war. The number of troops required sounds remarkably limited when viewed in the light of the magnitude of the subsequent Rwandan crisis. While such measures may not have avoided the crisis or prevented the conflict, they would certainly have meant a crisis of considerably lower proportions than that of the summer of 1994. This is the critical lesson of the Rwandan experience—modest measures used in a timely fashion may mean the difference between a stable situation and one which spirals out of control.

Two different arguments for a rapid reaction capability are drawn from this experience. First, had the United Nations been able to launch even a preliminary mission at the time of the signing of the peace accord, a number of the factors that contributed to the Rwandan crisis may have been avoided. Second, had a rapid reaction capability been available at the United Nations, this could have been used to support the UNAMIR operation as the crisis began to unfold in April 1994, possibly deterring a further deterioration of the situation.

Angola

The situation in Angola provides a different example of the case for acting early and quickly. After the collapse of the election process and the renewal of fighting there, negotiations began in Abidjan in April and May 1993, in an effort to get the peace process back on track. The two sides reached agreement on a blueprint for a new peace process, but they would only sign on to the plan if a ceasefire could be ensured. The parties to the conflict, still deeply distrustful of each other, requested a UN military presence in Angola to verify and support the ceasefire. A UN presence would provide a buffer, a way of separating the parties and providing them with a mechanism through which events and accusations, which might undermine a ceasefire, could be filtered.

The Security Council was willing to consider authorizing a new UN operation in Angola but only after a ceasefire was in place. Margaret Anstee, the Secretary-General's Special Representative in Angola, then faced what she termed a "chicken and egg" situation.

> The Security Council required agreement at Abidjan before "Blue Helmets" could be considered. UNITA wanted an assurance of at least an immediate, symbolic presence of Blue Helmets before they would agree to the terms for a ceasefire set out in the Abidjan Protocol. The reality was even worse than that. I was told that I must warn both sides that, even if they agreed to a ceasefire, no UN troops could, for practical reasons, be made available until six to nine months later. Not surprisingly, I had two nightmares in Abidjan: one was that I would fail, which was what happened; the other was that I would succeed because then I could not see how a ceasefire would be monitored and supported.[6]

While there are no guarantees of success, especially in a situation where such deep mistrust exists between the parties to a conflict, had a rapid reaction capability been available, it could have been used to support a ceasefire in Angola thus facilitating a consolidation of the peace process and paving the way for the future use of peacekeeping troops as part of that process. It could also be argued that a rapid reaction capability could have been used when UNITA refused to accept the election results, to insert a UN presence quickly in an effort to prevent a return to fighting, and to uphold the election results or at least facilitate ongoing negotiations about what should happen next.

How Might Rapid Reaction Work?

In general, the types of situations which would benefit from a rapid reaction response are characterized by a high level of uncertainty, and a state of crisis or imminent conflict. Events are moving quickly, or threaten to move quickly, without external intervention. These situations are likely to have a substantial humanitarian component though this may not always be the case. Humanitarian or environmental emergencies, without any accompanying conflict, may also warrant a rapid reaction response.

In most instances of rapid reaction, the consent of the parties will have been obtained, and a request for a UN presence will have been made. In some instances, however, not all parties may have given consent, such as in the case of a failed state where the government has collapsed and no group has a legitimate claim to govern, as occurred in Somalia.

This raises questions about the degree of armament and rules of engagement for a rapid reaction operation. This will vary depending on the situation. In some instances, the simple fact of a UN presence is enough to achieve the initial objectives of the mission and, consequently, a relatively small-scale, modestly armed operation will be sufficient to the task. In other cases, the tasks given to the mission may include a higher likelihood of the use of force, and the mandate and armament level will reflect that. The key is that, with a rapid reaction capability, the United Nations would have flexibility in determining the level of its response.

Rapid reaction tasks might include: assisting, monitoring and facilitating cease-fires and negotiations; securing communications, and/or airfields for humanitarian or other follow-on operations; establishing safe areas for threatened groups; and assessing the situation and gathering information to be provided to the Security Council.

Since the idea behind rapid reaction is to respond before crises escalate or before peace agreements disintegrate, a highly successful rapid reaction response might have little to do beyond monitoring and consolidating the situation on the ground, thereby deterring and/or preventing further destabilizing developments while waiting for follow-on forces and humanitarian support if needed.

Specific examples of situations in which a rapid reaction capability might be used include:

- as a vanguard force for follow-on peacekeeping operations;
- to counter/deter an imminent border incursion;
- to consolidate and enforce peace agreements, immediately on their signing;
- to separate warring or potentially warring factions;
- to deal with large-scale refugee flows in situations of potential or ongoing conflict;

- to distribute aid and other forms of relief;
- to help in failed state situations where there is an absence of any form of government control;
- to shore up peacekeeping operations in trouble; and
- to re-establish ceasefires or to deal with violations of peace agreements.

A rapid reaction capability, either in its vanguard or crisis response form, would be deployed on the decision of the Security Council. Once deployed, the rapid reaction capability operation would be run by the Secretariat.

Reflecting the multi-dimensional nature of United Nations peace operations, the UN's rapid response capability would also be multi-dimensional. It is for this reason that the focus is on developing a rapid reaction *capability* as opposed to a rapid reaction *force*. A fully developed rapid reaction capability would give the United Nations the ability to draw on military and other resources in the mix required to suit the situation. Humanitarian, political and other resources included in the initial phase of the response can act as a precursor to further resources to follow later and as liaison with organizations and agencies which may already be in place.

However, the crises and situations likely to be faced by a rapid response mission, by virtue of their uncertain and crisis nature, are likely to require a response that is primarily military. The more the situation is driven by conflict, the more an emphasis on military components will be necessary in the initial response phase. Somalia, Rwanda and Haiti provide examples of this. In each case, the humanitarian and political crises were of such a scale, and so completely intertwined with the political conflict, that a military response was the only effective way of asserting a UN presence, protecting and ensuring the delivery of humanitarian aid and providing stability.

At the other end of the spectrum, where conflict plays little or no role in creating or complicating a humanitarian or other international crisis, the military role may be considerably smaller, used primarily for the purpose of facilitating rapidity and effectiveness in the operation, rather than for dealing with a military situation on the ground.

A rapid reaction capability refers, as well, to the ability to ensure rapidity in implementation procedures. Optimum response to crisis situations requires an overlap of the decision-making and implementation processes. This means that, for maximum rapidity, elements of the response mission are warned and begin preparations for action while the decision-making process is ongoing, rather than waiting for a Security Council decision before preparatory action is taken. In addition, as many arrangements as possible are made in advance. This would include, for example, soliciting troop and equipment contributions so that time is not wasted in that process.

To achieve this, the United Nations could develop and gain acceptance of a new set of crisis procedures which would be used when a rapid response crisis was declared. The ability to move to the use of crisis procedures would allow regular procedures to be speeded up or alternative procedures to be used. In essence, an extraordinary situation is said to exist and extraordinary procedures are called into play. This would allow more of an overlap in decision-making and implementation procedures than occurs on a regular basis and would provide a way of overcoming procedures which usually take a considerable amount of time.

Conclusion

The overall purpose in developing a rapid reaction capability is to decrease response time and increase efficiency when it is most critical: in responding to a crisis or establishing the conditions for further United Nations action. These broad outlines of a rapid reaction capability describe the gap that is to be filled and the basic principles guiding the proposals for specific measures.

A final argument for a rapid reaction capability is found in the United Nations Charter. In large part, the impetus for a rapid reaction capability at the United Nations comes from the greater recognition given by Member States to the original intentions of the Charter and their accompanying willingness to act to uphold those principles. The development of a rapid reaction capability is simply the next step in accepting and acting on the responsibilities contained in the Charter. The argument for the need for a rapid reaction capability has as its base Article 1 of the Charter which states:

> The Purposes of the United Nations are:
>
> 1. To maintain international peace and security, and to that end: to take effective collective measures for the *prevention and removal* of threats to the peace, and for the suppression of acts of aggression or other breaches of the peace, and to bring about by peaceful means, and in conformity with the principles of justice and international law, *adjustment or settlement of international disputes or situations which might lead to a breach of the peace...*

Notes

1. *Secretary-General Boutros Boutros-Ghali, Agenda for Peace*, paragraph 51, United Nations, June 1992.

2. Paul LaRose-Edwards, *United Nations Internal Impediments to Peacekeeping Rapid Reaction*, Department of Foreign Affairs and International Trade, 2 April 1995, pp. 18-19.

3. A/50/60, paragraph 11.

4. *Ibid.*, paragraph 12.

5. *The United Nations and the Situation in Rwanda*, Reference Paper, United Nations, Department of Public Information, April 1995.

6. Margaret J. Anstee, "Angola: the Forgotten Tragedy, A Test Case for U.N. Peacekeeping," *International Relations*, vol. XI, no. 6, December 1993, p. 502.

7. Article 1(1), Charter of the United Nations, emphasis added.

Proposals for UN Standing Forces: History, Tasks and Obstacles

Adam Roberts

From the time of the formation of the UN, the question of standing forces and certain variations thereof has been intermittently discussed. It has arisen in response to very different problems, and the proposed UN forces have been envisaged as having very different forms and functions. This paper reviews past proposals for standing forces; outlines some proposals made in the 1990s, including those for an individually recruited UN brigade, and for a UN rapid reaction capability drawing on national contingents; summarizes the 1995 Dutch and Canadian initiatives; seeks to identify the different practical tasks that UN standing or rapid reaction forces have been envisaged as serving; considers the implications of the 1994 Rwanda crisis, which reinforced calls for standing forces; lists some of the problems regarding the creation and operation of such forces; and offers some conclusions about how the question of improving the UN's response capability might be approached.

As this paper indicates, there are many grounds for scepticism about proposals for UN standing forces. However, the seriousness of the problems which such forces are intended to address is real. By almost universal consent, some improvement in the international community's rapid response capability is needed. The nub of the issue is: What is realistically achievable in a world where the demand for UN rapid response forces is likely to be huge, the interest of states in responding to that demand is not unlimited, and the capacity of the UN to manage crises effectively is often questioned?

Consideration of Standing Forces in the Cold War Years

In the UN Charter, Articles 43 to 48, which are part of Chapter VII, envisaged forces being at the disposal of the Security Council exclusively in the context of enforcement operations. These provisions have never been implemented. From the earliest years the Security Council has not in fact had armed forces at its disposal in the manner apparently envisaged in the UN Charter.

Professor Adam Roberts is Montague Burton Professor of International Relations at Oxford University, and a Fellow of Balliol College.

In 1946-47, the UN's Military Staff Committee was set up and asked to examine the question of contributions of armed forces to the Security Council. It duly published a report which reflected significant disagreements among the Permanent Five about the size and composition of national contributions. The whole enterprise was abandoned.[1] This was part of a broader failure to implement the provisions of Chapter VII specifying an ambitious scheme for collective security.[2] In the first 50 years of the UN, agreements under Article 43 of the Charter, necessary to place national forces at the general disposal of the UN, have never been concluded.

More modest ideas for standing forces were put forward at various times. In most cases this was not for enforcement operations as envisaged in the Charter, but for different purposes. Thus in 1948, Secretary-General Trygve Lie proposed the creation of a small guard force

> which could be recruited by the Secretary-General and placed at the disposal of the Security Council and the General Assembly. Such a force would not be used as a substitute for the forces contemplated in Article 42 and 43. It would not be a striking force, but purely a guard force. It could be used for guard duty with United Nations missions, in the conduct of plebiscites under the supervision of the United Nations, and in the administration of truce terms. It might also be called upon by the Security Council under Article 40 of the Charter, which provides for provisional measures to prevent the aggravation of a situation threatening the peace.[3]

This proposal was not acted upon. Peacekeeping forces developed, especially from 1956 onwards, along different lines: they were composed of national contingents which were made available for UN service on an *ad hoc* basis. From the earliest years this system proved, sometimes but by no means always, to be slow and cumbersome. As a result, proposals for a "UN force" were extensively discussed at the UN in the late 1950s, including in the General Assembly. They became coupled with the idea of stand-by arrangements as a means of making a quick response possible. John Foster Dulles' letter to Dag Hammarskjöld of 18 November 1958 is an early example of the enthusiasm of states for stand-by forces: "As you know, the United States ... has a strong interest in the early establishment of standby arrangements for a United Nations Peace Force." He went on to mention the need for consultations

> with a view to determining the terms and circumstances under which Member States would make available personnel or materiel for UN field missions. I understand further that it is your hope that such consultations will lead to indications by governments on the provisions they might wish to make within their own armed forces so that it would be possible to place units in UN service on short notice. Moreover, I am informed that you intend to maintain a group

within the Secretariat to carry forward advance planning and to carry on consultations with governments.

I hope that you will be able in the near future to make significant progress in this direction. I want to assure you that the United States is prepared to assist you in every feasible manner in strengthening the capacity of the United Nations to discharge its responsibility for the maintenance of international peace and security, a task to which you have already contributed so much.[4]

In the three subsequent decades, virtually all developments in the UN were in the direction of relying on, and periodically attempting to improve, stand-by arrangements for UN peacekeeping forces. The UN Special Committee of Peacekeeping frequently discussed the issue with a view to improving the UN's rapid reaction capability.

The Proposals in *An Agenda for Peace*

In *An Agenda for Peace,* published in June 1992, Secretary-General Boutros Boutros-Ghali responded to the new situation in which the UN had vastly increased potential for reaching decisions about action; increased obligations; and a perceived need to act faster, or more forcefully, than had sometimes been possible in the Cold War years. This report contained three distinct proposals touching on the question of standing forces:

1. The idea of *Article 43 agreements* for making armed forces available to the Security Council was revived. This was in a brief two-paragraph discussion of "Use of Military Force", which sought to resuscitate what was termed "the concept of collective security as contained in the Charter". The report proposed "bringing into being, through negotiations, the special agreements foreseen in Article 43 of the Charter".[5] Their purpose was "to respond to outright aggression, imminent or actual"; but Boutros-Ghali conceded: "Such forces are not likely to be available for some time to come."[6]

2. *Peace-enforcement units* were proposed, mainly or exclusively to buttress peacekeeping forces by providing a capacity to respond to ceasefire violations. The principal task of such units, to restore and maintain a ceasefire, was one which "can on occasion exceed the mission of peace-keeping forces and the expectations of peace-keeping force contributors." The report proposed the use of such units "in clearly defined circumstances and with their terms of reference specified in advance. Such units from Member States would be available on call and would consist of troops that have volunteered for such service. They would have to be more heavily armed than peace-keeping forces and would need to undergo extensive preparatory training within their national forces."[7]

3. As far as the provision of peace-keeping forces is concerned, the report highlighted the importance of *stand-by arrangements* whereby Member States

would specify "the kind and number of skilled personnel they will be prepared to offer the United Nations as the needs of new operations arise."[8]

Although they pointed in the same general direction, none of these proposals was for a permanent UN standing force. In response to these three proposals, only the last aspect—stand-by arrangements for peacekeeping forces—has seen progress along the lines envisaged, and even that progress has been ambiguous. The UN stand-by arrangements for peacekeeping, although significantly developed from 1993 onwards, retain national control over the availability of national units.[9] These arrangements have helped in finding forces for many peacekeeping missions. However, they failed conspicuously in the 1994 Rwanda crisis, as will be described later.

Proposals for Standing Forces from 1993

Since early 1993, there have been many proposals for standing forces under UN control. These have developed because the opportunities for effective action seemed much enhanced at a time when the veto was being used only rarely in the Security Council; and because the UN's slow responses to some of the crises of the post-Cold War world seemed to show a particular need for more rapid or more forceful reaction.

Voluntary Individually-Recruited UN Force: the 1993 Urquhart Proposal

The idea of a standing UN Volunteer Military Force comprising professionals recruited on an individual basis was advanced by Sir Brian Urquhart in June 1993. The central issue to be addressed was the increasing difficulties faced by UN peacekeeping. Two aspects of this were: weakness in face of violent harassment (as in Cambodia and Angola); and delays in getting states to contribute forces to an urgent UN mission (as in Mozambique and Somalia). The former Yugoslavia exemplified both aspects:

> Above all, the tragedy of Bosnia has shown that international organizations are not able to deal effectively, and when necessary forcefully, with violent and single-minded factions in a civil war. The reluctance of governments to commit their troops to combat in a quagmire is understandable. Yet the Bosnian Muslims, among others, have paid a terrible price, and the credibility and relevance of international organizations are dangerously diminished.[10]

What was the exact nature and function of the proposed force? He indicated that he was thinking in terms of "a five-thousand-strong light infantry force" that might cost in the region of $US 380 million a year to maintain and equip. As Urquhart succinctly wrote at around the same time:

> Recent UN experiences provide a good argument for at least considering the establishment of an immediately available elite UN force directly recruited from volunteers worldwide. Hitherto the Security Council has lacked the capacity to deploy a convincing

military presence at the outset of a crisis before the situation has disintegrated and become uncontrollable. In fact, the first Secretary-General, Trygve Lie, suggested such a force for precisely this purpose in 1948, in the early stages of the first Arab-Israeli war.

There are numerous possible objections to such a force. However, there is one overwhelming argument for it. It might give the Security Council (and the Secretary-General) the capacity to display strength and determination at a point where larger disasters could be avoided. If the Security Council is to retain its credibility and relevance in the kind of low-level conflicts in which it is now widely involved, it urgently needs a capacity for immediate "peace-enforcement" action.[11]

It is clear from the above that this proposal, like some others (including the 1995 "Netherlands Non-paper"), is not limited to peacekeeping as traditionally understood, nor is it limited to the role of a quick reaction force, to be replaced by regular peacekeepers as soon as possible. A standing force along these lines is seen as giving the Security Council (and, more debatably, the Secretary-General) a capacity for a fast military response in certain crises: for example, in assisting a state threatened by external attack, or in enforcing a ceasefire in an incipient international or civil war. Such a deployment might be without the consent of at least one of the parties to a conflict, and it might be carried out before there was a ceasefire agreement.

A UN Rapid Reaction Force: The Boutros-Ghali 1995 Proposal

The terrible experience of Rwanda in 1994, outlined in the next section, gave a new impetus to the debate about standing forces. In early 1995, in his *Supplement to An Agenda for Peace,* Boutros-Ghali suggested that a rapid reaction force was needed. Whereas many other proposals have envisaged a broader range of tasks, going well beyond peacekeeping, Boutros-Ghali's proposal was located firmly in the context of the problems of availability of troops and equipment for peacekeeping forces. His proposal immediately followed a reference to the failure of stand-by arrangements over Rwanda in May 1994:

> In these circumstances, I have come to the conclusion that the United Nations does need to give serious thought to the idea of a rapid reaction force. Such a force would be the Security Council's strategic reserve for deployment when there was an emergency need for peacekeeping troops. It might comprise battalion-sized units from a number of countries. These units would be trained to the same standards, use the same operating procedures, be equipped with integrated communications equipment and take part in joint exercises at regular intervals. They would be stationed in their home countries but maintained at a high state of readiness. The value of this arrangement would of course depend on how far the Security Council

could be sure that the force would actually be available in an emergency. This will be a complicated and expensive arrangement, but I believe that the time has come to undertake it.[12]

The Security Council's response to *Supplement to An Agenda for Peace* is similarly confined to the question of peacekeeping; and it suggests that there is no significant support there for such a rapid reaction force. The essence of its response on this point is in this passage:

> The Security Council shares the Secretary-General's concern regarding the availability of troops and equipment for peace-keeping operations. It ... reiterates the importance of improving the capacity of the United Nations for rapid deployment and reinforcement of operations. To that end, it encourages the Secretary-General to continue his study of options aimed at improving the capacity for such rapid deployment and reinforcement. The Council believes that the first priority in improving the capacity for rapid deployment should be the further enhancement of the existing stand-by arrangements, covering the full spectrum of resources ...[13]

This statement, although a dampener on proceedings, does not necessarily preclude all further debate on the Security Council about a possible rapid reaction force. Two circumstances could reopen the matter. First, if there is a failure to improve stand-by arrangements for peacekeeping, the question of a rapid reaction force would probably have to be addressed again. Second, members of the Security Council do in practice accept that some operations have gone beyond traditional peacekeeping in various ways; and, if this situation continues, there might yet be a need to discuss a new type of UN force, perhaps along the lines of the peace enforcement units that had been advocated in *An Agenda for Peace* in 1992.

The 1995 Netherlands Non-paper

In September 1994 both the Canadian and Dutch foreign ministers made speeches at the UN General Assembly in which they reported the view, widely held in the UN system, that the presence of a brigade of UN forces in the Rwandan capital, Kigali, in May 1994 might have saved up to half a million lives. Hans van Mierlo, the Dutch foreign minister, added:

> If the deployment of a brigade could have prevented the indiscriminate slaughter of many hundreds of thousands, what then prevented us from doing so? Let us face it: the reason for our inaction was neither lack of means nor time. The reason was that under the circumstances no government was prepared to risk the lives of its citizens. The physical danger was considered too high.[14]

He proposed the establishment of a small international all-volunteer force to enable the UN to save lives in situations such as Rwanda. This was subsequently developed into a more definite proposal, discussed in the 1995 "Netherlands Non-paper", for a UN Rapid Deployment Brigade. This is along similar lines to the 1993 Urquhart proposal, but in several key respects more fully developed. The Netherlands document explores "the possibilities for creating a permanent, rapidly deployable brigade at the service of the Security Council", with "an immediately deployable strength of between 2,000 and 5,000 men". It envisages that the personnel should be recruited on an individual basis, and that its annual running costs might be in the region of $US 300 million —or perhaps $250 million if member states procured equipment, basing, housing etc. Its starting point, like Urquhart's, is a void in the UN peacekeeping system: the time-lag between a Security Council decision to deploy peacekeeping forces and their arrival in the area of operations.

The proposed UN Rapid Deployment Brigade, like the force proposed by Urquhart in 1993, would have a wide variety of possible tasks, some of which go beyond even an expanded definition of peacekeeping and encompass forceful intervention. For example, the tasks of the Brigade are envisaged as including preventive deployment on the territory of a party which feels threatened; intervention in some internal conflicts, possibly without the formal consent of the *de facto* rulers, especially to prevent or stop crimes against humanity, mass murders and genocide; and acting as an advance party for agencies providing humanitarian relief, or providing them with military protection. Further, the "Non-paper" does not rule out the possibility that the Brigade could be deployed within the wider framework of a multinational enforcement operation, as over Kuwait in 1990-91.[15]

The 1995 Canadian Study

The 1995 Canadian Study on "Improving the UN's Rapid Reaction Capability" was first announced in the speech of Foreign Minister André Ouellet to the UN General Assembly in September 1994. It starts from the same problem as other proposals, namely the slow UN response to urgent crises. This study is less wedded to a single organizational military form (volunteer force v. national contingents), and seeks to "elaborate the component elements of a rapid reaction capability in a generic sense", of which one important element will be "the nature of standing forces, options for their development and a discussion of their potential utility".[16] By its nature, therefore, it involves looking at a wide range of options: these include not only a standing UN force of whatever kind, but also the strengthening of UN decision-making and logistic capabilities, trying to make the stand-by arrangements for peacekeeping forces work better, examining the role of regional arrangements and individual countries, and so on. Some of these issues are mentioned further at the end of this paper.

Lessons of the Rwanda Tragedy in 1994

The disaster of war, genocide and vast refugee flows in Rwanda in 1994 did more than any other crisis to generate support for proposals for a standing UN force. As Major-General Roméo Dallaire, the UN Force Commander in Rwanda at the time of the mass killings, has put it:

In Rwanda, the international community's inaction was, in fact, an action which contributed to the Hutu extremists' belief that they could carry out their genocide.

...UNAMIR could have saved the lives of hundreds of thousands of people. As evidence, with the 450 men under my command during this interim, we saved and directly protected over 25,000 people and moved tens of thousands between the contact lines. What could a force of 5,000 personnel have prevented? Perhaps the most obvious answer is that they would have prevented the massacres in the southern and western parts of the country because they didn't start until early May—nearly a month after the war had started.[17]

Many other observers have argued similarly that when the large-scale killings of Tutsis by the Interahamwe militias began on about 7 April 1994, a quite modest sized international military force could have stopped the slaughter. This is a serious argument, which has clearly played a significant part in the development of the various proposals for UN forces made in 1995 by Boutros-Ghali and by the Dutch and Canadian governments.

There could also be a legal obligation on the UN to take rapid action in respect of acts of genocide. The 1948 Genocide Convention, Article VIII, specifies that any contracting state "may call upon the competent organs of the United Nations to take such action under the Charter of the United Nations as they consider appropriate for the prevention and suppression of acts of genocide...".

In briefest outline, the background to the UN's authorization of forces over the Rwanda crisis was that in 1993 there was an increase of fighting in Rwanda, mainly between the predominantly Hutu government and its opponents in the Rwanda Patriotic Front (RPF). The RPF was supported principally by the Tutsi minority, many of whom were in exile, and was operating mainly from Uganda. Attempts to organize a political settlement centred on the Arusha accords, signed on 4 August 1993 after long negotiations by representatives of the Rwanda government and the RPF. These accords sought to achieve an end to the war between these two parties, and to establish a broad-based transitional government. There were repeated difficulties in implementing the accords. The deaths of the Presidents of Rwanda and Burundi in a suspicious air disaster at Kigali on 6 April 1994 became the trigger for systematic killings of Tutsis in Rwanda, which began immediately afterwards. Up to half a million Tutsis are believed to have died. During April a huge number of Tutsis fled, mainly to Tanzania.

In response to these events, and to support attempts to reach a political settlement, three UN-authorized forces were established:

1. The first UN force to be established was the *United Nations Observer Mission Uganda-Rwanda (UNOMUR),* a small military observer group which operated on the Ugandan side of the Uganda-Rwanda border for almost exactly one year from August 1993 to verify that no military assistance was reaching Rwanda.

Its authorized strength was 81. It was established on the basis of Security Council resolution 846 of 22 June 1993. It took into account the Arusha accords which were eventually signed on 4 August 1993.

2. The second UN force, *United Nations Assistance Mission for Rwanda (UNAMIR)*, was set up in November 1993, on the basis of Security Council resolution 872 of 5 October 1993. Originally, its authorized military strength was 2,548 military personnel. It operated within Rwanda, a principal function being to facilitate the implementation of the Arusha accords of 4 August 1993. It had 2,539 military personnel at 31 March 1994. In April 1994, following the outbreak of mass killings, the Security Council decided, controversially, to reduce UNAMIR's strength to 270 personnel.[18] By 13 May it had in fact been reduced to 444.[19] Then in May 1994, in response to revelations of the full horror of events, the Council belatedly expanded UNAMIR's mandate to enable it to contribute to the security and protection of refugees and civilians at risk, and its authorized strength was increased to 5,500 troops.[20] Not one of the 19 governments that had undertaken to have troops on stand-by for UN peacekeeping agreed to contribute to this force under these arrangements.[21] UNAMIR thus appeared to be ill-supported and ineffective. Despite continued difficulties, the number of UNAMIR personnel was increased in subsequent months, especially after the RPF victories in June and July, and stood at 5,522 by 31 December 1994.

3. Following the failures surrounding UNAMIR, on 22 June 1994 the Security Council accepted an offer from France and other member states to establish a temporary operation inside Rwanda under French command and control. This became the French-led *Operation Turquoise* in western Rwanda in summer 1994. The Council stated that in accepting the French offer it was acting under Chapter VII of the Charter, and it authorized France to use "all necessary means to achieve the humanitarian objectives" set out in earlier Security Council resolutions.[22] The deployment of the French under UN auspices actually exacerbated some of UNAMIR's problems, as the French role was seen (rightly or wrongly) as favouring the government (largely Hutu) forces, and preventing the RPF from achieving total victory throughout the country.

On 4 July 1994 the RPF captured Kigali, the capital of Rwanda. This led to a new flood of refugees, this time Hutus seeking to avoid the anticipated retribution of the country's new masters. Many of these refugees went to camps inside Rwanda. Over one million of them fled the country, mainly to camps established just inside Zaire, at Goma and Bukavu. In 1994 the United States sent troops to help run these camps. The UN continued to encounter severe problems in getting states to provide contingents for peacekeeping forces in these refugee camps on the borders. Boutros-Ghali sent out appeals to 60 governments for troops and equipment for a peacekeeping force to protect 1.2 million Rwanda refugees in camps in Zaire, and did not get a single positive response: a repeat of the frustration of May 1994.[23]

Particular reasons why the Rwanda experience was seen as pointing in the direction of some kind of UN standing or quick reaction forces include the following:

- The Interahamwe, the main group carrying out the killings in 1994, did not constitute an impressive military force. Its Tutsi victims might well, therefore, have been saved by a modest-sized external military force.

- The weakness of existing UN stand-by arrangements for peacekeeping forces was demonstrated in Rwanda. As in Somalia in December 1992, so over Rwanda in May 1994, the UN failed to secure national contingents for a UN force in any reasonable time-frame, and then had to authorize a single country to act in respect of an urgent humanitarian crisis. Such a system of authorization involves an implied reproach to international organization, yet in the absence of some kind of UN rapid deployment force it may be the only way of addressing certain endemic conflicts and failures of government.

However, there must be some doubt as to whether the principal lesson of the Rwanda disaster has to be that the UN needs a standing military force. Possible counter-indications might be:

(a) The UN did already have some forces (UNOMUR and UNAMIR) in the area. The problems were that it was fearful of the risks to them, conscious that their original mandates were of declining relevance, uncertain how to use them in a rapidly deteriorating situation, and only able to achieve very limited results with them.

(b) Large forces—more than a brigade—might in fact have been required to stop the widespread and systematic genocide.

(c) It is hard to be confident that in 1993, or in May 1994, the whole of any UN standing force would have been available for immediate service in Rwanda: it might have been already fully occupied in several crises elsewhere.

(d) Even if a UN standing force had been sent to Rwanda, it might have been there at the "wrong" time. Such a force might have become involved in Rwanda during the crises there in 1993; and might then have had to leave later that year under proposed arrangements in which it would have a purely vanguard role, preparing the way for more regular UN peacekeeping forces. Thus it might have left before the genocide began.

(e) It is not immediately clear what exactly the mandate for a larger UN force in Rwanda should have been. Should it have established safe areas for Tutsis, and if so could it have prevented them from becoming involved in the war on the side of the RPF? Should it simply have supported the RPF forces, as some advocated?

(f) A particular problem with the appeal for forces for UNAMIR in May 1994 may have been that it was not coupled with a clear indication of what particular forces were needed for what particular actions. It is possible that had there been a clearer request, geared to a clear central purpose (e.g. to establish safe areas for Tutsis), the outcome might have been different.

(g) Some actions to stop the genocide that were advocated but not undertaken, such as jamming the inflammatory government radio stations, did not themselves need large number of troops. (However, they might have exposed the UN peacekeeping forces in the area to reprisals, and thereby increased the need for armed protection.)

(h) A principal UN weakness, exposed by the Rwanda problem, is the lack of a flexible range of options between the peacekeeping mode (with its emphasis on impartiality and consent) on the one hand, and enforcement against aggression on the other. This may need attention at least as much as the question of standing forces.

(i) A further UN weakness exposed by the Rwanda crisis is the way in which some governments vote for a resolution on the Security Council, but are then unwilling to take even the minimum of action to put their money where their mouth is.

Behind all these particular problems lies the larger and more terrible one that there was simply a lack of solid interest and definite will to do much about Rwanda. Actual and potential troop-contributing states were reluctant to take risks with their troops' lives in what was perceived as a very uncertain cause. There was a sense of hopelessness at the UN and in national capitals as to whether the Tutsis could be saved from genocide, and whether any approximation of a stable political order could emerge in Rwanda. The bitter experience of intervention in Somalia, from which the US and other powers were in the process of extricating themselves at the very time the Rwanda crisis erupted in 1994, added to the mood of caution. Finally, the international community's inaction in this crisis owed something to the unfortunate fact that it erupted at the very time when both the US government and the UN Security Council were attempting to devise guidelines for the circumstances in which peacekeeping operations should or should not be established. The criteria laid down in these documents put much emphasis on preconditions, such as a stable ceasefire between belligerents, that were not present in Rwanda.[24]

For the UN, the lessons of the Rwanda catastrophe are complex. They must include consideration not only of the question of standing forces, but also of other related matters such as the quality of decision-making by the Security Council and the need to advance beyond the *ad hoc* approach which marked all the UN's decisions over the crisis; the question of whether the UN should sometimes simply take sides in a civil war; and the importance of strengthening the role of regional international bodies, so that the UN is not asked to bear a huge range of burdens alone.

On 22 April 1995, the killings of large numbers of internally displaced Hutus at Kibeho camp inside Rwanda by forces of the Rwanda Patriotic Army, in the presence of UNAMIR troops, further confirmed the inadequacy of UN responses in situations of extreme communal violence. On this occasion, as before, at least part of the problem was not so much the availability of forces, but their lack of authorization and willingness to act forcefully in a dangerous situation.

In neighbouring Burundi there were many killings in early 1995, prompting further calls for a UN rapid reaction capability to prevent a recurrence of the Rwandan tragedy. However, the government there has indicated that it does not want any UN investigation or peacekeeping operation, so the question of whether or not to further develop UN practice in the area of humanitarian intervention is raised sharply by this case, and is at least as important (and difficult) as the question of a UN standing force.

Problems Regarding the Proposals for UN Standing Forces

There have been many lines of criticism of the various proposals, described earlier, for standing UN forces. Obviously they do not all apply equally to all proposals. The problems that have been identified might be briefly summarized under the following headings:

1. The *practical tasks* envisaged for UN standing forces have been numerous and varied. They have included particularly: preventive deployments in threatened countries or regions; entering situations of incipient crisis to prevent, for example, the outbreak of civil war or genocide; reinforcing harassed peacekeeping forces and providing them with enhanced enforcement capability; and protecting humanitarian relief efforts. If these tasks remained on the agenda of a standing force, it would likely be required for more crises than it could manage. This problem is not only quantitative, but also qualitative: the variety of types of military expertise, equipment and force structure required would be beyond a single specially constituted UN force on anything like the scale that has been envisaged for it.

2. The common factor in most of the crises in Africa and elsewhere which have stimulated recent proposals is the problem of *civil war and the failed state.* This presents three main difficulties so far as quick international military action is concerned: (i) Such problems are not generally susceptible to a quick in-and-out military action, and indeed may require a longer commitment than UN member states have seemed willing to envisage; (ii) There may be a need for outside bodies to take on heavy administrative responsibilities on a long-term basis, possibly in a trustee-like role; and (iii) Such problems do not always engage the real interests of outside states; the impulse to intervene is primarily humanitarian, or reflects a legal obligation under the Charter, but can hardly in today's circumstances be seen as part of an emerging global scheme of collective security.

3.   The *early injection of a military force into a crisis may not necessarily avert tragedy.* It is possible, but not entirely self-evident, that war in Bosnia, disaster in Somalia, or genocide in Rwanda, could have been averted by such means.

4.   If, as is sometimes proposed, a UN standing force were to have the role of *pioneer/pathfinder for subsequent peacekeeping forces contributed by states in the normal way,* and were scheduled to withdraw after, say, four to six months, it is far from certain that the standing force would still be on the spot when its services were most urgently needed.[25] In Rwanda, it might have become involved in 1993 and left by April 1994.

5.   The *problems of using or threatening force in connection with ongoing peacekeeping or humanitarian operations* remain serious. They include risks to the UN's reputation for impartiality, and dangers of UN or related personnel on the ground being taken hostage. While there is often a strong case for use of force, and there remains a need for some coherent doctrine on this matter, the experiences of Somalia and Bosnia must induce caution about the likelihood of these problems being quickly overcome. In proposals made in 1995, there has been some down-playing of earlier ideas that a standing force could act as a main means of using coercive force to back up UN peacekeeping operations. The difficulties encountered over uses of force in support of UN objectives in Bosnia no doubt contributed to this caution.

6.   There are worries that the existence of the force would only *encourage the Security Council to intervene* more frequently, thus increasing the already serious problem of the UN's over-commitment.[26] As evidenced by important statements issued in May 1994, the actual tendency of both the UN Security Council and the US government has been to try to set firmer criteria so that the UN will be more discriminating, not less, about the situations in which peacekeeping forces get involved.[27]

7.   There remain *doubts about the suitability of the Security Council* as a military decision-making body. Its structure—including both its composition and the existence of the veto power—is not ideally suited to running fast-moving military operations. It lacks resources in certain spheres, including intelligence. Its judgement and possible bias have been very heavily criticized among Group of 77 members.[28] There is a real fear that talk of a quick reaction capacity would mean in practice the North intervening in the South. As a result of these concerns, any placing of military power more directly in the hands of the Security Council (or indeed the Secretary-General) is likely to be resisted. The tension between the General Assembly and the Security Council is a real problem in the UN, and the fears that the Security Council may acquire powers which the General Assembly views as belonging in its sphere have been manifested over several issues, including the financing of the International Criminal Tribunal for the Former Yugoslavia.

8. The record suggests that there is a general *resistance among governments to the idea of endowing the UN with an independent military capacity,* preferring to maintain a definite power (which they retain through existing stand-by arrangements) to say Yes or No to particular military operations.

9. The proposal for a small quick reaction force risks an *under-estimation of the size of forces required for certain urgent tasks.* In Somalia and Bosnia, doubt has been cast on the capabilities of even quite large professional forces to carry out difficult tasks. Moreover, any standing force acting in a vanguard role would require a strong back-up capacity. Sooner or later such a force would appeal for help, and something would have to be available.

10. Although it is possible that a UN volunteer force could, as its proponents have argued, be *more prepared to sustain casualties* than national contingents, many of which have been extremely nervous about any losses in UN peacekeeping service, it is not self-evident that this would be so: soldiers might still be reluctant to take considerable risks in conflicts far from home, and in causes that are debatable; and those in charge of such a force might be similarly cautious.

11. The *financing* of a standing UN force, whether volunteer or composed of national contingents, would be difficult. Some states have ruled out the standing force option on what are basically financial grounds. As France put it in 1993: "Since it is clear that the Organization cannot today afford to maintain a standing force, it is indispensable for the Member States to establish forces which can be mobilized rapidly."[29] It is indeed not obvious that governments, which have denied the UN any general right to draw on parts of their armed forces, and have in many cases kept the UN (and especially its peacekeeping operations) on a ludicrously short financial leash, would be willing to pay the large sums involved.

12. At a time when there are multiple pressures to see a wide range of problems tackled on a *regional rather than global* basis, a UN rapid reaction capability might create a strong presumption in favour of the UN taking on problems, and actually weaken pressures to see more crises handled by regional organizations. That regional approaches have inherent problems is undeniable, but to tilt the balance too far away from regional responsibility could be to seriously overload the UN.

13. There is some risk of *the UN and the office of Secretary-General being seen as a primarily military in function,* when some of its greatest achievements, whether in the field of good offices or of peacekeeping, have been on the basis of negotiations and consent of the parties; or, as with some enforcement and other actions, on the basis of force being authorized by the UN but handled by states. Many events of recent years suggest that too direct an association with military force, which inevitably involves tragedies and failures of

many kinds, could seriously undermine the UN, and more especially the Secretary-General's reputation and capabilities.[30]

Conclusions

These problems suggest that building up a standing military force directly under the Security Council may not be the best way to approach the difficult problem of maintaining respect for the UN, or even of enhancing rapid reaction capabilities. The inherent difficulties of multilateral raising and management of military force, and the dangers of raising false expectations in that regard, need to be recognized.[31]

The fundamental question has to be addressed: Why have the various past attempts at getting standing, or even stand-by, forces yielded such slim results? In the early years of the UN, the most obvious reason for the failure to implement the Charter provisions for forces directly under Security Council control was the inability of the Permanent Members of the Security Council to reach agreement across the Cold War divide. However, this may be a superficial explanation. There appears also to have been an underlying reluctance on the part of all states either to see a major transfer to the UN of their power to use military force, or to see their own forces committed in advance to participate in what might prove to be distant, controversial, and risky military operations without their express consent and command. Put more simply, states continue to be jealous of their powers, and to act in accord with what they perceive as national interest.

The system of stand-by arrangements has survived over four decades because it has solid merits as well as some defects. It has enabled states to retain control over their armed forces and the uses to which they were put; and it has reflected the UN's need to have substantial reserves potentially available, even if not all are needed at a given time.

The failure to implement the many proposals for standing UN forces should not be seen as anything like a complete abandonment of efforts to develop collective uses of armed force. On the contrary, the UN era has seen three striking variations on the collective security theme, each of which responds to difficulties in the pure idea of collective security. The three variations are: regional arrangements and alliances; UN authorizations of the use of force under the leadership of a single state; and international peacekeeping forces. As in the 1950s, so in the years since 1992, it is the development of peacekeeping that has led to the strongest pressure for strengthened stand-by arrangements, and also for the establishment of standing UN forces.

The history of international organization is full of episodes in which high ambition has led to disappointment and adverse political reaction. The way in which *An Agenda for Peace* has been followed by the US document PDD-25, by the anti-UN mood in the USA, and by the much more cautious *Supplement* document, is one example.

None of this is a reason to abandon the effort to get a better quick reaction capability under UN auspices. Several contemporary crises seem to confirm that the problem of how to organize prompt and effective action under UN auspices remains important. However, in the interest of achieving solid progress, there is a case for directing attention to less ambitious, but more realistic, goals than a standing UN military force. These might include a wide range of measures, many of which have been proposed in UN reports and debates in recent years:

- Further strengthening the under-staffed Department of Peacekeeping Operations at UN Headquarters in New York.

- Maintaining a permanent planning unit, from which the senior military and civilian staff of any individual operation might be drawn promptly once it is decided to set up an operation.

- Improving the quality of military advice available to the Security Council and the Secretary-General.

- Developing a proper logistic capability for peacekeeping forces.

- Enhancing the existing stand-by arrangements, for example by establishing a dialogue with governments about political willingness to supply forces, and about the time-scale of political decisions; and by encouraging joint training and exercises by the stand-by forces of different countries.

- Developing a system whereby states which deploy troops rapidly can be assured of their release in less than six months.

- Working out a concept for UN operations which are distinct from both peacekeeping and enforcement against aggression, or encompass elements of both approaches.

- Being prepared in particular instances to authorize operations led by one country or by a group of states, as distinct from sticking with the basic pattern of UN control of most operations—states being by nature better than large multilateral organizations in reacting rapidly to fast-moving situations.

- Looking again at regional arrangements, and UN cooperation with them, with a view to developing a system for more rapid reaction within regions, taking full advantage of regional capacities in that regard.

- Developing the UN's capacity to provide police and administrative services, conceivably including development of a UN police force.

Proposals along such lines build on a system which, imperfect as it undoubtedly is, is already developing. They represent the most likely, and perhaps also the best, way forward.

Notes

1. Report of the Military Staff Committee, "General Principles Governing the Organization of the Armed Forces Made Available to the Security Council by Member Nations of the United Nations", UN Doc. S/336 (1947). For an account based on British archives of the UN discussions in 1946-48, see Eric Grove, 'UN Armed Forces and the Military Staff Committee', *International Security*, Vol. 17, No. 4 (Spring 1993), pp. 172-82.

2. See e.g. Fernand van Langenhove, *La Crise du système de sécurité collective des Nations Unies 1946-57* (The Hague, 1958).

3. Trygve Lie, Introduction to his Annual Report for 1947-48, UN Doc. A/565 (1948), pp. xvii-xviii.

4. Letter from US Secretary of State John Foster Dulles to UN Secretary-General Dag Hammarskjöld, 18 November 1958. I am grateful to Brian Urquhart for making a copy of the letter available to me, and for having drawn attention to it in his article "UN Peacekeeping Was and Will Remain Invaluable", *International Herald Tribune*, Paris, 17 February 1995, p. 6.

5. Boutros Boutros-Ghali, *An Agenda for Peace: Preventive Diplomacy, Peacemaking and Peacekeeping,* Report of the Secretary-General Pursuant to the Statement Adopted by the Summit Meeting of the Security Council on 31 Jan. 1992, New York, June 1992, paras. 42 and 43.

6. *Ibid*, para. 44.

7. *Ibid*, para. 44.

8. *Ibid*, para. 51.

9. "Stand-by Arrangements for Peace-keeping: Report of the Secretary-General", UN Doc. S/1994/777 of 30 June 1994, para. 2. This short document (2 pp. plus 2 pp. of bar charts) failed to mention the May 1994 debacle over the raising of troops for UNAMIR.

10. Brian Urquhart, "For a UN Volunteer Military Force", *New York Review of Books,* 10 June 1993, p. 3. See also the comments in subsequent issues.

11. Brian Urquhart, "The UN and International Security After the Cold War", in Adam Roberts and Benedict Kingsbury (eds.), *United Nations, Divided World: The UN's Roles in International Relations,* 2nd edn. (Oxford, 1993), p. 102.

12. *Supplement to An Agenda for Peace,* para. 44

13. "Statement by the President of the Security Council", UN doc. S/PRST/1995/9, 22 February 1995, p. 2. France reportedly wanted a more positive response to the Secretary-General's ideas on a rapid reaction force, but failed to get sufficient support.

14. Hans van Mierlo at UN General Assembly, 49th session, 27 September 1994.

15. The Netherlands Non-paper, "A UN Rapid Deployment Brigade: A Preliminary Study", The Hague, revised version, April 1995, Section I.5. The original (January 1995) version of the paper had envisaged all these tasks, but had also indicated that the Brigade could carry out peace enforcement—including "armed action against military units, for instance against a party who breaks an agreed cease-fire agreement."

16. "Improving the UN's Rapid Reaction Capability: A Canadian Study", a 6-page preliminary document issued by the Government of Canada in early 1995.

17. General Roméo Dallaire, speech at Hague Colloquium, 23 March 1995, written text, pp. 3 and 14.

18. SC Res. 912 of 21 April 1994.

19. Figures from UN, *United Nations Peace-keeping Information Notes*: Update May 1994, UN, New York, 1994, pp. 164-6.

20. SC Res. 918 of 17 May 1994.

21. *Supplement to An Agenda for Peace: Position Paper of the Secretary-General on the Occasion of the Fiftieth Anniversary of the United Nations,* UN doc. A/50/60, 3 January 1995, para. 43.

22. SC Res. 929 of 22 June 1994.

23. Julia Preston, "UN Drops Effort for Rwanda Refugees", *International Herald Tribune,* Paris, 25 January 1995.

24. On these two documents, see note 27 below.

25. The Netherlands Non-Paper states: "Deployment of the Brigade will always have to take place at very short notice and be of limited duration. When deployed in a UN peace-keeping operation, the Brigade will have to be the first one in and the first one out of the area of operations. Deployment of the Brigade will therefore always have to be accompanied by simultaneous decision-making and preparations for its replacement by Stand-by Units, an international peace-keeping force composed of national troop contributions, or an integrated multidisciplinary mission, including civil administration, monitoring of elections and human-rights observance, police support, humanitarian expertise, political negotiation and mediation, etc." Revised version, April 1995, Section I.5.

26. Brian Urquhart, "Prospects for a UN Rapid Response Capability", paper presented at Vienna Seminar of International Peace Academy, 2-4 March 1995, p. 4.

27. See Statement by the President of the UN Security Council, UN doc. S/PRST/1994/22 of 3 May 1994, 5 pp., discussing the Secretary-General's report "Improving the Capacity of the United Nations for Peace-keeping", UN doc. S/26450 of 14 March 1994; and T*he Clinton Administration's Policy on Reforming Multilateral Peace Operations* (Washington DC: US Department of State Publication 10161, May 1994), 15 pp. This US document, issued on 5 May 1994, is virtually the text of Presidential Decision Directive 25, less some appendices.

28. See e.g. the record of the UN General Assembly's debate on the Report of the Security Council (A/49/2), starting on 31 Oct. 1994, UN doc. A/49/PV.48, pp. 1-29.

29. Statement of France, 28 July 1993, in response to *An Agenda for Peace,* in "Improving the Capacity of the United Nations for Peace-keeping: Report of the Secretary-General—Addendum", UN doc. A/48/403/Add.1/Corr.1, 2 November 1993, p. 6, para. 11.

30. See especially Giandomenico Picco, "The U.N. and the Use of Force: Leave the Secretary-General Out of It", *Foreign Affairs,* Vol. 73, No. 5 (September/October 1994), pp. 14-18.

31. A well-argued attack on the capacity of international institutions to provide a collective security system in the post-Cold War world, and a warning of the pernicious effects of excessive reliance on institutional approaches, is John J. Mearsheimer, "The False Promise of International Institutions", *International Security,* vol. 19, no. 3 (Winter 1994/95), pp. 5-49.

Military Staff in an International Organization

J.K. Dangerfield

Although the international composition of United Nations peacekeeping operations complicates the daily work in the field and brings with it some loss of efficiency and economy, it is arguably their greatest strength. Their multinational character assures all concerned that these operations will carry out the mandate entrusted to them by the Security Council objectively and fairly, representing the political will of the international community as a whole rather than any partial interest.

> *Improving the capacity of the United Nations*
> *for Peace-keeping*
> Report of the Secretary-General
> A/48/403, 14 March 1994

In October 1972 "Canada proposed that the Military Staff Committee, supported by an 'International Headquarters Staff' established under the Secretary General, be used to advise the Security Council on the mandate of a peacekeeping mission and to undertake periodic reviews of the peacekeeping mission to ensure continuing compliance with the mandate."

> *Prometheus Unborn: The History of the*
> *Military Staff Committee*
> Jane Boulden
> Canadian Centre for Global Security
> *Aurora Papers* 19
> August 1993

Lieutenant-General (Retd) J.K. Dangerfield, Canadian Army, was formerly Director of the International Military Staff, NATO.

NATO Acronyms

NAC	North Atlantic Council
DPC	Defence Planning Committee
IS	International Staff (civilian)
IMS	International Military Staff
MC	Military Committee
SACLANT	Supreme Allied Commander Atlantic
SACEUR	Supreme Allied Commander Europe
SHAPE	Supreme Headquarters Allied Powers in Europe

Aim

The aim of this paper is to present a case study on the operation of an international military staff using the North Atlantic Treaty Organization as a model, and suggesting how this model might be adapted to the United Nations.

The Levels of Headquarters

Any headquarters is based on the principle of responsibility. Responsibility is normally divided and thus the headquarters are at different levels to reflect this division of labour. A traditional separation, at least in the military sense, is:

Political: This is the level where consultation takes place, diplomacy is practiced, economic, political and military advice is rendered, options are weighed, political decisions are taken and political guidance for implementation is formulated. In the NATO context this is the North Atlantic Council and the Defence Planning Committee at NATO Headquarters in Brussels, Belgium. (The Nuclear Planning Group is also a major committee, but is not considered further in this paper).

Strategic: This is the level where the political/military interface takes place, particularly in crisis management and defence planning. The key here is that it truly must be an interface where political imperatives are clearly enunciated but, at the same time, taking due consideration of the military implications of those imperatives. The politicians direct, the military advises. Political guidance is then translated into military directives by a military staff. In the NATO context, the national politicians direct via their ambassadors on the Council, military advice is provided by the national Chiefs of Defence through their military representatives on the Military Committee, and staff support is provided by an international military and civilian staff, all situated at NATO Headquarters in Brussels.

Operational: This is the level where military directives are translated into coherent, complete military operational plans. It is the senior level of the military chain which possess all the resources needed to implement the political decision and is the focal point where responsibility and resources must match. In the NATO context, it is also the level where national inputs begin to lose influence in favour of organizational (and multinational) imperatives and procedures. For NATO an example would be SHAPE (Supreme Headquarters Allied Powers Europe) Headquarters in Casteau, Belgium.

Tactical: This is the level responsible for implementing the operational plan or a proportion of it. It is the field headquarters. An example is the ACE Mobile Force (Land) the standing multinational headquarters of which is situated in Heidelberg, Germany.

NATO Headquarters

NATO Headquarters is composed of four basic components: the Secretary-General, the national delegations (with political/diplomatic, financial and military sub-components who, along with the Secretary-General or his representative, make up the committee structure), the International Staff (primarily long-contract civilians but also civilians seconded from their nations, who are responsible for policy development), and the International Military Staff (primarily military personnel seconded from Member States).

NATO's Political Level

There are two principal political organs of NATO. The first is the North Atlantic Council (NAC) with all 16 Member Nations represented and which can meet at Head of State or Government, Foreign Minister, or Head of Delegation (Ambassador) level. The second is the Defence Planning Committee (DPC), with 15 Member Nations (France chose not to be represented on this Committee when it withdrew from the military structure of NATO) and which can meet at Head of Government, Defence Minister, or Head of Delegation level. Both are chaired by the Secretary-General as a non-voting member. The Chairman of the Military Committee sits as an advisor on both the NAC and the DPC.

Committees of NATO, with very few exceptions, operate on consensus with all nations (15 or 16) unanimously agreeing to proposals. In essence, every nation has veto powers. At the senior political level (NAC and DPC), consensus is sought through consultations, and the good offices of the Secretary-General. Frequently, and especially recently, consensus has been difficult to achieve. This has resulted from the deeper and deeper involvement of NATO in non-traditional roles and missions such as the programmes with the Central and Eastern European countries, and in peacekeeping operations. Both these examples are highly political with nations often having opposing views. Another complication is the unique situation of France, which has declared that it wishes to be fully involved in any NATO peacekeeping considerations. NATO, of course, conducts its peacekeeping planning using NATO's integrated military structure and chain of command, neither of which has had French representation. Hence many innovative changes had to be made to longstanding procedures and precedents. For example, the DPC, which is responsible for military plans and force structure, now does not meet to consider these (or other) issues if they are related to peacekeeping, that is conducted by the NAC. One significant implication of this is that NAC is Foreign Ministry oriented while DPC is Defence Ministry oriented. Nations have had to adjust their *modus operandi* to accommodate the fact that NAC is now doing what would normally be DPC business.

The "French situation" also presents complications in the political/military interface (see below). France does not want NATO's integrated military structure (a structure to which France does not contribute) to be used to control peacekeeping operations. Instead it wants the NAC (advised by the Military Committee) directly to control the "field" headquarters which would be *supported* by NATO's integrated military structure but not *commanded* by it.

Another significant factor at NATO's political level is the interaction of the "circles within circles" which come to play in situations such as that in Bosnia-Herzegovina. Here, there are nations of the UN Security Council and nations which are not; some Troop Contributing Nations (TCN) and some nations which are not represented in UNPROFOR; and nations of the "contact group" and those not in the group. Interestingly, there are non-TCN in the "contact group", and some TCN *not* in the "contact group". This has led to at least two situations in the political decision-making process. It is not axiomatic that a nation which supports a specific resolution in the UN will render the same degree of support in the implementation of that resolution by a regional organization, such as NATO, and vice versa. The use of air power in support of UNPROFOR is an example. Second, the consensus rule and the "circles within circles" can mean that a NATO resolution is of the lowest common denominator and noticeably less than specific. Both of these present challenges at the next level down—the strategic level.

NATO's Strategic Level

Actions at this level involve all four of the basic components of NATO Headquarters—the Secretary-General, the Member Nations, the civilian International Staff (IS) and the International Military Staff (IMS).

The principal activities at this level are:

- Interfacing the Organization with the Nations and other world and regional organizations;
- Developing long-range strategic concepts and plans;
- Force planning, force proposals, organizational structure and long-term defence planning;
- Production and reviewing policy guidance on the full range of NATO functions such as logistics, infrastructure, financial, personnel and armaments;
- Standardization;

- Crisis management to include the provision of command, control and information capabilities;

- Preparing assessments and studies, and operational contingency planning; and

- Translating political direction and guidance into operational guidance (and in some cases operational plans) for use by subordinate headquarters.

The major difference between the political level and the strategic level is that in the latter there is political interface with the military, and with the staffs that support both the political and military structures. It should be viewed as a whole, although not always working that way in practice.

The Military Committee is the highest military authority in the Alliance and has these main responsibilities:

- Providing the NAC and DPC with international military advice and recommendations;

- Conveying NAC and DPC decisions to those responsible for their implementation; and

- Providing executive overwatch of the integrated military structure and, in particular, its execution of political decisions.

The Military Committee (MC) operates on the basis of consensus and is composed of the Chiefs of Defence of the 14 nations which make up NATO's integrated military structure, and a senior representative from Iceland (which has no military). France has a general/flag officer as a non-voting observer (but see below for its status on peacekeeping issues). At the Chiefs of Defence level, the MC meets at least three times a year and more frequently during a crisis situation (such as Bosnia). At the military representative (Milrep) level, it routinely meets weekly and often much more frequently, both formally and informally. The Chairman of the Military Committee (CMC) is an ex-Chief of Defence, appointed by the Military Committee for a three year secondment, and is a non-voting member of the Committee. As previously mentioned, the Chairman attends all NAC and DPC meetings and, providing he has consensus, represents the views of the national Chiefs of Defence in those forums. The Milreps are senior general/flag officers accredited to their national delegations, normally for a period of three years, and whose role varies from nation to nation. Some receive their instructions *solely* from their Chief of Defence, others receive them from their Ministry of Defence, yet others receive interdepartmentally coordinated instructions. Some are fully integrated into their national delegations, some are quite separate. Thus it is possible, but rare, for a nation to vote one way in the MC and vote another in the NAC (in essence, a Chief of Defence being overruled by his political masters).

The Chairman of the Military Committee has a key role in the development of strategic options and direction. Going upward, he desirably, and normally, operates on consensus and represents the formal collective view of the Chiefs to the NAC and DPC. If he is unable to achieve consensus in the MC, he formally provides his personal view, which is clearly stated as such, and is fully transparent to the nations. He also has a specific role as advisor to the Secretary-General, which in crisis situations is often presented informally and as a personal view pending MC consideration. Going downward from NATO Headquarters to the Major NATO Commanders, he must operate on consensus and, if he is unable to achieve this in the MC, he must return to the NAC or DPC for guidance.

The stresses and strains at the political level which come into play when NATO considers peacekeeping (the role of France and "circles within circles") are quite naturally present in the MC. By informal precedent and not by formal amendment, France has become a "full" voting member of the MC as regards peacekeeping in general and Bosnia in particular. Also, understandably, nations with troops on the ground in Bosnia and Croatia tend to have specific and focused military viewpoints and cannot abide generalities where lack of clarity puts those troops at risk. Consensus building under these circumstances is hard work and the MC has done admirable work over the course of the last two years of the Bosnia crisis.

The two staffs of NATO headquarters—civilian and military—operate somewhat differently. The civilian International Staff consisting of about a thousand personnel organized into five main divisions (Political Affairs; Defence Plans and Policy; Infrastructure, Logistics and Civil Emergency Planning; Defence Support; and Scientific Affairs) is responsible to the Secretary-General and is, therefore, able to offer assessments and recommendations that are uninhibited by national positions and, indeed, may not even be known to the nations. The International Military Staff on the other hand has no executive authority unless specifically given that authority by the MC. It is responsible directly to the CMC and the MC, and any formal recommendations or assessments passed on to the political organs of the Organization must first have the consensus blessing of the MC before they are transmitted. Despite this seeming anomaly, the system works.

NATO Headquarters International Military Staff (IMS)

The IMS is the executive agent of the MC and consists of about 170 officers, 160 non-commissioned officers, and 100 civilians. The military posts are categorized as either quota, non-quota or host nation.

Quota posts are allocated to nations according to an agreement between the Milrep of the nation concerned and the Director of the IMS based on the requirements of the MC-approved manning tables. Each post has a job description, together with the qualifications required. Staff planners must be graduates of their national staff colleges and, desirably, also graduates of the NATO Defence College. Officially, a thorough working knowledge of one of the two official NATO languages is required and some knowledge of the other language is desirable. In practice, a thorough knowledge of English is necessary to be effective. Once nations have agreed to a quota, they submit the curricula vitae of the personnel nominated to fill the positions. The Director of the IMS reviews the qualifications and accepts the nomination or rejects it if the nominee is not qualified. So far as is practicable the posts allocated to a nation are evenly distributed among the IMS. All personnel assigned to the IMS work exclusively in an international capacity. The normal tour of duty is three years. Of the 330 military posts in the IMS, about 210 are quota posts assigned to nations.

Non-quota posts are normally those at division, branch and section chief level and are open to all nations which are members of the MC. Appointment to all non-quota posts requires the approval of the MC. Approval of appointments to general/flag officer posts is invariably taken in committee by majority vote, while approval for posts lower than that rank is taken out of committee. A nation can hold only one of the most senior posts at any one time (except for a short period of overlap). Officially, not more than two general/flag officer posts may be held by one nation at any one time, but in practice few nations have ever been represented in two general/flag officer posts at the same time.

The organization of the IMS is typical of any military staff at this level. The Director acts as a Chief of Staff, is empowered to act on behalf of the MC on routine matters, and, in case of urgency, to take executive action on behalf of the Committee. He is represented on all the committees of the headquarters and attends the Secretary General's meetings of Assistant Secretaries-General. He supervises six staff divisions and the Situation Centre, each having traditional responsibilities, viz:

Intelligence Division: NATO has no integral intelligence gathering capability but this Division, using the intelligence provided by national authorities, is responsible for monitoring the military capabilities and actions of countries posing an actual or potential threat to NATO, and receiving, collating, analyzing, and disseminating the all-source intelligence required to keep the NAC informed of current situations.

Operations Division: It defines and manages contingency reactions to international crises where NATO interests are involved, and coordinates NATO multinational training (it should be noted that this Division has provided a Liaison Officer to UN Headquarters in New York for the past two years).

Plans and Policy Division: It develops long-term strategic concepts, the military contribution to Allied defence policy, force proposals and goals, and arms control and disarmament.

Logistics and Resources Division: It develops policy and courses of action for logistics, manpower, finances and infrastructure, and civil emergency planning.

Communications and Information Systems Division: It manages NATO's command, control and information systems, and the interoperability of automatic data processing techniques to NATO functions and activities.

Armaments and Standardization Division: It develops armaments policy and co-ordinates standardization activities.

Situation Centre: It serves as the central agency for the receipt, exchange and dissemination of current information and intelligence.

The Operational Level

In NATO this level is manifested in the headquarters of the two Major NATO Commanders—Supreme Allied Commander in Europe (SACEUR) and Supreme Allied Commander Atlantic (SACLANT), who command the integrated military structure. Their headquarters have the acronyms SHAPE and ACLANT respectively. Because of the span of control, SHAPE is much larger than ACLANT (about 800 personnel compared to about 400). While there are national liaison missions attached to both headquarters, the staff of the headquarters operates on an international basis similar to the IMS at NATO HQ. In essence the headquarters are organized along traditional military sub-components (Personnel and Administration, Intelligence, Operation and Training, Long-range Plans and Policy, Logistics, Civil Affairs, and Communications). Both SACEUR and SACLANT attend high level NAC and DPC meetings and are permanently represented on most NATO committees, including the MC.

This is the highest level of command. The MC at NATO HQ is a committee and the highest collective military authority, but it does not command. SACEUR AND SACLANT are individuals who have been appointed to command the troops placed at their disposal by the nations. This command relationship is predetermined in most instances and may be graduated. ("Full command," as one would expect, covers all aspects of operations and administration, and exists only in national services.) The command relationship includes "Operational Command", where the NATO commander is given command of the national troops and may assign missions or tasks to individual components of those troops. In other words he may "break up" national contingents, assigning geographically and functionally different tasks to sub-components. This level of delegation is common for longstanding contingency plans.

It also includes "Operational Control", which is assigned for a given mission (limited by function, time or location) but the NATO commander may not assign tasks to sub-components of national contingents. A task is given to the national commander who may use all, or a portion, of his troops. Normally the national commander is responsible for logistics. This level is common for less clearly defined contingencies where the nations wish to maintain more control. An *unofficial* variation which is sometimes used is "Under Operational Command (or Control) except for.....". Nations may put restrictions on the degree of delegation they give to NATO commanders by using the "except for" clause when normal procedures do not satisfy their concerns. Examples could be deployments or redeployments, cross border movements, etc.

In any military organization unity of command is a principle which is ignored at great risk. Simply stated, there has to be one person, and one person only, in charge, and the troops need to know who he or she is. In NATO this is SACEUR or SACLANT or one of their subordinate commanders. Once a nation has agreed to the mission and assigned forces at the political level, it rescinds its control of those forces to a NATO commander and the international integrated chain of command. Of course, a nation can still influence the destiny of its forces at the political and strategic levels, but it is implicit that they will not interfere with operational decisions at the operational and tactical levels.

The Tactical Level

This is a "field" headquarters where operations are conducted. It is normally small, mobile and more concerned with operations than politics. In the past it was mainly a single nation entity (exceptions being formations like ACE Mobile Force or Standing Naval Forces) but more recently there have emerged more and more multinational formations with international headquarters commanding them, e.g. ACE Rapid Reaction Corps (ARRC).

Some Observations Arising from the NATO Experience

POLITICAL DIRECTION

A mission may not necessarily be successful merely because it is clearly enunciated, but it cannot be overemphasized that the mission is doomed without such clarity. Regardless of the difficulty of achieving consensus, the mission statement (in whatever format—resolution, declaration, proclamation, manifest, communication, etc.) must be unambiguous and unequivocal. Striving for this clarity will also provide cement to the political will. It goes without saying that the mission must be achievable and this implies solid military advice before the final political decision is taken. Additionally, the need for secrecy versus public knowledge will always be a difficult choice.

POLITICAL/MILITARY INTERFACE

Rarely will the political direction be in a format that is readily transferable to the military as operational guidance. A mechanism is needed to provide the two-way dialogue necessary to draft this guidance. A body such as the NAC, usually made up of diplomats representing politicians, is not a good organization to exercise control over all the details of a military operation. However the NAC using the MC is a relationship that works well. It is important to note that the MC is a body operating *outside* of the international staffs but (operating on behalf of the NAC) it is able to task them and receive support from them.

COMMAND, CONTROL AND COMMUNICATIONS

Command and control is exercised through a chain of command. It is a two-way system—instructions going downwards, feedback going upwards. NATO's command structure is based on an integrated (international) military structure that is, in the main, present on a day-to-day basis. The line of authority is practiced and well known to all. Communications are fast and secure—visual, voice and print.

THE COMMANDER

Selection of the most senior commanders is a political prerogative, but, once that decision is made, the nations place their troops under that commander and do not interfere with his operational decisions. The commanders receive their operational guidance from the MC but they have direct access to a political authority (the Secretary-General) if needed. The commanders have complete authority over all combat, combat support, and service support elements, and their units do not report to more than one headquarters in operations.

INTERNATIONAL HEADQUARTERS

Standing headquarters composed of seconded national personnel have many advantages but they are based on one highly political imperative—organizational acceptance of a mission implies that each nation that accepts the mission also agrees that its personnel can continue to serve in the headquarters that is going to execute that mission. When that mission is connected to a treaty obligation, as in NATO, this should not be a problem. However if the mission is not directly connected to the Treaty, then new political factors and national constitutions come into play.

Language of work is a difficult problem. Diplomatic enterprises, written correspondence and committee work will be in the official languages. The fact of life, however, is that day-to-day work will be carried out in a language in which *all* can function, and for the military in NATO that language is English, particularly as one moves further down the chain from NATO Headquarters. This implies that all nations have some kind of scheme to train their personnel in the working language.

Standards and Standing Operating Procedures are an absolute necessity in an international headquarters. Much effort is devoted to getting all nations to agree on doing a task the same way (Standard NATO Agreements). Once agreement is reached, the nations are encouraged (and most comply when it is applicable to them) to adopt the same practice in their *national* systems. This means that personnel who are seconded to a NATO position will have a large degree of familiarity with the NATO procedures because these personnel are likely to have seen those procedures in their own system. The format to issue operational orders is an example, where the same basic format will be used in every NATO headquarters and in a very large percentage of national headquarters.

Training and readiness are connected. NATO expends many resources in NATO-wide and multinational courses and exercises to learn and practice its procedures and to test its plans. Schools such as the NATO Defence College in Rome, with six-month courses for senior staff officers, and the SHAPE School in Oberamergua, with multiple shorter courses for specialists, are key to the interoperability of the national personnel. Everyone is singing from the same sheet of music and because of this, and the frequent practice, response times are reduced and readiness is increased.

Contingency planning is an everyday activity in a NATO headquarters. Obviously one cannot predict with any kind of precision what events may come to pass, but if one wants to reduce response time, and give troops the best chance of success, one must prepare, prepare, and prepare. Brainstorming possible political objectives and then gathering information, developing concepts, preparing possible courses of action, determining resource requirements and availability, followed by good old-fashioned staff work on movement tables, administration, supply, communications, etc., in the end will provide a product that is seldom used. When it is needed, however, it is a gift from heaven. A good permanent staff is a requisite to its production.

Discipline is another consideration in an international headquarters. Discipline is an essential element of command, and the ability to respond to breaches of discipline is a necessary tool for a commander. Nowadays, few nations will allow their personnel to be disciplined by an officer from another nation. Thus, in NATO, notification of breaches of discipline are passed to the senior national officer of the personnel involved for his action. This is the exception to the internationalization of personnel serving in a NATO headquarters.

The United Nations

Obviously it is not feasible to change the political structure of the UN, and it would be naive to believe that radical changes in policies and procedures could be made, but there is certainly scope to improve the decision-making capabilities, the political/military interface, the operational command and control, and readiness and responsiveness.

First, however, one must apply the principle of "if it ain't broke, don't fix it". Based on current writings and comments one could draw up a list of things that may be "broke":

- The Security Council adopted 78 resolutions in 1994! Many of these were peacekeeping oriented and many constituted the only formal "directive" to the chiefs of mission. Many of these had two failures: they were unimplementable and they lacked clarity. Both failures could be solved, or at least improved, by interactive dialogue with experts during the drafting stage. The lack of clarity could be improved by being less stereotyped in the format of the decision (resolution) and putting it in plain English—less "whereas" and "therefore", and more detail.

- The distinction between the levels of command "must be kept constantly in mind in order to avoid any confusion of functions and responsibilities. It is as inappropriate for a chief of mission to take upon himself the formulation of his/her mission's overall political objective as it is for the Security Council or the Secretary-General in New York to decide on matters that require a detailed understanding of operational conditions in the field."[10]

- "There has been an increasing tendency in recent years for the Security Council to micro-manage peacekeeping operations."

- "Another important principle is unity of command....[there must not] be any attempt by troop-contributing Governments to provide guidance, let alone give orders, to their contingents on operational matters."

- "As regards the availability of troops and equipment, problems have become steadily more serious. .... For example, when in May 1994 the Security Council decided to expand the United Nations Assistance Mission for Rwanda (UNAMIR) not one of the 19 Governments that at the time had undertaken to have troops on stand-by agreed to contribute."

- "An additional lesson from recent experience is that peace-keeping operations, especially those operating in difficult circumstances, need an effective information capacity."

- "The division of labor must be clearly defined and agreed in order to avoid overlap and institutional rivalry where the United Nations and a regional organization are both working on the same conflict."

- "Guidance to the field must ... be coordinated, in order to ensure that chiefs of missions do not receive conflicting instructions from different authorities within the Secretariat."

- "Members States would like to see ... ready availability of trained Secretariat staff to undertake and/or support early warning and conflict resolution functions".

- "At the time the Security Council decides to establish a peace-keeping operation, it is often uncertain as to where the required resources will come from, or if they will be adequate.....One way to reduce this difficulty is to have a more precise understanding between the United Nations and each Member State regarding the capabilities the latter would be prepared to make available, should it agree to contribute to an operation."

- " ...a United Nations operation must function as one integrated unit. Given language barriers and differences in training and organizational culture, this is difficult enough to achieve, but it cannot be achieved at all if the operation is divided by contradictory orders from different authorities."

- The United Nations headquarters has operational security leaks. As an example, see General Lewis MacKenzie's comments.[11]

The list goes on, but from the above one can draw conclusions.

1. *Decision-Making.* Security Council resolutions are drawn up by the missions (normally one of the Permanent 5) and may, or may not, be based on a report

of the Secretary-General. Frequently, however, the Secretariat is not involved until after the fact.

2. *Military Advice.* Paradoxically, at this time when UN missions are becoming more "military" and in some areas are near-war, military advice to the Security Council is limited unless coming on invitation from the Secretary-General's Military Advisor, from the lead nation, or informally from the "interested" military advisors.

3. *Staffing.* There is little long-range planning (although a planning section has recently opened in DPKO). Resource management is seldom connected to decisions except in the general sense of budgets. Integration of political and military, and of functions (intelligence/information, operations, logistics, finance, etc.) has not yet been optimized. Collaboration in problem solving between the specialist staffs of the Secretariat and those of the missions is limited.

4. *Command and Control.* No formal process exists which harmonizes strategic planning, political decisions, operational guidance, and mission execution. National interests override the international structures and authority. Distinctions between strategic, operational and tactical levels of control are blurred.

5. *Responsiveness and Readiness.* Efforts to create a common training curriculum and introduce standard operating procedures have begun, but have not yet been fully implemented by many national authorities within their systems. There are no stand-by headquarters, equipment or forces. Every mission is *ad hoc*.

Recommendations

Only a few of the following recommendations are technical or mechanical, and consequently easily implemented. The significant recommendations will require a willingness on the part of the Secretary-General and the Secretariat to give up some of their "autonomy" and a political will from the Member States (particularly the Permanent 5) which may not be present at this time. However, it should be possible to build on the lessons learned in Rwanda to convince the international community (in its broadest sense) that the *status quo* is not good enough.

Recommendation One: Close the gap between the Security Council and the Secretariat.

Using the NATO analogy, the Security Council should give broad political guidelines and then *task* the Secretariat to conduct contingency planning (options, resource requirements, risks, etc.). The Secretariat then would be required to provide a coherent and integrated report back to the Security Council through the Secretary-General *before* the Security Council took its decision.

Recommendation Two: Ensure the political decision always *has full clarity.*

This can be done in a number of ways but one approaching "fail-safe" (from the point of view of the Member States) is again to task the Secretariat to produce operational guidance which would then be vetted by the Security Council Member States (perhaps by a subordinate committee, see below).

Recommendation Three: Provide aggregated *military advice to the Security Council.*

This can come from within the Secretariat, from a separate body reporting directly to the Security Council, or both. There is great merit in having a high ranking international military body (such as NATO's Military Committee) reporting directly to the Security Council. The UN has a major problem in this regard because of the existence (so to speak) of the Military Staff Committee (MSC) under the Charter. The ill-fated MSC is not only ineffective, but is politicized because of its linkage to Article 43 of the Charter, and to a mandate perceived to be exclusively for Chapter VII operations.[12] Sadly, the chances of providing essential collective military advice would be better if the MSC did not exist and one could start with a clean sheet.

With a clean sheet, one would create a "Security Council Military Committee", which:

- would be loosely modelled after NATO's Military Committee;
- would be composed of one representative from each of the Security Council Member States, chaired by either an elected non-voting member, or (more likely) a voting member rotating among the Permanent 5;
- would advise the Security Council on the military aspects of any proposal;
- would receive staff support from, and give guidance to, the Secretariat;
- would scrutinize (on behalf of the Security Council) the operational guidance which would be prepared by the Secretariat following a Security Council decision (if that decision concerned military operations);
- would conduct periodic reviews (with the assistance of the Secretariat) of military operations and report to the Security Council.

If one *must* operate with the Military Staff Committee today, it should be recognized that it has no relationship with the Secretariat. Recall that in October 1972: "Canada proposed that the Military Staff Committee, supported by an 'International Headquarters Staff' established under the Secretary-General, be used to advise the Security Council on the mandate of a peacekeeping mission and to undertake periodic reviews of the peacekeeping mission to ensure continuing compliance with the mandate. The International Headquarters Staff, consisting of civilian and military members appointed by the Secretary-General, would be responsible for the day-to-day conduct of the operations."[13] The assumption is that the MSC would still operate outside of the Secretariat (i.e. from the Permanent 5 missions) but would be able to task the Secretariat. One could perhaps assume that the MSC ("supported by an International Headquarters Staff") would have a separate staff, but this would be counter-productive. There is merit in this proposal today, as there was in 1972, but there are certain conditions that should be met if this solution is to come close to meeting today's challenges:

- The mindset of "the Charter says so" must be overcome. The link of the MSC to Article 43 and exclusively to Chapter VII operations must become less strict. If the inability of the MSC to implement Article 43 remains the obstacle for it to carry out a broad interpretation of Article 47, and it is perceived that the MSC's work is limited to enforcement operations, then nothing has been solved in today's context, and military advice will continue to be lacking.

- The Charter states that "Any Member of the United Nations not permanently represented on the Committee (the MSC) shall be invited by the Committee to be associated with it when the efficient discharge of the Committee's responsibilities requires the participation of that Member in its work".[14] Today this will be influenced from two quarters—the "other" members of the Security Council, and troop contributing nations (TCN) for specific UN missions. Nations will not want a powerful MSC conducting business which affects them, either because they are *also* a member of the Security Council and want the same military responsibility as the Permanent 5, or they are contributing troops to a mission and want control over the instructions that are given to those troops. There are few politically acceptable options open and they do not necessarily contribute to efficiency. One option may be:

- Leave the core membership of the MSC as it is in the Charter (the Permanent 5);

- *As a matter of routine* invite the representatives of the other members of the Security Council to meetings which are discussing options and mandates (advice to the Security Council);

- *When appropriate* invite representatives of TCN to discuss mission-specific issues (eg. operational guidance);

- Agree that the Secretary-General allow "his" Secretariat directly to support a committee of Member States (Permanent 5/Security Council);

- Ensure that the Secretariat is willing to accept that a committee of Member States (other than the General Assembly/Security Council) can task them and is interposed for military matters between them and the Security Council.

Only an optimist will believe that the above conditions can be met. A pessimist would design a less ambitious (and less efficient) option. One such option would be to leave the MSC as is, but call upon it to render advice on military matters in general and not just Chapter VII issues. Without a staff to support it, this could only work on a "lead nation" basis, with the work being done within a mission (hopefully in consultation with the Secretariat). The result would lack an integrated conclusion because no mission can duplicate the span of control of the Secretariat (political, economic, financial, legal, humanitarian, operational, etc.). Nevertheless, sometimes incomplete advice is better than no advice.

Another option, of course, is to rely on the Secretariat to provide military advice.

Recommendation Four: Harmonize the military staffing with the civilian staffing within the Secretariat.

The Secretariat has roles and tasks that go far beyond the conduct of "military operations". Within the Department of Peacekeeping Operations (DPKO), however, arguably the bulk of the tasks are connected to some kind of military operation (although many civilians will disagree with this opinion) and in some instances connected to operations that are near-war. Within DPKO, the military and civilian staffs are, in the main, integrated. Aside from the Secretary-General's Military Advisor there is no clearly defined military staff. Proponents of integrated staffs will argue that this produces politically acceptable options faster. Opponents will argue that you don't get "pure" military advice. The arguments are spurious. Any strategic level headquarters must balance political imperatives with military risks and this can only come from frequent and trusting dialogue between the two. What is absolute is the requirement to integrate the military *functions* into the problem solving/decision process. This can only be accomplished with *sufficient* military staff being *organizationally* responsible for those functions. This is particularly important in long-range contingency planning and in control of current operations. With today's problems it is ludicrous for the UN to continue to treat military intelligence (as opposed to information) as some kind of repulsive device. A commander (or Chief of Mission) without military intelligence is blind.

Recommendation Five: With the full or partial adoption of the previous recommendations, formally *ratify a command and control mechanism (such as NATO's "operational control", but mean it) which will allow national interests to be fully considered at the strategic (UN Headquarters) level, but leaves the direction of operations to the mission Commander who is responsible to* one *political authority.*

Recommendation Six: Organize at least one standing multinational tactical headquarters able to respond quickly to a crisis (either Chapter VI or Chapter VII).

There is no purpose in having nations nominate stand-by units which would be available in a matter of days if it will take weeks and months to put in place the headquarters that will direct their operations. A standing headquarters modelled after NATO's Headquarters ACE Mobile Force (Land) would provide:

- A commander and staff who have planned and trained together, and will have developed cohesion;

- A quick response capability (assuming that they have the basics of equipment—vehicles and communications);

- A contingency planning capability;

- A training mechanism (conduct exercises, write curriculum and doctrine, train the trainer, etc.);

- A validation mechanism (standards, standing operating procedures).

There are two significant obstacles to this proposal. The obvious financial obstacle must be weighed against the alternative of not having a standing headquarters ready to go—and paying the price of a Rwanda or a Bosnia. The second obstacle is the political problems associated with deciding which nationalities will be represented in the headquarters and then guaranteeing that those nations will allow their personnel to deploy whenever and wherever the headquarters deploys. The second obstacle could be alleviated by having more than one headquarters, but this presents an irreconcilable situation vis-à-vis the financial problem.

Although there are possible sub-options to this recommendation, they present more risk. For example:

- Rather than permanently manning a full headquarters staff, man only a cadre with the rest of the staff remaining in their national systems on a stand-by basis. As a minimum the cadre must consist of the Chief of Staff (who would be the acting Commander), and principal staff officers for intelligence, operations, plans, training, and logistics.

- Base the communications unit on a national system that would remain in its country except for operations and exercises.

- Do both of the above.

Obviously a fully manned and ready headquarters complete with communications and equipment is the best solution. The fact remains that, without this capability, every mission will remain *ad hoc* and will require months for organizing, deploying, training, and operating.

Recommendation Seven (perhaps naive): Place less emphasis on the perceived practical differences between Chapter VI operations (Pacific Settlement of Disputes) and Chapter VII operations (Action with Respect to Threats to Peace, Breaches of the Peace, and Acts of Aggression).

There are differences in the two Chapters from the political, legal, and economic points of view; the principal ones being that in Chapter VI the disputing party (or parties) initiates the action, and in Chapter VII the Security Council may initiate the action. However, these differences can become political dogma which impairs UN crisis management. Recall that Secretary-General Boutros-Ghali wants to reactivate the Military Staff Committee, but *only* for Chapter VII. Also recall that he believes it essential immediately to create a rapid deployment force for

Chapter VI, but is of the opinion it "would be folly to do so at the present time" for Chapter VII. If one were to have only one criterion—how do we *best* conduct international crisis management—this limiting dogma about the Chapters VI and VII makes no practical military logic.

Recommendation Eight: Standardize, particularly training. Create regional schools and travelling training teams.

The UN has made great strides in the past few years in developing a common training curriculum, standard rules of engagement, and operating procedures (although the mission-specific procedures tend to abridge the standard ones). The task now is to validate and implement them. This can best be done by setting up regional training schools and by travelling training teams. Schools (such as the one already set up by the Nordic countries) would train the trainers of their national forces (who are on stand-by) in such things as:

- The United Nations: how it works, legalities, principles, roles, etc.;
- UN missions: case studies, lessons learned, procedures;
- Command and Control;
- Administration and Logistics;
- Operations: observation, escort, protection, reporting, negotiating, etc.; and
- Conduct of Area Studies.

The Schools could be like mini-missions (international and UNHQ controlled and funded) or, more likely, schools set up (and funded) by regional organizations, groups of nations, or a single nation (perhaps with some UN assistance).

UN travelling training teams are another method of training the national trainers. These would be controlled by UNHQ, operate on a UNHQ approved curriculum, and visit national forces that are on stand-by. Desirably these international teams would be permanent, made up of seconded officers and NCOs who would be very familiar with their subject. They could come from the standing headquarters of Recommendation Six. Less desirable, but workable, would be teams formed for specific limited times (say two months, twice a year) which would operate to a schedule, then return to their national systems. Either way, the teams could be UN funded or, more likely, offered by nations.

Conclusion

"Consistency by members of regional organizations who are also Member States of the United Nations is needed in dealing with a common problem of interest to both organizations".[15] There are many questions today about NATO's perceived diminishing role and political mandate, but it does have an efficient crisis management/ problem solving/command and control capability. The UN on the other hand is increasing its role and political mandate but, arguably, does *not* have an efficient crisis management capability. In this latter regard, with less inter-organizational rivalry and more political will, the UN could profit by adopting many of NATO's procedures.

Notes

1. *A Supplement to An Agenda for Peace*, p. 10.

2. *Ibid.*, p. 10.

3. *Ibid.*, p.10.

4. *Ibid.*, p.11.

5. *Ibid.*, p.11.

6. *Ibid.*, p.21.

7. *Ibid.*, p.22.

8. *Implementation of the Recommendations contained in 'Agenda for Peace'.* General Assembly A/47/965,15 June 1993, p. 2.

9. *Improving the capacity of the United Nations for Peace-keeping*, General Assembly A/48/403, 14 March 1994, p. 4.

10. *Ibid.*, p. 7.

11. Maj. Gen. Lewis MacKenzie, *Peacekeeper: The Road to Sarajevo*, Douglas & McIntyre, 1993, pp. 310 and 324.

12. For a full discussion of the Military Staff Committee and a complete expose of its ineffectiveness see Jane Boulden, *Prometheus Unborn: The History of the Military Staff Committee*, Aurora Papers 19, Canadian Centre for Global Security, August 1993.

13. *Ibid,* p. 23, and A/SPC/152 10 October 1972.

14. United Nations Charter Article 47(2).

15. *A Supplement to an Agenda for Peace*, p. 21.

Multinational Rapid Reaction Forces: Applying NATO's Experience to the UN Rapid Reaction Requirement

A.G. Christie

NATO Acronyms

ACE	Allied Command Europe
AMF[A]	Allied Command Europe Mobile Forces [Air Component]
AMF[L]	Allied Command Europe Mobile Forces [Land Component]
APOE	Airport of Entry
C2	Command and Control
C3I	Command, Control, Communications and Intelligence
COMAMF[L]	Commander AMF[L]
CPX	Command Post Exercise
DPC	Defence Planning Committee
FTX	Field Training Exercise
HNSU	Host Nation Support Unit
IALCC	International Air Lift Control Centre
IALCE	International Air Lift Control Element
IRF	Immediate Reaction Forces
LO	Liaison Officer
MNC	Major NATO Command
MNFs	Multinational Forces
MSC	Major Subordinate Command
NCF	NATO Composite Forces
PSC	Principal Subordinate Command
RR MNF	Rapid Reaction Multinational Force
SPOE	Seaport of Entry
STANAGs	Standing Agreements
TOEs	Tables of Organization and Equipment

Major General (Retd) A.G. Christie, Canadian Army, was formerly Commander of Allied Command Europe Mobile Forces—Land Component (AMF[L]), NATO.

Aim

After reviewing the multinational rapid reaction forces available within the NATO force structure, this paper will examine the organization and operations of the Allied Command Europe Mobile Force - Land Component within the NATO force structure, identifying those "lessons learned" which might be applied to the UN requirement for multinational rapid reaction forces.

Components of Rapid Reaction

Rapid reaction depends upon an efficient, well-defined crisis-management process which includes or produces:

- the political/diplomatic and military advice necessary to arrive at a timely decision;

- a supporting staff well trained in the requisite procedures;

- a responsive potential threat identification means;

- timely decisions on action to be taken;

- an unambiguous system for command and control of committed forces;

- clear, concise employment mandates to committed forces;

- a library of contingency plans for deployment and employment of designated forces under a number of type-scenarios;

- *Well trained forces* which are both structured to meet the operational requirement and are at an appropriate state of operational readiness and deployment preparedness to react to the strategic requirement;

- Transport resources and infrastructure to support the proposed deployment within the time frame dictated by the strategic and operational requirements;

- *Integrated logistics support* which can meet immediate force needs on deployment, has the internal resiliency to meet unforeseen requirements, can sustain the force in-theatre for an indefinite period of time with minimum restructuring, and is both cost-effective and efficient.

None of these component elements can be generated quickly; it takes time, generally measured in months and years rather than hours, days and weeks, to establish each; to develop and refine internal procedures for each element, and then to integrate each of them into an efficient, effective, and responsive organization. If any element is missing or its activities not sufficiently coordinated, then the degree of reaction will be substantially denigrated.

NATO Multinational Forces (MNFs)

The NATO force structure includes a number of rapid reaction forces of differing strengths and composition which are held at varying degrees of readiness. In the early 1960s NATO formed two forces to meet perceived threats to its flanks:

- Allied Command Europe Mobile Forces [AMF] consisting of two supporting elements: Allied Command Europe Mobile Forces [Land Component] (AMF[L]), and Allied Command Europe Mobile Force [Air Component] (AMF[A]).[1]

- Standing Naval Force - Atlantic (STANAVFORLANT).

Since the late 1980s, due to the diminishing risk scenario and subsequent reductions in stationed standing forces in Europe, NATO authorities have authorized the establishment of the following MNFs:

- NATO Composite Force (NCF) to compensate for the withdrawal of the Canadian Air/Sea Combat Group assigned to North Norway;

- Standing Naval Force - Mediterranean (STANAVFORMED) to replace the "On-Call Naval Force - Mediterranean" on a more permanent basis in view of the increased risks to European stability in the Mediterranean basin;

- Allied Rapid Reaction Corps (ARRC) to offset partially the readiness reductions experienced in NATO's Central Region resulting from the downsizing of forward stationed standing forces;

- Immediate Reaction Forces [Land] and [Air].

The mission assigned to each NATO rapid reaction force varies according to its specific role and force structure, but each carries with it two basic functions; first, a deterrent obligation, and second, in the event that deterrence fails, a combat responsibility. In every case, the force mandate and chain-of-command are clearly defined, contingency plans are in being, and are regularly practiced under varying scenarios and climatic conditions.

In the 1960s the initial NATO MNFs[2] were established to display NATO solidarity, especially on the Alliance's flanks, by deploying quickly to the threatened area to deter aggression, and as a last resort, if deterrence were to fail, to assist national forces in the defence of NATO territory. These MNFs have exercised extensively over the past 30-plus years and, as a result, have built up extensive experience and data bases upon which to draw in deciding what works, and what does not, under various scenarios. As many similarities exist between the deterrent operations anticipated for the AMF[L] and UN peacekeeping operations, the UN should carefully examine to what extent the NATO experience could benefit UN planning, especially in the areas of force structuring, crisis management and decision-making procedures, contingency planning, and command and control of this rapid reaction MNF.

Force Planning and Development

NATO is fortunate to have a very well-defined and disciplined force planning and development process which was designed to permit both nations and NATO commanders to plan the orderly definition, acquisition, deployment, integration and employment of defence resources. Commanders at every level annually[3] review their defence requirements for personnel, equipment, and infrastructure by national element to meet the long term threat/risk assessment and forward their returns through the chain of command to NATO HQ. As these requirements progress through the staff system, they are reviewed, consolidated, and prioritized at each level of command. NATO HQ then engages each member nation in the defence review process to determine how the operational requirements can best be met. Although this process may be slow in the estimation of some,[4] it does ensure that properly structured, balanced forces are available to meet Alliance defence needs in consonance with national resource availability.

AMF[L] FORCE STRUCTURE

The AMF[L] is a balanced, task-organized, integrated, cohesive and well-trained force constantly held at seven days notice to move with good CI and logistics support capabilities. It draws upon a base of 12,000-13,000 personnel of whom approximately 6,000-8,000 would be deployed to any one of its seven pre-assigned contingency areas. Recently the AMF[L] has been tasked to "be prepared to engage in 'out-of-area' peacekeeping missions under NATO control".

As contributing nations only maintain units on a permanent stand-by basis, the HQ AMF[L] is the only element under continuous NATO command. Thus the HQ becomes the key element in the planning, deployment, and employment equation.

HEADQUARTERS AMF[L]

A relatively small unit composed of 45 permanent staff officers and support personnel organized along continental staff lines, HQ AMF[L] is located in Heidelberg, Germany, fairly central to its contingency deployment areas and units, and offering easy access to the international air transport network. When deployed, the staff is increased by an additional 48 pre-designated and trained augmentees from contributing nations to permit 24/7 operations.[5] In addition, the HQ also has a limited, theoretical capability to divide itself into two smaller HQ, each with decreased Command, Control, Communications and Intelligence (C3I), to deal with simultaneous threats on both flanks of Allied Command Europe.

This permanent HQ provides a major degree of stability to the contingency planning for, and training of the force. As such it acts as a clearing house and repository for all information concerning the AMF and ACE land/air rapid reaction matters. Other NATO and national HQs involved in rapid reaction endeavours actively contribute to, and draw upon, this extensive information base. The UN planning staff might well profit from tapping this accumulated corporate knowledge and experience as it revises its rapid reaction concept.

When not deployed, HQ AMF[L] reports directly to SACEUR, and has, for all intents and purposes, Major Subordinate Command (MSC) status—although it is not designated as such. Due to the nature of its mission and force structure it must maintain very close relations with the MSCs and Principal Subordinate Commands (PSCs) in whose areas it may be called upon to deploy and the Ministries of Defence of both contributing and potential host nations.

AMF[L] UNITS

For operations the AMF[L] is task-organized as a light air-portable brigade composed of the following major type units, although the mix of national contingents will vary by contingency area:[6]

Combat Units
- three to five infantry battalions,
- a light armoured reconnaissance squadron;

Combat Support Units
- a composite, multinational light artillery regiment/battalion,
- an augmented combat engineer company,
- a composite tactical aviation unit;

Command and Control Units and Elements
- HQ AMF[L] and HQ company,
- a radio communications squadron,[7]
- a line communications company,[8]
- a field security section,
- tactical air and aviation support detachments, and
- a HQ liaison and communications helicopter platoon;

Combat Service Support
- a logistics support battalion,
- a movement control squadron,
- a field hospital,
- a multinational MP platoon,
- a host nation support unit, and
- national support elements from each of the contributing nations with deployed units.

In addition, miscellaneous specialized elements and detachments are assigned by contributing nations, as required and requested, to meet specific contingency requirements (e.g. veterinary services, blood collection and transfusion teams, etc.).

The AMF[L] force structure is constantly evaluated on the basis of the experience gained as a result of exercises and the emergence of new technologies. There is always the temptation to add elements, equipment and/or stocks to enhance overall force capabilities without identifying offsetting reductions. When considering the constantly evolving structure of a "rapid reaction" MNF, such as the AMF[L], the planner is constantly engaged in a struggle to match the "operational need" to allocated transportation resources. Therefore it is essential that every element of the force structure, whether a personnel element, weapon, or stock item, is assigned a priority and whenever a new capability is introduced an offsetting weight and cube must be identified and deleted from the force structure.

One method considered to counterbalance this constraint and improve operational capability was the regional stockpiling of selected vehicles and ammunition. As "high-cube" items or dense, heavy commodities, they are very costly to transport by air. Nations, however, were reluctant to provide and maintain these valuable equipments and stocks in some remote area where there was only a possibility that it would be used. As a consequence, the AMF[L] has had to accept a limitation on its tactical mobility to fit the immediate requirement for 15 days of combat stocks into the available initial airlift. Although the UN may not have the problem of transporting large quantities of ammunition to contingency areas, it would do well to consider carefully the advantages and disadvantages of regionally stockpiling of vehicles and equipment before taking a decision to commit funding.[9]

EMPLOYMENT CONSTRAINTS

In addition to the constraints imposed by transport resources, nations also imposed various constraints on the commitment of their contingents. Nations did not impose these limitations lightly, and it was important that all elements involved in the planning for force employment understood the rationale for their imposition. Almost every troop unit had some form of constraint on their employment; thankfully most were minor in nature and did not affect the force's operational effectiveness. Others were more serious and required replacement of the unit prior to deploying to specific contingency areas or under certain climatic conditions. To ensure the maintenance of force readiness to meet all contingencies, a system which designated primary and secondary troop units for each contingency area was established; thus if the primary unit was unavailable another was on stand-by to replace it. In the case where the AMF[L] had only one unit to fulfil a specific function, it was imperative that no constraints were imposed by either the contributing or host nations on their employment. Therefore, early in the process of structuring of a UN Rapid Reaction MNF, it is vital that potential contributing nations explicitly define any constraints which they will impose on the employment of their national contingents. Similarly, when MNF deployment is being considered, and prior to a Security Council decision being taken, the potential host nation(s) must identify any constraints which they wish to have imposed upon MNF composition or operations.

Interoperability

Inevitably, whenever the subject of interoperability within an MNF arises, the discussion quickly moves to, and concentrates on, the associated subjects of standardization and specialization. Although these two subjects are indeed important, a number of other areas should be examined which, the AMF[L] experience indicates, have an equal or higher cost-benefit.

COMMON PROCEDURES

Being a NATO MNF gives the AMF[L] a significant interoperability advantage as all elements operate within a single tactical concept and doctrine, use the same glossary of military terms, and have adopted a common, comprehensive set of standing operational, tactical, and logistical support agreements [STANAGs]. From this base the AMF[L] has developed a set of very detailed "standard operating procedures" (SOPs) for internal use, which are far more comprehensive than those normally found within a national force, to insure against misinterpretation of procedures. While these form a solid foundation for interoperability, nothing contributes more to the smooth operation of the force than "personal contact" and an ambitious training programme, points which the UN should not overlook in its considerations.

INTEGRATED AND CROSS TRAINING

The AMF[L] training programme guaranteed one major force deployment on a field training exercise [FTX] and one "Reconnaissance/Study Period" or command post exercise (CPX) on the North and South flank annually. Platoons and detachments were exchanged between units during FTXs so that they could achieve a better understanding of other contingents, their equipment capabilities and methods of operation. This programme was so successful and valuable that HQ AMF[L] found itself coordinating a continuing training exchange programme during non-exercise periods at the request of contributing nations.[10] This cross training produced some noticeable, and unanticipated, collateral benefits. As troops, commanders, and national staffs became better acquainted and more at ease with these skills which previously had been viewed as a specialty of a particular contingent, the value of developing similar skills was recognized and began to be included in the national programmes. As a result the AMF[L] gained greater flexibility in the operational employment potential of these units.

COMMON TRAINING STANDARDS

Each contributing nation annually issued national training standards to be achieved by its unit(s). These varied widely: in some cases they were focused on the unit's AMF[L] mission; in others they were more general in content. Therefore, after consulting with contributing nations, and as a part of the formation's annual training programme, HQ AMF[L] began issuing minimum common training standards to be achieved by individuals and units by contingency area for inclusion in national training programmes. This proved to be a very cost-effective method of achieving a higher state of operational readiness, while at the same time ensuring that all units could engage in specific activities at the same level of effectiveness.

FIRE SUPPORT TRAINING

Each nation contributing an infantry battalion also contributed a mortar platoon and an artillery battery to provide fire support to the AMF[L].[11] Unfortunately each platoon and battery was equipped with a different mortar or artillery piece and national firing procedures varied. As each was a valued element in the force coordinated fire plan, it was essential that these elements be brought together to train under the force Artillery HQ. Consequently all indirect fire elements were concentrated annually for an extensive artillery practice camp which exercised every permutation and combination of observer, firing unit, and controlling element possible. In addition to the annual training, two shorter concentrations were held annually during the deterrent phase of FTXs for participating units.

During all of the aforementioned, aircraft from both AMF[A] and host nation squadrons were fully engaged in providing integrated air support to mixed artillery and mortar fire support programmes. As a result, it was not unusual for an infantry unit to be supported by the guns and mortars of at least one other nation, ground support aircraft from a third, all controlled by a fire observation team from a fourth.

TRAINING OF COMMANDERS AND STAFF

While the integrated training of units is essential to achievement of combat readiness standards, it is equally important that commanders and staff officers are presented with comparable integrated training opportunities to improve not only their skills but also to develop a better understanding of the nature of the environment in which they might be called upon to operate. This was accomplished in three ways:

- An annual one-week Commanders Study Period which was devoted to resolving planning, training and interoperability issues. Participants included all unit commanders, HQ AMF[L] staff branch chiefs, representatives of MSCs, PSCs, and contributing and host nation headquarters involved in force planning.

- A similar annual one-week Logistics Study Period was conducted for logisticians from both contributing and host nations as well as SHAPE and various MSC and PSC headquarters.

- Reconnaissance/Study Periods and CPXs conducted in contingency areas were exploited extensively as "learning opportunities" for both commanders and staff.

We found that we gained double value for every dollar spent in these types of endeavours; not only was the operational aim of the activity accomplished, a very significant training benefit accrued. This aspect should be actively pursued by the UN when considering MNF training requirements.

LANGUAGE DIFFICULTIES

Even with all the effort which went into the area of interoperability, some problems inevitably occurred as a result of misunderstandings due to language difficulties. In the AMF[L], where English was the working language and less than one-third of the strength was therefore working in its native tongue, language fluency and military vocabulary shortfalls from time to time created difficulties, and invariably at the most critical point of an operation. Many words and operational terms when translated directly into another language assume a different meaning. As a matter of course we took great pains to use simple unambiguous English words and phrases and we provided far more explanation than normal in all documents and orders to guard against misinterpretation. An additional measure to simplify communication was, wherever possible, to use formatted messages, reports, and returns.

As non-English speaking units used their own language internally, a requirement existed to have a cadre of personnel within each sub-unit who could also understand, and be understood in, English. Most nations offered additional training, and in some cases financial incentives, to their AMF[L]-assigned personnel to reach a reasonable level of English language proficiency. As an added insurance policy, HQ AMF[L], in cooperation with both contributing and host nations, developed a small pamphlet for use at the junior leader/soldier level, which was issued to all ranks, containing almost 500 basic sentences, phrases and military expressions in the 10 languages which could be encountered during AMF[L] deployments. When every other means failed, this simple lexicon seemed to fill the bill. With the extensive translation services available to it, the UN should consider adopting this simple communications expedient for future MNFs.

LIAISON

Both internally and externally, the AMF[L] depended upon Liaison Officers(LOs)/Teams to augment its modern communications systems and to enhance interoperability. A trained Liaison Officer/NCO can overcome the difficulties of language, can garner the spirit of what is occurring, and pass on the nuances of a situation. Face-to-face communications are far more effective than attempting to pass complicated instructions over a radio or telephone. Liaison team personnel from both contributing and host nations were specially selected and trained for their AMF[L] tasking. Most were trilingual, staff college graduates and were assigned to an AMF[L] liaison or staff function in their day-to-day national assignment. In addition to their normal information passage function, the liaison team proved a very cost-effective resource, worth its weight in gold, within an MNF to assist in avoiding potential problems involving national sensitivities, local lore and customs, and to tap for background information. If one accepts the expression "blessed is the peacemaker", a good LO should be considered as a double blessing.

STANDARDIZATION

There is no doubt that if all units in an MNF are similarly organized and equipped, the overall force support costs can be reduced. Prior to determining to what extent the equipment within the MNF should be standardized, three factors should be considered:

- First, unless external funding is provided, nations prefer to purchase equipment which is compatible with their overall national needs, can be procured from national sources, and for which they have a guaranteed or established support system. In essence this means that the MNF will often have to accept incompatible weapon and equipment suites which call up additional resources to operate and maintain unless the sponsoring organization is prepared to pay the full procurement bill.

- Second, even if it does pay for the equipment and deploys it to stand-by units, the sponsoring organization should be prepared to permit the equipment to be used for day-to-day training and be prepared to pay the additional maintenance bills associated with that use as well.

- Third, if standardized equipment is procured and stockpiled centrally in anticipation of use, the dollar cost of maintenance, updating and repair for stored equipment must be recognized and provided; and the time involved in withdrawing equipment from storage, readying it for use, deploying it, and then training the user to employ it, must also be recognized and built into the deployment flow chart.

Probably the best that the UN, like NATO, can hope to achieve is to have all equipments in any particular category interface satisfactorily and to achieve standardization within each unit—but even this will be an uphill battle especially in the case of less developed countries.

SPECIALIZATION

Depending upon the degree and nature of the specialization,[12] it can be either a force multiplier and cost-effective, or can reduce unit employment flexibility and create a force imbalance. Within a rapid reaction force (RRF), specialization might merit encouragement in some very specific areas, but should be discouraged in most others unless the RRF is unequivocally targeted for employment:

- in a specific type of terrain,
- under particular climatic conditions, and/or
- to counter a distinctive threat.

One should not confuse the terms *"specialization"* and *"enhanced skills"*. Due to the nature of its designated contingency areas and the number of units upon which it could draw, the AMF[L] did encourage contributing nations to enhance skills within assigned infantry units which increased their capabilities under particular terrain and/or climatic conditions, but discouraged all efforts to concentrate on a particular skill area to the detriment of general combat capabilities.[13]

All other units of the AMF[L] might be categorized as "specialist units" in that they contributed a particular skill and specialty set to the overall force capability. However, the functions each performed did not differ materially from those of similar "type-units" in other similar sized formations except for the types of equipment employed and the distances over which they were expected to operate.[14]

When discussing *specialization* with those involved in UN peacekeeping operations, the word appears to take on three very different meanings. In one context, it is used as discussed above; in the second, it appears to be used to differentiate between forces or units which have different "peacekeeping" functions (i.e. an infantry battalion employed to control a sector versus a military observer unit); and, in the third, in the context wherein a nation will *specialize* by providing only one particular type-unit. As a first step in determining to what degree specialization should, or should not, be accepted within a RR MNF, perhaps the UN should define what it means by *specialization.*

In the second context, a good case can be made for maintaining separate stand-by lists of units available for RR deployment on UN missions which do not require the deployment of a more traditional type RR MNF. Such units could be included as adjuncts to the RR MNF to provide collateral flexibility and an economy of effort element in particular situations; more conventionally a number of these *specialized* units could be grouped under an RR MNF HQ for a specific operation such as a monitoring mission.

With regard to *national specialization,* this option may be very attractive to planners due to the inherent consistency of its organizational structure, method of operation, and training standards which could be expected. Nonetheless, it should be approached with caution as an unacceptable degree of dependence on one nation, or group of nations, could result.

Unfortunately, there are no easy answers to this *specialization* conundrum; only difficult decisions which must be faced.

AMF[L] Operations

The AMF[L] is a SACEUR strategic resource employed by NATO's Defence Planning Committee at the operational level in a tactical role to discharge a political-military mission.

AMF[L] Mission

The mission of the AMF[L] is to deter aggression by the display of NATO solidarity and resolve by rapidly deploying to a threatened area on a NATO flank, and, in the event that deterrence fails, to assist in the defence of NATO territory in conjunction with other NATO and national forces. The three mission elements, to deploy rapidly, to deter aggression, and to defend, call up a combination of force requirements which are unique within NATO forces.

NATO/AMF[L] RAPID REACTION CONTINGENCY PLANNING PROCESS

Within NATO, the authority to select and approve contingency employment missions for the AMF[L] rests solely with the DPC. This body considers planning proposals from, and solicits the advice of, Major NATO Commanders (MNCs), the NATO Military Committee, and Member Nations—especially potential host nations—prior to issuing general planning guidance. This broad direction is then developed into a contingency plan in four stages:

Stage One. The responsible MNC, MSC, PSC, HQ AMF[L], and the host nation set out the strategic and operational planning parameters to include:

- the general area in which deterrent operations are to be conducted,

- designation of the host nation formation with which the AMF[L] will operate,

- a proposed AMF[L] force structure which includes consultation with possible primary and secondary troop unit contributing nations;

- potential APOEs and SPOEs to support the proposed deterrent operation area, and

- any special factors which must be taken into account.

Stage Two. The responsible PSC, host nation military authorities and HQ AMF[L] then define the mission specifics, assemble a planning data base, and carry out a detailed reconnaissance of the contingency area, after which the HQ AMF[L] develops an outline draft operational plan in conjunction with the local host nation military HQ.[15] This draft is then circulated to all HQ involved from MNC downwards for coordination and revision as required. During this stage, contributing nations confirm their commitments and join the planning process.

Stage Three. Once the "Draft OPLAN" has been "agreed in principle", a detailed and integrated joint reconnaissance of the contingency area is conducted by HQ AMF[L], the PSC, and the designated host nation HQ. All primary and secondary AMF[L] unit commanders and staffs are included along with representatives from the MNC, MSC, and International Air Lift Control Centre (IALCC) on the NATO side, and representatives from host nation military and civilian authorities.[16] In this stage a detailed plan encompassing all aspects of the deployment, deterrent and combat employment plans are coordinated and any outstanding problem areas are identified and resolved. The "Draft OPLAN" is then circulated for review and concurrence by the various NATO HQs and both host and contributing nation authorities, prior to approval-in-principle by the MNC and DPC. Subsequently, the plan is tested through the medium of both CPX and FTX, if possible, and then published as an MNC OPLAN.

Stage Four. This stage is the open-ended maintenance of the OPLAN and includes its review, revision and updating:

- after every AMF[L] CPX, FTX, or reconnaissance/study period conducted in the contingency area;

- whenever the political and/or military situation the contingency area changes markedly;

- whenever significant changes to the units and formations or their capabilities of either the AMF[L] or host nation forces occurs; but

- as a minimum, on a regular biannual basis.

Suffice to say that this contingency planning process, which includes both political and military input and spans the strategic, operational and tactical levels of planning, can be both time consuming and frustrating, but is absolutely vital if the rapid reaction MNF is to be deployed and employed in a timely manner during a period of tension. While time-consuming and staff manpower intensive, this process ensures that the OPLAN remains a current, credible document.

In preparing contingency plans, those involved should recognize that:

- the attainment of the strategic goal must remain paramount;

- deployment infrastructure and transport resource constraints will probably be the most difficult areas to be resolved;

- to secure local military and civilian support, MNF deterrent and operational employment planning must take cognizance of both local military and non-military factors and sensitivities;

- any in-country logistical support and procurement arrangements must be devised to minimize the impact on the local economy; and

- honesty, openness, and the ability to compromise where possible in negotiations are essential ingredients to the success of the mission.

Contingency planning and training to implement these plans will consume the bulk of a RR MNF HQ's time and efforts. Detailed planning for contingency employment is one of the four cornerstones of rapid reaction. If any one of the cornerstones is weak, or less than complete, a reduction in reaction capability will result. While detailed contingency planning may be appropriate for the NATO scenario, a more generic approach may well be a more appropriate route for the UN to travel.

NATO CRISIS-MANAGEMENT, DECISION-MAKING AND THE AMF[L]

NATO's crisis-management and decision-making processes have evolved and undergone constant refinement over the past 45 years. The resulting procedures incorporate an unambiguous delineation of corporate authorities and responsibilities; an excellent system to collect, collate, analyze, and integrate intelligence; and a clear chain of command and control of the executive elements. At the apex of this process, the Defence Planning Committee (DPC) is charged with taking timely political-military strategic decisions on behalf of the Alliance. It is the sole body within the NATO structure empowered to deploy the AMF[L].

A request to the DPC for the deployment of the AMF[L] can be originated by either SACEUR or a host nation[17] based upon strategic and tactical intelligence that a threat to NATO territory exists. On receipt of the request, the DPC, supported by the joint efforts of the political/diplomatic International Staff and the International Military Staff, begins its consultation process with Alliance Nations and the NATO Military Committee to obtain a consensus decision on the measures it will employ to react to the perceived threat. Concurrent with these political-military discussions, SACEUR immediately takes a number of military measures to enhance the readiness of the rapid reaction force, of which the major actions are:

- Contributing nations[18] are alerted, and requested to activate their assigned primary and/or secondary contingents;

- Contributing nations in turn alert their assigned units and transport resources, and then confirm their readiness and deployment status to HQ AMF[L] and the International Airlift Control Centre (IALCC);

- Small advance elements of HQ AMF[L] and the International Air Lift Control Element (IALCE) deploy to the proposed contingency area to initiate reception arrangements;

- The proposed host nation alerts and deploys its Host Nation Support Unit (HNSU) to the designated APOE and SPOE; and

- Contingency OPLANS are reviewed, updated as necessary, and confirmed in light of the evolving military and political situation.

Throughout the above:

- SACEUR has gradually been reducing the "notice to move" limitation on HQ AMF[L] and its units;

- The IALCC and HQ AMF[L] engage in constant dialogue with nations to make final adjustments to the composition and planned flow of air, sea and land transport resources[19]; and

- adjustments to force organization are made as necessary.

Once consensus has been forged, the DPC directs SACEUR to deploy the AMF[L], including within this direction:

- the time by which AMF[L] deterrent operations are to commence;

- the time by which the AMF[L] is to be complete in the contingency area;

- the latest political-military assessment of the situation; and

- the Rules of Engagement (ROEs) under which the AMF[L] is to operate initially.

SACEUR in turn repeats this decision to HQ AMF[L], contributing nations, the host nation, and all MSCs and PSCs and confirms, *inter alia,* the following information:

- the contingency plan option to be implemented, if applicable,[20]

- an intelligence update for the contingency area;

- command and control arrangements,

- force composition/task organization, and

- allocated transport resources.

When compared to the above, the UN crisis-management and decision-making processes appear to lack the inherent necessary delineation of responsibility and authority, as well as executive and supporting staff structure to manage crises in a timely manner. To improve its responsiveness, the UN should consider the following remedial actions:

- develop an early warning system to identify and track threats to international stability;

- institute an internal means of providing comprehensive, independent military advice to the Security Council, the Secretary-General, and the UN Secretariat;

- rationalize the UN staff system concerned with planning, implementing and supporting peacekeeping operations;

- establish a "24/7" operations centre at UN headquarters in New York, empowered to manage crises on behalf of the UN and in which political, diplomatic, military and military staffs are represented and integrated;

- develop, with nations, a list of committed stand-by units which could be employed on peacekeeping duties at short notice, and establish a reporting system to monitor the status of these units;

- authorize the establishment of a standing RR MNF HQ to provide a responsive command and control element to implement Security Council mandates; and, in the light of the above,

- review and refine the UN's crisis-management and decision-making procedures.

AMF[L] DEPLOYMENT

The rapid deployment of the AMF[L] is one of three components of its mission statement and is critical to the maintenance of its credibility as a deterrent instrument. Pre-planning of the deployment, early warning, provision of adequate transport and infrastructure resources, and coordinated concurrent activity are key elements to the success of the deployment phase of the contingency operation. The success of the deterrent operations phase depends in part on the initial impressions imparted to the potential aggressor, the host nation, and the international media. The apparent beehives of activity, at both points of embarkation and disembarkation, must appear to be orderly, coordinated and yet conducted with zest; the flow of personnel, equipment and stocks should challenge the flow potential of allotted transport resources, infrastructure and reception facilities; but must never degenerate into congestion or confusion.

Contingency deployment pre-planning begins in the force structure development process. When considering the structure of an RRF, the planner is constantly engaged in a battle between the operational need and the transport requirement to move each force element. The AMF[L] had to accept initial limitations to its tactical mobility to fit the immediate operational requirement for combat stocks into the available lift. The possibility of establishing regional stockpiles to speed up deployment, reduce transport requirements and to redress these transport induced equipment and supply shortfalls has been studied on a number of occasions. Each study quickly determined that nations were prepared to pay the additional costs involved and accept the resulting operational limitations rather than tie up valuable resources to provide and maintain valuable equipment and combat stocks in some remote area when there was only a possibility that they might be required. All enhancements to the basic agreed force structure had to be measured against a scale which divided equipments and elements into "vital", "necessary", and "desirable" categories. Where a new requirement was added, an equivalent offset had to be found which could be dropped off the other end of the scale.

Coordination and control of the movement of the AMF[L] is complicated as it could involve, depending upon the contingency area, 350-850 C-130 aircraft equivalents and up to five ships to move all its personnel, equipment, and 30 day stocks of stores, consumables and ammunition. Due to meticulous pre-planning, close coordination and an excellent control system, it worked surprisingly well.

Success commences with the initial planning for each contingency area by:

- determining the operational requirements for each movement line item and then eliminating the excess from the movement requirement;

- organizing the flow of personnel, equipment, stocks, and ammunition into priorities for arrival; and then

- prioritizing "filler" cargo that can be used to maximize the carrying capacity of each aircraft without impeding the rational flow of the force elements and the ability to secure it on arrival.

The importance of the IALCC and IALCE in managing the air flow cannot be overemphasized. Each aircraft and its load is positively controlled by the IALCC at SHAPE and the IALCE throughout its transit to the APOE and return to home base. This information and confirmation of load flow ensured that the requisite personnel and equipment were available to handle each aircraft on touchdown and congestion minimized in both the airfield transit and reception areas was minimized. Although they further complicate the movement plan, the following additional measures were included in the coordinated movement plan to relieve APOE congestion:

- designated airfields along the routes where aircraft could be diverted, as necessary, either for servicing in case of aircraft malfunctions and/or the transfer of loads to smaller aircraft,

- alternative airfields if for some reason the APOE has to close, and

- servicing airfields to reduce time delays and congestion at the APOE.

Close liaison with both national and international air traffic control organizations are absolutely necessary during both the planning and execution of the deployment phase to obtain and confirm overflight clearances, and to optimize flight routings if the flow is to be maintained as planned. The IALCC and IALCE managed this aspect for the AMF[L] as well as coordinating customs clearance of aircraft and their loads in conjunction with both the host nation and the AMF[L] movement control element.

To maximize aircraft flow through the APOE and minimize congestion, HQ AMF[L] established the following aircraft handling guidelines:

- C-130 and C-141 type aircraft were allowed 30 minutes from touchdown to exit taxi to discharge their loads of personnel and cargo;

- C-5As were scheduled for 50 minutes on the apron;

- commercial passenger aircraft, depending upon the type, were normally allotted 30-45 minutes for turn around;[21] and

- not more than six aircraft were permitted in the unloading area at any one time.

To further avoid congestion, aircraft servicing and refuelling at the APOE were minimized. Aircrew changes and servicing were normally carried out at another airfield 1-2 flying hours away; and only those "snags" which would hazard aircraft operation were authorized for repair at the APOE.

The AMF[L] movement control element, in addition to its duties at the APOE, was also responsible for the coordination and trans-shipping of sea cargo from the SPOE[22] to the AMF[L] Base Area by rail or road. The same general principles drove this element's operations as those of the IALCE at the APOE. The major problem areas encountered at the SPOE were security, customs clearance, materiel handling, and coordination of trans-shipment arrangements. The relatively small SPOE movement control detachments always required significant augmentation by host nation labour, security, and transport resources to be effective. However, considering the number of airframes which could be saved by the timely arrival and forwarding of each shipment of high cube/density equipments and stocks, the payback was very high.

In view of the success record of the AMF[L] in planning and executing deployments, the UN planning staff should consider adopting a similar system of planning, coordinating and operating future UN MNF deployments.

AMF[L] Deterrent Operations

The purpose of deterrent operations is to deter aggression by displaying Alliance solidarity and resolve, and, therefore, these AMF[L] activities were generally conducted overtly, although paying due regard to the requirements of operational security. Deterrent operations had two different but complementary functions. On the one hand, measures to deter aggression were conducted along or close to the frontier and were directed towards the potential aggressor; while on the other, measures were undertaken throughout the contingency area aimed at the local population and host nation forces. Both categories were designed to be non-provocative in nature, attract high visibility, and demonstrate Alliance resolve and commitment, but were significantly different in form.

Frontier operations consisted of deterrent patrolling in the main, and initially involved a minimum of one-third of the AMF[L]'s combat strength, i.e. one company from each battalion, known in AMF[L] parlance as "Key Companies". The concept employed was to deploy the Key Companies[23] directly from the APOE forward to designated patrol bases and then to mount mobile section and platoon-strength patrols throughout the border area[24] in accordance with the OPLAN and ROEs as set out by the DPC to demonstrate NATO presence, to report any aggressor activity, and to encourage the local inhabitants to maintain their normal routines. In some instances this last role required patrols to act as protective elements for agricultural activities, escorting medical teams, etc. All activities however were governed by the ROEs. Maximum contact with the local population was encouraged, not only through patrolling, but also through participation in local events. Reporting directly to HQ AMF[L], the Key Companies recognized the importance of their tasking and that the rapid passage of accurate, complete information, surrounding both activity and non-activity in their areas, could have direct implications not only on their local situation but on the defensive posture of the Alliance as a whole.

Joint patrols with host nation forces were conducted wherever and whenever possible to further demonstrate solidarity. At the very least, a liaison team, with intimate knowledge of the patrol area was located at each AMF[L] Key Company patrol base.

Throughout the remainder of the contingency area, the balance of the AMF[L], as it arrived in the ensuing six-day period, began training to improve their knowledge of the local terrain, to refine operational procedures (both internally within the AMF[L] and jointly with host nation forces), and to support the local "hearts and minds" campaign. Great emphasis was always placed on this last activity, which included *inter alia* weapons and equipment demonstrations, briefings to local groups on NATO, the AMF[L] and their cooperation in host nation defence efforts, provision of free medical clinics and services, and involvement in local improvement projects by engineer elements. In this regard, activities were jointly coordinated by HQ AMF[L] and local military and civilian authorities and each FTX left behind visible reminders of NATO presence such as road improvements, wells, etc.

Deterrent patrolling and other deterrence activities continue until:

- the threat of aggression disappears, and the AMF[L] is withdrawn by the DPC;

- a point is reached in the NATO Formal Alert System where deterrence is deemed to have failed and the AMF[L] is integrated into the Regional General Defence Plan; or

- based upon the situation in the contingency area, the DPC changes the AMF[L] ROEs with regard to adopting a defensive posture.

RULES OF ENGAGEMENT[25]

During the deterrence phase all operational activity is governed by the ROEs established by the DPC. These ROEs are uniform for all contingency areas with individual setting for each "Rule" being set out by the DPC at the time that AMF[L] deployment is authorized. An outline of the AMF[L] ROEs is attached at Figure 3.

Only the DPC has the authority to change the ROE settings. Therefore to ensure speedy, timely response to requests for changes, NATO developed a formal ROE change process which is based upon "silence procedure", i.e. unless one voices disagreement to a request within a specific timeframe, agreement is assumed. The HQ originating a change request sends its request directly to SACEUR, and the DPC and NATO Military Committee at NATO HQ, with copies to all other HQs concerned. Any HQ in the chain has the opportunity to object, but must provide its rationale for non-agreement and the negative implications the ROE change will have on the operational situation in its area of responsibility if approved. As a consequence COMAMF[L] ensures that his HQ is constantly consulting with other concerned HQ to ensure that each request is fully coordinated where possible prior to submission.

Throughout this period, NATO HQ, SHAPE, and the MSC, PSC, and host nation HQ, all endeavor to keep the AMF[L] Commander (COMAMF[L]) up to date on the political and military strategic, operational and tactical intelligence assessments and operational readiness states to ensure that any assessment of the situation in the deployment area can be evaluated in the wider deterrence context.

The justification and timing of each request are two very important factors in its handling. All HQ must be manned by decision-makers on a 24/7 basis to deal with these requests if lives are not to be hazarded. In the event of an operational emergency COMAMF[L] has the authority to "exercise requisite operational judgement to guarantee the safety of his force". This does not mean that he can change the ROEs *per se,* but does authorize him to take specific self-defence emergency measures on a one-time limited duration basis to ensure that elements of his force are not hazarded. Any decision to take such action outside the ROE system rests upon a balance of trust between the DPC and its AMF[L] Commander, with the DPC understanding the situation extant at the time, and the COMAMF[L] understanding the implications that his action could have, not just in his area of operations, but on the Alliance position as a whole.

While the NATO system works well for the AMF[L], it may not be appropriate for a UN RR MNF considering the present state of the UN crisis-management/decision-making process. Nevertheless, the UN urgently needs to revise its method of controlling operations and, therefore, its ROEs for deployed forces. Perhaps a good place to commence would be the establishment of the "24/7" operations centre recommended above, manned by an integrated diplomatic/civilian/military staff with authority to take action within specific parameters, and direct access to the Security Council for those outside these conditions.

AMF[L] COMBAT OPERATIONS

In the event that deterrent operations fail, the AMF[L] assumes a combat role alongside the host nation forces under the direct operational control of the PSC HQ. In this role it has limited capabilities to conduct sustained operations against heavy mechanized forces due to its force structure. However, properly sited in the correct terrain, it could give a very good account of itself. The decision to withdraw the AMF[L] rests with the DPC, with requests for such action coming from contributing nations, SACEUR or the host nation.

MNF Command, Control and Communications

COMMAND AND CONTROL ARRANGEMENTS

Command and control arrangements, unless carefully defined, smoothly handled, and applied uniformly, can create situations, almost innocently, which will degrade an MNF's operational ability so severely as to render it ineffective. To lessen the chances of this occurring as a result of misunderstandings, NATO has adopted a standard series of graduated command and control levels which define command and control authorities and responsibilities explicitly. When applied to AMF[L] operations they resulted in the following command and control arrangements.

- Contributing nations at all times retain national command of their contingents but assign operational command of units, on arrival in the contingency area, to SACEUR, who in turn assigns tactical command of units to COMAMF[L].

- During the deterrent phase of operations, the AMF[L] remains under SACEUR's operational command, but will normally be "chopped" to the tactical control of the MSC in whose area it is operating.[26] The AMF[L] also closely coordinates its operations with the applicable PSC and host nation HQ and forces.

Considering the problems which have arisen in some of its operations in the past, the UN might wish to:

- review the NATO system with a view to adapting it to UN requirements; and

- have troop contributors agree to vest specific command and control (C2) authorities in the UN command structure.

MANDATES/MISSION STATEMENTS

The mission statement of a force is the mandate under which it operates and, as such, must be a clear, concise statement of the tasks to be performed and include any limitations to be imposed on its freedom of action to execute those tasks. In this regard the DPC, in employing the AMF[L] in a political/military context, always explicitly defined its mandate to the Force Commander. This clarity was achieved because the mission statement was always drafted by an integrated diplomatic/civilian/military staff team which ensured that the proposed mandate was both complete and acceptable to all three staff groups prior to submission. Sadly, this degree of coordination and clarity does not appear to exist within the UN structure. However, unless the UN begins to consider military factors in the drafting of future mandates, UN missions will continue to lack adequate direction, authority and responsibility to effectively meet the aspirations of the international community.

AMF[L] COMMUNICATIONS

High quality, reliable and flexible communications are the lifeline of a RR MNF such as the AMF[L]. Immediately upon deployment, communications backbones are quickly extended and put into operation using both in-place civil and military networks and additional links established by AMF[L], host nation and NATO agencies.

With the advent of satellite communications, the initial set-up of this very complicated circuitry has simplified this operation and made it more reliable. These communications links with between HQs are absolutely vital if instantaneous passage of information and direction is to be of any value to both political and military authorities at all levels of command and control.

All units are linked to HQ AMF[L] by redundant VHF, VHF (Secure), and HF radio provided by detachments of the Force Signals squadron. As well, telephone and teletype circuits are provided as back-up systems to all units by the Force Line Company when time permits.

The HQ AMF[L] is not a monolith and breaks into four elements on deployment:

Main HQ: During deterrent operations, located in the Force Assembly Area in an area close to the local host nation HQ. During operations, located in the forward tactical area.

Alternate HQ: Normally co-located with the HQ of one of the major units, but may be deployed forward to the deterrent patrol area to enhance the control of deterrent patrolling or if communications between the Force Assembly Area and the deterrent patrol areas of Key Companies becomes difficult.

Rear HQ: Located in the Force Administrative Area and collocated with the Logistics Support Battalion HQ.

HQ AMF[L] Base Area: Normally located at the APOE with a detachment at the SPOE.

Each of the above has access by secure and insecure telephone, teletype and data links directly into the NATO-wide telecommunications network through the AMF[L] Line Company facilities established at the HQ AMF[L] Base Area. One circuit of each type is restricted to the use of the Commander and Branch Chiefs to guarantee instantaneous access for consultations.

A UN RR MNF will probably require similar communications to the AMF[L], at least during the initial stages of its deployment. The value of secure communications links cannot be over emphasized, especially for links from the deployed HQ to UN headquarters and to major units engaged in operations.

Integration of Service Support

GENERAL

The nature, quality, and equality of the service support provided have a significant impact on the operational effectiveness of an MNF. While, within NATO, logistics is a national responsibility, within the AMF[L] we could not afford the luxury of separate lines of communication for each national contingent *per se*, and therefore the logistics system was integrated wherever and whenever possible and practicable. When an MNF is deployed, particularly in remote areas with little supporting infrastructure or facilities, logistics becomes one of the most important factors governing a commander's options and in maintaining force morale. The organization and integration of service support should not be neglected, left solely to logisticians, or assumed to be available from contractors. Well structured, resilient, and integrated service support units are absolutely essential to the maintenance of the operational effectiveness of the force *ab initio,* and cannot be cobbled together as an afterthought, or hired off the street—at least initially.

The AMF[L] was indeed fortunate to have a very professional Logistics Support Battalion and two extremely well-equipped and superbly manned field hospitals upon which to build its service support organization.

LOGISTICS

The Logistics Support Battalion provided the logistics support backbone for the AMF[L]. It supplied all common-user commodities and services, such as POL, veterinary and finance services and bulk purchase and distribution of non-combat consumables and fresh rations[27] to all contingents within the Force on either a repayment or restocking basis. This unit also provided a core maintenance and recovery capability to all elements of the Force with national contingents providing non-common-user parts and technical support as necessary. Each national contingent also had a National Support Element, collocated with the Logistics Support Battalion, but remaining under national command, which was responsible for:

- the provision of non-common user items, national ration supplements, and national personnel accounting and administrative services;

- providing maintenance support, repair and spare parts for non-standard national vehicles and equipment; and

- acting as the national link between the contributing nation and its deployed contingent.

In addition, a Host Nation Support Unit [HNSU] was always provided to the AMF[L] on its arrival in each contingency area. This unit provided additional liaison detachments and linguists for each AMF[L] unit, guard platoons for various HQ and support locations, heavy lift transport, and a labour company, as well as local intelligence, psyops, NBC and MP service support detachments.

As a consequence of detailed, solid planning, a sublimation of national self-interests combined with liberal measures of good humour, camaraderie and common sense, the standard of deployed logistics support provided to the AMF[L] was unparalleled within NATO. The "personal contact" relationships built up during training were identified as a major contributing factor to this success and, therefore, a meaningful force multiplier. As a result the flow of goods and services within the Force was optimized and duplication was minimized. Unfortunately, at the present time the internal AMF[L] logistics arrangements are in a state of disarray as the Logistics Support Battalion fell victim to recent UK downsizing efforts. As no other nation has volunteered to fill the gap created, COMAMF[L] is still trying to cobble together a replacement—without too much success.

MEDICAL SERVICES

At least one major medical unit was always deployed with the AMF[L]. Both field hospitals were specially organized, equipped, and staffed to provide a full range of medical and surgical services to an MNF which would be deployed in relatively isolated and primitive locations under extreme climatic and field conditions. The German hospital specialized in supporting cold and temperate operations on the North Flank, while the Italian hospital specialized in Mediterranean littoral and mountain operations. Each hospital had a holding capacity of 100 patients and contained an element with special training to prepare patients for aeromedical evacuation to national medical facilities if they could not be returned to duty within a reasonable period of time. The preventative medical and hygiene services which can be provided by this type of field hospital are extremely important assets, both to maintain the health of the Force and to contribute to any "hearts and minds" campaign involving the local populace.

Regional Rapid Reaction MNFs

One of the options under consideration to accelerate the UN response to crisis situations is the establishment of regional rapid reaction MNFs. This concept certainly has a great deal of merit, but is unlikely to be attained in the short term due to the lack of resolve, financial resources and ability to achieve consensus within regional security organizations (RSOs). Until these difficulties can be overcome, the role of RSOs will remain limited in scope.

If RSOs decide to commit the resources necessary to establish regional RR MNFs, they will be faced with not only the same problems faced by the UN at present, but also a lack of expertise in organizing operations involving military forces. Perhaps this could work to their advantage. They could begin, as a first step, by establishing a multinational planning staff to develop a concept for the use of a regional RR MNF, followed by a RR MNF HQ to develop the supporting force structure requirements, SOPs and training standards before embarking upon training and employment. The UN should consider the partial underwriting of such a programme for those regions which require financial assistance, and look on such payments as insurance premiums to lower possible claims in the future. Until RSOs create their own RR MNFs they will have to rely on centrally-funded and provided UN resources.

In the interim, RSOs can, and should be encouraged to play a greater role in enhancing the UN's RR capabilities. Much of the contingency planning information required by a RR MNF exists at present in RSOs. As well, they could play a greater role in providing:

- regional early warning assessments, and,

- identification and monitoring of both non-governmental and governmental assets existing within the region which could be drawn upon in the event that international intervention is deemed necessary.

Multifunctional/Multidisciplinary Force Structures

Although NATO MNF contingency plans do not include these types of forces directly, a number of similarities with possible UN operations exist and have been exercised.

- Deterrent patrolling, although limited to only one side of a frontier, is very similar to the activities carried out by UN disengagement monitoring activities;

- The "hearts and minds" and public awareness activities conducted as an integral element of any AMF[L] contingency operation are not dissimilar to the activities of UN non-military and NGO agencies, albeit on a much smaller and less publicized nature; and

- Cooperation with local administrative, police, development and procurement authorities essentially parallel those of UN MNFs although much reduced in scope.

Some analysts are of the opinion that multifunctional MNFs cannot be effective due to the differing organizations, concepts, missions and methods of operation involved. While this view should not be dismissed out of hand, greater efforts should be pursued in which the UN's overall efforts could be integrated and operating costs reduced. In this writer's opinion, based upon the AMF[L] deterrent patrolling experience, the integration of both types of forces operating in the same region could generate overall savings in both effort and cost, while increasing effectiveness, as each element of the overall force would be deployed in accordance with the most cost-effective assignment of troops to tasks. Thus observer detachments could be reinforced by recognizable formed bodies of troops—and vice versa—as, when, and where necessary to accomplish the overall force mission, to defuse local tensions, and/or to stabilize a situation. Coordination of the operations and support of both types of force elements falls well within the normal functions of the HQ staff.

Cooperation with, and support of, non-military UN and NGO agencies by a MNF does not present major difficulties to the military force, although it introduces new factors to be considered in planning. Although the "G-5" Staff Branch[28] is normally the smallest staff element in the HQ, it could easily be augmented by both civilian and military staff to provide the additional expertise and staff capacity to assume and execute greater responsibilities. To formalize a relationship linking these military and civilian entities under a single HQ, consideration should be given to attaching the non-military UN and UN-sponsored NGO entities "for local support" to the UN MNF. This link would permit the UN, through the MNF HQ:

- to coordinate more efficiently the support being delivered on its behalf;

- to provide administrative support to those designated civilian personnel supporting UN operations; and

- to provide military resource support and services, when not required for their primary military function, to authorized civilian entities and their operations to deal with surge requirements.

Thus humanitarian relief agencies and civil police elements, for example, would be provided with a direct input channel into the force operational tasking process. This should ensure greater coordination in allocating and tasking of all elements involved in the delivery of services as resources would be available to be grouped in the most cost-effective manner to achieve the desired results.

UN Force Structure and Development

Unlike NATO, the UN has no force structure and development process. On each occasion that the UN activates a "peacekeeping" force, the force is cobbled together based upon perceived requirements, previous experience and the anticipated locally available support. In the past this has resulted in desired force structure parameters being stated in terms of x-number of type units of a particular size and with general capabilities. Nations are then requested to contribute units to meet these requirements. Unfortunately the units contributed do not always match the stated requirement.

Recent staff initiatives within UN headquarters to develop standardized Tables of Organization and Equipment (TOEs) for stand-by forces is a good first step to bring a degree discipline to the UN force planning process. Unfortunately the team drafting these proposed TOEs has concentrated its efforts in preparing a myriad of establishments to meet ancillary and specialized support needs rather than tackling the "front end" operational requirements. Perhaps the next phase in this project should be the development of TOEs for light armoured reconnaissance, artillery/mortar locating, area surveillance, and light air defence elements required to bolster force capabilities and credibility in situations such as the UN operation in Former Yugoslavia.

The development of an integrated or joint HQ establishment, and its subsequent activation and maintenance, would, without doubt, enhance the UN's reaction capability more than any other planning action.

- As seen from the NATO/AMF[L] experience, such a HQ could be assigned the task of developing a concept of operations for various "type" UN missions, and defining the force element capabilities requirements, and the minimum individual and unit training standards to be attained if the type-mission is to be successful.

- Inclusion of UN civilian staff within the HQ to undertake parallel, coordinated development of the non-military support establishment requirements is considered essential if planning benefits are to be maximized.

- While there may be strong pressure to deploy this HQ shortly after its formation, this should be resisted until it has had the opportunity to develop staff procedures and SOPs for use both within the MNF and between it, UN headquarters and other UN agencies. The HQ should also have time to conduct training with its communications and administrative support elements, and to practice its deployment and employment procedures within at least a few varying scenarios. Without this preparation, the HQ could lose its credibility which would be difficult to regain. The UN can shorten the time required to bring this HQ to an acceptable state of readiness by drawing upon the experience of the HQ to accomplish these goals.

- At the outset, the HQ should confine its operational planning to the development of generic contingency plans for "probable type" missions which could then be adapted to meet specific situations. As the RR MNF HQ acquires corporate experience and gains access to a global data base to support detailed planning requirements, UN headquarters should transfer responsibility for contingency planning to it.[29]

Professional competence, dedication and personal integrity must be the paramount considerations for selection of personnel to man the HQ; other considerations, such as regional representation, while important, cannot be permitted to replace the pursuit of excellence.

The value of a RR MNF rests in its ability to react rapidly to contingency situations, and therefore it should never be deployed for operations for more than the time necessary to stabilize the situation, and to organize and deploy a task-organized replacement force to replace it. Ideally three, but as a minimum two, forces are necessary to maintain this operational readiness posture. Due to the UN's financial position, the most that one can realistically expect is the creation of a RR MNF HQ to plan for, and execute contingency operations using national RR stand-by units made available to the UN for a specific operation. If this is to be the case, the UN should carefully consider expanding the staff and HQ units support base within the proposed RR MNF HQ organization to permit rapid regeneration of command and control capabilities, albeit on a reduced scale, during any deployment of the primary HQ elements.

Conclusion

The proliferation of regional conflicts flowing from national, ethnic, economic and religious tensions have replaced the more limited confrontations between power blocs and their surrogates experienced in the period from 1945-90 in the global arena. Unfortunately the UN has neither the resources nor the organizational structure at present to deal effectively with these more localized crises in a timely manner. As a consequence, its credibility has suffered. Unless action is taken to redress this situation quickly, the UN, as a force for to promote peace and stability, will soon become irrelevant.

A wholesale revamping of the UN's crisis-management system to enhance its ability to take timely action is unlikely to occur in the short-term due to the intransigence of certain members of the Security Council. Nevertheless, and in the absence of a major overhaul of its security apparatus, the UN could adopt a number of measures which could substantially improve its reactive ability. These fall generally into three areas: establishment of a rapid reaction capability; a restructuring of the Secretariat to enhance crisis response, and greater integration of planning and operations of UN agencies and resources. Actions for consideration in the short-term which will have an immediate return should be:

- The creation of an integrated RR MNF HQ, and associated HQ support elements, to plan for, and initially implement and command contingency operations, if only on a generic basis;

- The establishment of a stand-by catalogue of units which Member States have agreed to maintain and provide to the UN and which includes unit capabilities and employment constraints;

- The inclusion in the UN Secretariat of a "24/7" operations centre capability organized, equipped and manned to provide early warning of impending crises, coordinate and control crisis-management actions, and support deployed missions;

- The establishment of a mechanism to inject independent, integrated diplomatic, military and civilian advice into the drafting of future mission mandates; and

- The institution of clearly defined command and control channels for future operations.

These proposed remedial solutions do not constitute a panacea for the UN's inability to generate rapid responses to emerging crises. They will however provide a modicum of relief from the lethargy and complacency which appears to exist today.

NATO's RR MNFs may not meet all of the UN's needs. However, by building upon NATO's experience in generating RR MNFs to both deter and combat aggression, the UN could move toward a more pro-active role in the maintenance of international stability. The challenges for the UN, while great, are not insurmountable; the alternatives are unacceptable to those who suffer or will die as a result of the UN's inability to react rapidly and deal effectively with emerging crises in the future.

Figure 1
Units Assigned To AMF [L] By Nations [1983-90]

UNIT	BE	CA	GE	IT	LU	UK	US
Infantry Battalion	x	x	xx	x	x	x	x
Lightly Armed Reconnaissance Squadron						x	
Light Artillery Regiment							
Regimental HQ						x	
Battery	x	x	x	x		x	x
Air Defence Section	x	x	x	x		x	x
Combat Engineer Company (+)							x
Composite Aviation Unit							
UTTH Aviation Company			x				
Medium-lift Aviation Squadron						x	
HQ AMF(L)							
Staff Personal	x	x	x	x		x	x
HQ Company	x	x	x	x		x	x
Radio Squadron						x	
Line Company			x				
Field Security Section							x
Tactical Air Support Section		x	x	x		x	x
Tactical Avn Support Section			x			x	
HQ C&L Helicopter Platoon							x
Logistics Support Battalion						x	
Movement Control Squadron (-)						x	
Field Hospital			x	x			
Casualty Treatment Company							x
Multinational MP Platoon							
Headquarters						x	
Platoons	x	x	x	x	x	x	x
Veterinary Section				x			x
Blood Collection/Transfusion Team			x	x			

Figure 2
Commitment of Contingents by Area [1983-90]

Contingency Area	BE	CA	GE	IT	LU	UK	US
N1 - Norway		p	h	p	p	p	s
N2 - Denmark	s		p/h	p	p	p	s
S1 - Turkish Thrace	p		p	h/s		p	p
S2 - Northern Greece	p		p	h/s		p	p
S3 - Southern Turkey	p		p	h/s		p	p
S4 - Northern Italy	p		p	h/s	s	p	p
S5 - Eastern Turkey	p*		p	h/p	s	p	p

p = primary; p* = primary (summer only); s = secondary; h = hospital

Figure 3
Detailed Rules of Engagement (ROE) for the
Allied Command Europe (ACE) Mobile Force (Land) (AMF(L))

Rule One: Authority to move element of AMF(L):

OPTION ALPHA: No authority granted to conduct deterrent operations. AMF(L) to stay in designated staging area.

OPTION BRAVO: Authority granted to conduct deterrent operations as detailed in appropriate contingency plans.

OPTION CHARLIE(1): Authority granted to withdraw Key Companies to the staging area.

OPTION DELTA(1): Authority granted to cease deterrent operations and move Force to assembly area.

Rule Two: Treatment of infiltrating civilians and of subversive elements committing suspicious or hostile acts:

OPTION ALPHA(1): Passive Policy. Observe and report. Inform local authorities. Problem to be handled by host nation. If attacked, *use minimum force for self-defence only.*

OPTION BRAVO(1): Active Policy. Co-ordinate with local commanders. If the situation requires, hand them over to host nation authorities u*sing the minimum force* necessary to control the situation.

Figure 3 (cont'd)

Rule Three: Type of defence against cross-border fire or fire from the sea:

OPTION ALPHA(1): Passive Policy. Observe and report. Withdraw if necessary to preserve own force.

OPTION BRAVO(1): Active Policy. For self-defence, return fire as appropriate to the circumstances, *using minimum force* necessary to control the situation; cease fire immediately if the enemy ceases fire.

Rule Four: Type of conduct against hostile ground force elements which have infiltrated and violated NATO territory by land, sea, and air:

OPTION ALPHA(1): Passive Policy. Maintain contact through observation. Determine identity and intentions. Report upon developments but do not open fire unless fired upon first or *in self-defence using minimum force necessary.*

OPTION BRAVO(1): Active Policy. If appropriate, stop hostile element and advise it is on NATO territory. If the hostile element fails to leave NATO territory, *use minimum force* necessary to eject them or disarm them before handing them over to the host nation authorities.

Rule Five: Type of defence against hostile aircraft over NATO territory:

OPTION ALPHA(1): Passive Policy. Passive air defence measures only.

OPTION BRAVO(1): Active air defence in accordance with control orders issued by the local air defence commanders. *Use minimum force necessary* to control the situation and *in self-defence.*

Note: (1) SACEUR may be delegated the authority to approve changes by the Defence Planning Committee after the approval of initial changes.

Notes

1. The AMF (A) had no HQ as assigned squadrons, when deployed, are integrated directly into the regional air command structures. HQ AMF (L) was responsible for coordinating AMF (A) activities with ATAFs.

2. AMF (L) & (A) and STANAVFORLANT.

3. Major reviews are conducted every two years with updates and adjustments taking place in the off years. Special major reviews can be submitted at any time if the risk scenario changes substantially.

4. The formal defence review process has a minimum reaction time of 2 years plus procurement time from input (statement of requirement) to output (introduction).

5. The HQ AMF (L), even with augmentation does not have a Political Advisor on staff. This requirement however has always been provided by SACEUR's office when needed.

6. See Figures 1 & 2 for an overview of AMF (L) assigned stand-by units and their contingency area allocations.

7. Responsible for the provision of all formation-level VHF, UHF and HF radio communications within the AMF (L).

8. Responsible for the provision of all internal and external telephone, teletype, microwave and satellite links for the AMF (L).

9. See below.

10. Unfortunately due to the distances involved, Canada was unable to fully participate in this programme during non-exercise periods, although it did provide excellent winter indoctrination programmes in Canada for both the HQ AMF (L) and the Luxembourg battalion, both of which were equipped with Canadian arctic clothing and equipment.

11. Except for Luxembourg which had no artillery resources within its one battalion army.

12. For the purposes of this paper, "specialization" is defined as "to be modified for a particular purpose or type-mission to the extent that significant limitations on general purpose employment may result."

13. For example, the CA, IT, LU, UK, and US battalions maintained a higher degree of winter warfare skills than other units; the IT, UK, and US battalions, mountain warfare skills; the CA battalion, mechanized infantry skills; etc.—but in addition to, and not to the detriment of, their general purpose light infantry specialty. Conversely the GE AB infantry battalions specialized in anti-armour operations; as they were organized into two large anti-armour companies and standard two infantry companies, it was difficult to exploit their capabilities in all assigned contingency areas.

14. For example, the GE "Line Company" was organized on a TOE not dissimilar to an equivalent GE "Divisional Line Company" except that its vehicles were procured specifically for the air-portable role and it operated a distinctive mix of both strategic and tactical communications equipment to meet the AMF [L] requirement.

15. Normally not below the Corps HQ level, although detailed negotiations/discussions with subordinate formations are conducted to ensure all activities are coordinated.

16. For example,officials representing *inter alia,* but not confined to, national air traffic, customs, frontier/border forces, civil police, emergency services, civil administration, health and medical services etc.

17. Norway and Denmark on the NATO North Flank, and Italy, Greece, and Turkey on the South are designated as Host Nations.

18. Contributing Nations to the AMF Land Component are Belgium, Germany, Italy, Spain, the UK and USA. As a result of post-Cold War force restructuring, Canada and Luxembourg have withdrawn their contingents and the UK has reduced the size of its contingent; negotiations for inclusion of additional contingents from Norway, Denmark, Greece and Turkey are ongoing. As a result of NATO restructuring, the AMF Air Component has been absorbed into the IRF (Air); Contributing Nations were Belgium, Canada, Germany, Italy, the Netherlands, the UK and the USA.

19. Concurrently the IALCC has confirmed the availability of air transport resources with Contributing Nations for the movement of their contingents, and, where shortfalls may exist, canvasses other Alliance nations to determine and procure their air frames to.

20. Some AMF[L] contingency plans contain more than one employment option.

21. Use of civilian type passenger aircraft in either the "cargo" or mixed "passenger/cargo" mode [e.g. B-707, DC-8, and Airbus aircraft] by some nations inevitably caused hold-ups/delays in the APOE throughput as the equipment to handle their "cargo packs" is generally not compatible with military air cargo handling equipment.

22. SPOEs were included in the planning for deployment for four of the seven AMF [L] contingency areas. In each case alternative air movement plans were "in being" in the event that time or the maritime did not permit sea shipment of equipment and stocks.

23. Key Companies were always scheduled as the first elements to arrive in the Contingency Area.

24. These patrols were supplemented by fixed observation positions when it was considered necessary to establish a more permanent presence on a particular potential line of advance.

25. Although ROEs are a C5 measure and should be included in that section, logic dictates that they are covered here under "Deterrent Operations".

26. In some contingency areas this authority devolved to the PSC level due to the distances and /or span of MSC command involved.

27. Even to the point of baking and distributing fresh bread which met national contingent specifications and tastes.

28. One of the responsibilities of the "G-5" Staff is "Civil Affairs".

29. Identification of potential contingency areas would remain a responsibility of UNHQ NY.

Enhancing UN Response:
Lessons from UNPROFOR

J. A. MacInnis

Introduction

First, what is UNPROFOR? Some facts and figures are relevant. The present strength of the mission is a shade under 43,000 with some 37,000 of these being military. A total of 35 nations have been represented in the mission, and some 22 of these contributed formed units. Like all UN peacekeeping operations, UNPRO-FOR is, of course, guided by Security Council resolutions; the Council has adopted over 50 resolutions which impact in some form or another on the operations of UNPROFOR.

The UNPROFOR mission is, not surprisingly, continually evolving as the priorities shift in response to the situation on the ground. However, in the most general of terms, there are, or at least were, three main components of the UNPROFOR mission:

(a) The provision of support to UN High Commissioner for Refugees (UNHCR) humanitarian assistance operations. At the moment, UNHCR provides assistance to over four million inhabitants in the former Yugoslavia; 2.7 million of whom are in Bosnia-Herzegovina. UNPROFOR's role in this operation ranges from actual delivery of food and shelter material, to convoy escort, to the monitoring of secondary distribution.

(b) The conduct of more traditional style peacekeeping especially along the zone of separation in the United Nations Protected Areas (UNPAs) in Croatia.

(c) Preventative peacekeeping in the former Yugoslav Republic of Macedonia.

HQ UNPROFOR, located in Zagreb, is headed by the Special Representative of the Secretary-General (SRSG) and consists of the military component; civil, police and political affairs, and the administration. UNHCR and the International Committee of the Red Cross (ICRC) heads of mission are also located there.

Major-General J.A. MacInnis, Canadian Army, is former Deputy Force Commander, UNPROFOR.

UNPROFOR reminds us that there are certain key aspects which set peace-keeping apart from more traditional military operations:

(a) First, military commanders are used to fighting clearly-defined, if not neces-sarily identifiable, enemies. In a peacekeeping mission, there are no enemies, only potential partners who have conflicting aims and interests. Notwithstand-ing the fact that his troops may be under fire, the UN commander must take an absolutely impartial and objective approach to all parties; he cannot, at any cost, take sides. It remains a fact of life that a peacekeeping mission can only be undertaken if all parties involved accept the presence and legitimacy of the UN force.

(b) On a related theme, there is not likely to be a military solution to a peacekeep-ing mission: there is no victory to be won by armed force. The only victory is that which occurs when a lasting peace is found.

(c) All military commanders seek to have a clearly identifiable end-state or goal upon which to focus their efforts and their resources. However, the peace-keeping scenario, with its missions to "establish conditions conducive to ne-gotiations" or "implement ceasefires between warring parties", hardly pro-vides the well-defined end-state which each commander desires. In many cases, the political authorities have not determined what that end-state will be. Hence, the military commander is often in the unenviable position of having to chart his own path.

(d) Political direction is provided to the force commander by the Special Repre-sentative of the Secretary-General. The SRSG must, however, act within the guidelines and directives issued by the Security Council, in the form of reso-lutions. These resolutions are, to put it mildly, often a reflection of divergent political views and as such are themselves occasionally contradictory or am-biguous. Thus the SRSG and military commander must wrestle with conflict-ing directions as to how to proceed.

(e) The multinational nature of a large peacekeeping mission such as UNPRO-FOR is, in itself, a contributing factor to that mission's performance. Not only does this result in a menage of equipment, procedures and capabilities, but it can be reflected in a lack of a common approach to a given problem. Simi-larly, the great variance in unit capabilities becomes, of necessity, a key factor in one's appreciation of the situation. To put it bluntly, some units are better than others.

(f) The role that is played by nationally-imposed employment limitations cannot be ignored and is a factor not normally encountered to the degree that is present in such a diverse mission as UNPROFOR. The more ambiguous the mandate, the tighter are the strings binding contingents to their capitals.

(g) Finally, the military component of UNPROFOR is composed of those units which the troop contributing nations have chosen to provide. The same is true for all missions. The fact that the Force Commander's number one reinforcement priority may well be engineer units is of little worth unless some nation chooses to provide such troops. The result may be, as is currently the case in UNPROFOR, a force which lacks certain key elements, such as logistics or engineers. It remains a fact that the Force Commander must use the force he is given and has little influence over its composition.

Each one of these key differences which set peacekeeping operations apart has an effect on the day-to-day conduct of operations.

There does appear to be a slowly growing realization of the differences between peacekeeping and peacemaking or enforcement operations. However, there still remains a large body of thought which seems to relate these differences mainly to equipment rather than to intention.

The closer a peacekeeping mission approaches peace enforcement, the more likely the mission is entering not a grey zone as some would have it, but rather a zone of paralysis wherein any mandate component, be it the delivery of humanitarian aid, the monitoring of weapons or simply mission self-support becomes difficult if not impossible to carry out. Peacekeeping and peace enforcement missions are, in fact, separate and distinct and not, as some might suggest, merely variations on a theme.

Peacekeeping and the Humanitarian Effort

UNPROFOR in Bosnia first established under UN Security Council Resolution 757 (1992) of 30 May 1992 was mandated "to create the necessary conditions for unimpeded delivery of humanitarian supplies to Sarajevo and other locations in Bosnia and Herzegovina". This mandate was later expanded, in resolution 776 (1992) of 14 September 1992, to include, *inter alia*, the following tasks:

- provide support to the UN High Commission for Refugees (UNHCR) in the delivery of humanitarian relief, particularly through the provision of convoy protection when so requested, and;

- providing protection for convoys of released detainees on request of the International Committee of the Red Cross (ICRC).

At least initially this mandate made sense; by the time of its coming into existence, it was clear that the international community was prepared neither to abandon Bosnia to its own fate, nor to intervene militarily. This humanitarian-based mandate allowed the community, working through the UN, to bring together two apolitical, seemingly impartial activities, in order to look after, in some fashion, the victims of the ongoing conflict while at the same time having in location a force of blue berets ready to exploit any hint of peace which might emerge. An added bonus would accrue if, by the very presence of UNPROFOR, UNHCR, ICRC and others, the level of conflict were to be lowered.

Almost three years have since passed, including two winters of quite intense conflict during which a working partnership among UNPROFOR, UNHCR, the World Food Programme (WFP), UNICEF, the World Health Organization (WHO), the ICRC, many non-governmental organizations (NGOs) and others have been forged. In the main, this partnership worked, but only as long as one overriding characteristic was present and was seen to be present, and that characteristic is "impartiality". To be successful in the execution of the humanitarian operation, the entire UN mission has to be seen to be impartial. The responsibility for this impartiality is twofold: first, the humanitarian agency must be impartial if aid is not to become a weapon in the conflict and second the escorting agency, in this case UNPROFOR, must be equally non-discriminatory. In essence, there must be a humanitarian-military bond in which the armed force is seen to be but a protective extension of the assistance operation.

Should the military force be required to take on other tasks which may put it in a position which would jeopardize its impartiality, then one of two results would ensue: either the military-humanitarian bond would become unglued, leading to a parting of the ways, or the impartiality of the humanitarian effort itself, through its perceived association with the military, would be questioned. I contend that both of these conditions have occurred to some degree in the former Yugoslavia, highlighting the incompatibility of, on the one hand, threatening the use of force and, on the other, attempting to continue to support the humanitarian operations.

A widely held expectation was that UNPROFOR and NATO were mandated and ready to fight to defend not only the as yet undefined safe areas, but also to ensure the unimpeded delivery of humanitarian aid. It is the inclusion of the latter mandate component which, in my view, dangerously linked the humanitarian effort and UNPROFOR to the ongoing conflict itself, to the point that there exists a belief that UNPROFOR and UNHCR have collaborated in the use of force to "punch through" humanitarian aid. This has never occurred.

This condition has led to the state of affairs whereby the media, many members of the international community, the warring parties and indeed, some members of UNPROFOR and the humanitarian relief organizations, are confused with the current state of affairs. Constant coordination, discussions, explanations and assurances are necessary in order to maintain the humanitarian operation and to retain a sometimes tenuous humanitarian-military bond in the former Yugoslavia.

In the experience of some humanitarian officials, the use of military and technical expertise for large and complex operations is a positive lesson learned; however, the use of the military for humanitarian access is more problematic. In the former Yugoslavia, the military component (aided and abetted by the parties to the conflict themselves) initially retained a tendency to link humanitarian with political and military issues with negative consequences. At the lower level, unfamiliarity with humanitarian procedures and principles, as well as an apparent lack of initiative and flexibility, required considerable time and energy to correct. Furthermore, with frequent troop rotation and wide disparity of capability and understanding among national contingents, these problems have a tendency to recur.

Uniformity of purpose and coordination among the humanitarian elements themselves was also lacking, thereby exacerbating the more difficult problem of military-humanitarian cooperation. The requirement, for example, to conduct detailed planning and preparation for convoy movement into insecure areas and impose control measures on movement came as a surprise to many senior humanitarian officials but was eventually accepted as being both necessary and prudent.

These problems of coordination of effort do not lie solely within the UN. There are many humanitarian agencies present in the former Yugoslavia apart from UNHCR and UNICEF and these run the gamut from highly professional, courageous and completely neutral groups such as ICRC and Care Canada, to those NGOs whose motives and performance are somewhat suspect.

The strengthening of humanitarian coordination is a very complex problem. Although there has been an increase in the exchange of information, much still remains to be done before true coordination, even within a mission area, can be said to have been accomplished. Success in coordination of the military-humanitarian effort within the former Yugoslavia has been achieved to a certain degree and should be exploited for future use. Too much success however has been based on personality and too little on procedures.

Allow me now to shift to the question of characteristics that peacekeeping forces must possess if they are to be successful. The one overriding characteristic which is applicable at every level, from a rifleman on observation post duty, to the Force Commander, to the force as a collective whole, is that of credibility.

Credibility has two principal components: capability and conduct, each of which is composed of sub-elements.

Under the heading of capability I have included three elements:
- combat effectiveness;
- equipment; and
- toughness.

Under the heading of conduct, I have listed seven elements:
- restraint;
- discipline;
- firmness;
- consistency;
- cultural sensitivity;
- rule of law; and
- impartiality.

A new one here is the respect for the rule of law, not only as it concerns the behaviour of peacekeepers themselves, although this is vitally important to overall credibility, but also the application of international legal instruments (international humanitarian law, international refugee law, and human rights). Respect for the rule of law is something which we in peacekeeping have taken for granted. With the expansion of the number of countries willing to participate in peacekeeping operations, however, and especially because of the changing nature of peacekeeping itself, we ignore this essential characteristic at our peril.

Nothing breaks down the credibility of a force faster than illegal or inappropriate activity on the part of its members. In this respect, the perception of wrongdoing can be as damaging as the proof of it. Peacekeeping forces must follow a three-track approach: first, to ensure that regulations and procedures are in place to thwart or at least dissuade those tempted to engage in improper activity; second, to educate the force to ensure that all members are aware of the conduct required; and third, to be seen to investigate in a serious manner each and every complaint or allegation made. The very fact that UNPROFOR has been seen to take allegations of improper conduct seriously has been, in my opinion, a boost to credibility. It is a fact, however, that certain contributors either have no means to discipline their personnel while on UN duty out-of-country, or no on-site means to carry out credible investigations into alleged wrongdoing by their peacekeepers. But the importance of this characteristic cannot be understated because the peacekeeper must not only be the model of respect for the rule of law as generally accepted, but also, for the law of war, and basic human rights.

The final and most important element in the conduct category is impartiality. Once a peacekeeping force loses its impartiality, then it becomes one of the belligerents. The force has to deal with each and all of the parties on an ongoing basis. Each of the parties must understand that they will be treated in the same manner as the others involved in the conflict.

Together, these seven sub-elements of conduct form an ethos or code of conduct by which peacekeeping should be carried out. This is, of course, easier said than done. A national army spends a great deal of time and effort instilling a sense of ethos within its ranks. How, then, does a multinational peacekeeping force, drawn from a number of nations, each with a different sub-culture or military ethos, develop its own such ethos? Part of the answer lies in the leadership imparted by the Force Commander and by the unit command structure. But I firmly believe that capability standards for peacekeepers and more importantly a universal code of conduct for peacekeepers has to be produced with some degree of urgency before a rapid response capability can be fully exploited.

Let me now turn to the subject of the current conflict environment and suggest one option as to how the tool called peacekeeping may be useful.

The type of conflict extant in the world today is the worst possible kind, ethnic-based and warlord driven. In his book, *Blood and Belonging,* Michael Ignatieff comments: "The key narrative of the new world order is the disintegration of national states into ethnic civil war; the key architects of that order are warlords and the key language of our age is ethnic nationalism."

Warlords and their warriors usually have no stake in peace; further, the longer the fighting continues the less redeemable they become. Their acts of violence are brutal and wanton, and usually conducted for their own sake. Tactics utilized in this kind of warfare are those of the guerilla, but are significantly enhanced by the warriors' total lack of restraint. Suffocation of this type of violence by standard military means is very difficult.

As the conflict continues, the home-grown warrior is joined by warrior-mercenaries from other lands. Meanwhile, as the societal structure crumbles, the victims become further exploited by internal and external criminal elements, leading to a state of affairs for which an imposed, or even a negotiated peace settlement will not necessarily mean the end of a conflict.

The hesitancy of the international community to impose or to attempt to impose a peace in this type of conflict is well known. The present contradiction between states' rights and the nationalist aspirations of component groups is unlikely to be resolved in the short term. Prevented on the one hand by public opinion from doing nothing, and on the other from imposing a military solution, the international community, working essentially through the medium of the United Nations, must strive for some middle ground in which either to achieve conflict prevention or, failing that, to achieve some degree of conflict containment or preferably resolution, and to conduct post-conflict rebuilding.

The first and greatest challenge is to produce a strategy which recognizes the warning signs, takes preventative measures, engages in conflict resolution activities or, at the very least, activities which moderate the effects of conflict, and follows up with a post-conflict agenda to reduce the risk of relapse. This process must be recognized as representing a continuum of effort and must be separate and distinct from operations in the field. In other words, peacekeepers, or a peacekeeping mandate, must not be used in an attempt to squeeze out a political solution. The contradictions and false expectations which plague current missions must be eliminated.

Second, while conflict prevention, containment and resolution tend to be the focus of attention, of equal if not greater significance is the need to protect, assist and support the victims of the conflict. Humanitarian assistance must be more than the delivery of foodstuffs and medicines. This should form the basis of the peacekeeper's mandate.

The third and final imperative is the need to strengthen the mechanisms by which crimes against humanity are investigated and through which the perpetrators are brought to justice. This last aspect, that of the application of international law to peacekeeping missions, is an area in which there is much work to be done, and it should be included in the peacekeeper's package.

Future UN mandates should:

- be based on humanitarian relief and/or assistance to refugees;

- include protection of human rights;

- include authority for the peacekeeping force to protect victims, assist aid organizations, and promote/enforce international humanitarian law, and;

- authorize the use of force for self defence only.

Force will be used, however, at the discretion of the commander, when faced with blatant human rights abuses.

It is precisely this type of mandate for which rapid response is most needed, not the benign, traditional, consent-based, conflict-free peacekeeping environment, nor an enforcement mission which requires and mandates peacekeepers to be warfighters and for which coalition or security based regional groupings are much more appropriate.

The type of peacekeeping intervention envisaged in Bosnia is neither traditional, that is, based upon the consent of *all* parties to the conflict, nor is it by any stretch of the imagination enforcement—it is however, much closer to the former in that it does have impartiality as a basic principle in order to build and retain a necessary bond between the humanitarian and military aspects of the mission as well as to prevent attempts to impose a solution by force.

This type of peacekeeping endeavour, in order to have any chance of success, must be carried out with precision and sophistication of a degree not seen to date. It presents operational, legal and behavioural challenges which must be addressed in order to enhance or to maximize the peacekeeper's greatest and sometimes only tool, and indeed his main source of protection—his credibility.

In summary, international intervention should continue, and should be humanitarian oriented with increased emphasis on international legal instruments. For military peacekeepers at the operational level, this means an added requirement to operate beyond the confines of traditional military operations. Peacekeepers must themselves be human rights monitors, if not enforcers; they must be schooled in the relevant international legal instruments such as human rights and refugee law; they must be fully conversant with the laws of war, specifically the Geneva Conventions and their additional protocols, and they must assist in ensuring their observation.

For peacekeeping leaders, it means functioning and decision-making in uncharted waters; it means being the antithesis of the warlord by being the champion of the rule of law and of peace. To misquote Dean Rusk, if the new world order cannot be perfect, at least it can be decent.

The United Nations Transition Assistance Group (UNTAG) in Namibia

M.K. Jeffery

Aim

This paper provides some background on UNTAG, and presents an assessment of the value that a UN rapid reaction capability would have had in the UNTAG situation.

Background

Namibia, originally South-West Africa, is a largely arid country about the size of Manitoba or Saskatchewan with approximately 1.1 million people. Approximately one per cent of the land is arable. The western coastline is one of the most inaccessible with its 200 km wide Namib desert. The central and southern plateaus are semi-arid, supporting sheep and cattle farming with the southeast bordering on the Kalahari desert. The north is open savannah suitable for cattle and some crops, and the northeast, along the Caprivi strip, is subtropical rainforest. There are 11 distinct ethnic groups within the country, the largest being the Ovambo in the north. The country is one of extremes. At one end is the cosmopolitan city of Windhoek, at the other you can find the mud huts of the Ovahimba or the wood dwellings of the Bushmen. Perhaps most significant from the perspective of the UNTAG mission was the size of the country and the distances required to be travelled, especially the 1600 km northern border.

The Namibian story has its start following World War I when South Africa was granted permission to govern the territory of South-West Africa under a mandate of the League of Nations. The years that followed saw a regular struggle between South Africa's attempts to annex the territory and the UN's intention to see it developed as an independent state.

Brigadier-General M.K. Jeffery, Canadian Army, was Chief Liaison Officer, UNTAG.

In the late 1950s, the South-West Africa People's Organization (SWAPO) emerged from the predominantly Ovambo people in the north of the country to pursue the objective of the liberation of the Namibian people and their lands. Operating out of bases in Tanzania, Zambia and later Angola, SWAPO infiltrated insurgents into Namibia starting in late 1965, reaching a peak in the mid 1970s. South Africa responded by deploying troops into northern Namibia and ultimately into Angola to halt the insurgency. The border war, as the South Africans referred to it, cost the lives of over 700 security force soldiers, over 1,000 Namibian civilians and an estimated 11,000 SWAPO and Angolan soldiers.

The UN Resolution

The UN plan for Namibia, first put forward in 1978 by the "contact group" of five nations (US, UK, France, West Germany and Canada), was focused on free and internationally supervised elections. The plan envisaged implementation of the resolution in four stages: the cessation of hostilities by all parties and the withdrawal or demobilization of the various armed forces; the conduct of free and fair elections to the constituent assembly; the formulation and adoption of a constitution; and the entry into force of the constitution and independence of Namibia. However, despite general agreement on the mandate, and approval as Security Council Resolution 435, it took 10 years to overcome the many hurdles to implementation. Finally implementation was approved on 16 February 1989.

Implementation of Resolution 435 was to commence on 1 April 1989. However, deployment of UNTAG was seriously delayed by the late approval, by the Security Council, of Resolution 632 on 16 February 1989 and the approval of the budget, by the Fifth Committee, on 1 March 1989. The resolution called for a minimum of six to eight weeks preparation time. Due to the delays however, only four weeks were finally available, requiring a major effort to deploy as soon as possible. Despite this, no attempt was made to delay the commencement of Resolution 435, and although some advancement of the deployments was achieved, it was insufficient to deal with the capability gap.

Deployment

All UNTAG personnel were transported to Namibia by air. Advance parties from the various contingents started arriving on 8 March. The first UN military observers arrived on 23 March and deployment forward was complete by 8 April. However the effectiveness of these troops, particularly the observers, was extremely limited. Communications were almost non-existent, vehicles were scarce and even the most basic commodities were in short supply. Only a few of the observers could conduct any patrols and most communications relied on the sparse and overloaded civil/military phone system.

The main bodies of all contingents deployed to Namibia throughout April. Vehicles and communications equipment, the majority of which came by sea, didn't start arriving until 15 April with the arrival of the Finnish battalion (FINNBATT) ship. But the last set of contingent equipment did not arrive until 1 May. The last ship containing a large number of civilian pattern vehicles, which represented an essential part of UNTAG's mobility, arrived on 23 May. As a consequence of these late arrivals and the distances personnel and equipment had to be moved once in Namibia, the force was not really operational until 1 June.

Organization

UNTAG was headed by the Special Representative of the Secretary-General, Mr. Martti Ahtisaari. He was assisted by a military force of some 4,500 troops, under the Force Commander, Lieutenant General Prem Chand, and a civilian component, which at its height was almost 3,000 strong. The civilian component included 1,500 civilian police monitors, staff to run 10 UN regional offices, electoral staff, staff from the UN High Commission for Refugees, and administrative staff.

The military force was based on three 850-man infantry battalions. The supporting units included an engineer unit, a signals unit, a medium helicopter unit, a medium air transport unit, two logistics units and a medical unit. In addition there were 300 UN military observers.

Operations

The UN resolution called for the UNTAG military force to monitor the cessation of hostilities by all parties and the restriction to base of all South African Defence Force (SADF) and South-West Africa Territorial Force (SWATF) troops. It was then to supervise the demobilization of all SWATF Troops and the withdrawal to South Africa of all SADF troops. These tasks were to be accomplished primarily by the military observers. The infantry battalions were to deploy to keep the borders under surveillance, prevent infiltration and guard the vital military installations along the northern border.

As stated earlier, the UN mandate was to take effect on 1 April 1989. By 31 March, the SADF and SWATF units had withdrawn into their bases and handed the patrolling of the Namibian northern border over to the South-West Africa Police (SWAPOL). Early on 1 April, armed soldiers from SWAPO's military organization, the People's Liberation Army of Namibia (PLAN), started to cross the border in the region of Ovamboland. This was not, as some believe, a total surprise. On 31 March, the SADF advised the Force Commander of the likelihood of this event. However, with no ability to confirm it, and with the UN's predisposition to mistrust the South Africans, nothing was done.

Fighting soon took place between PLAN and SWAPOL, and South Africa requested release of SADF troops to assist the police. Given the level of operational readiness of UNTAG, the UN had little option, and many SADF units were soon engaged along the border. With the lack of UN presence in the region, the events of the first few days are at best hazy and accounts vary greatly between the two sides. There is also much dispute over the intent of the SWAPO move. It is, however, clear that the confrontation was at times quite violent. It is estimated that some

1,800 to 1,900 PLAN soldiers crossed into Namibia, and during the fighting a total of 315 PLAN and 30 SADF/SWAPOL were killed.

During the fighting UNTAG tried to get UN observers and troops along the border at least to determine what was going on. Some observers and troops from the Australian and British contingents performed patrolling and monitoring duties along the Namibian/Angolan border. There were at times some serious confrontations with the SADF and SWAPOL.

Understandably, many questions were asked about UNTAG's ability to forecast or identify the movement of SWAPO troops within Angola. However, in addition to the administrative problems of deployment, this was beyond UNTAG's mandate. Under the Brazzaville Agreement, the monitoring of SWAPO was to be conducted by the Angolan military and UNTAG only established a liaison office in Luanda and a headquarters in Lubango for coordination purposes. Even though UNTAG representatives were deployed in Angola from 18 March, no indication of SWAPO activities was ever received. This reliance on Angola for monitoring SWAPO was to my mind a serious flaw in the UN plan.

The confrontation was to be UNTAG's most serious challenge, and could well have been the end of the process. I have no doubt that there were those on both sides who would have been happy to see the peace plan scuttled. In an attempt to get the process back on the rails a number of meetings of the Joint Monitoring Commission (JMC)—a grouping of the US, USSR, South Africa, Angola and Cuba—were held. Many attempts were made to withdraw the PLAN fighters and re-establish the situation that existed before 1 April.

Finally, it was agreed on 19 May at Cahama, Angola, that the necessary disengagement of forces had been achieved. Despite the difficulties this delay had imposed, the SADF now worked hard to get back on schedule. The majority of the SWATF troops were demobilized by 27 May, and by 24 June all but the 1,500 SADF troops permitted under Resolution 435 had been withdrawn. Thus this serious threat to Resolution 435 had been averted and the process was back on track. At this stage the main tasks of the UN military force had been completed. Their role from here on was to monitor the few remaining SADF personnel, provide overall security for the country and to support the civilian component of UNTAG.

Assessment of UNTAG

Despite the success of UNTAG, the reality was that, as a military force, UNTAG never achieved an acceptable operational level. It was plagued from the start with problems of organization, command and control. While this was not significantly different from other UN missions, the events of 1 April 1989 created such a crisis of confidence across UNTAG from which it never really recovered.

How does one reconcile that with the fact that overall UNTAG was a successful mission? Here we must consider the too-frequently misunderstood importance that the position and intentions of South Africa played in the mission. Here there are two major factors.

First, South Africa is a major regional power and at no time was there ever a threat to her ability to project power and influence events. Even at the height of the border war, South Africa's abilities were never in doubt. Only when a significant number of Cuban troops became engaged did South Africa have difficulties and even here the situation was militarily manageable. On the other hand SWAPO was never really a major threat and never obtained a power base within Namibia.

Second, by the time UNTAG was approved, South Africa wanted the UN resolution to work. For political and economic reasons it had decided upon the course to be charted for South Africa, and Namibia was an essential first step to show the world that it intended to comply with the agreement on Namibia and to act as a trial run for what would have to occur in South Africa. The result of these two factors was that, within reason, South Africa would have ensured that the objective was achieved, irrespective of what went wrong.

The reality was that the military component of UNTAG did not perform well. Irrespective of the problem posed by the late approvals of the mandate, it could have performed much better. It could have responded better to the crisis on 1 April, and much better over the course of the mission. As it was, much of the force was an unnecessary expense and at times an impediment to progress.

I will highlight just three major factors.

The Impact of Poor UN Planning

The first factor was the lack of initiative and reaction to the reality that UNTAG would never meet the 1 April deadline for implementation. Here, to some extent, the lack of options with respect to early deployment is understandable. However, it would seem that no attempt was made to get even a small effective force in the country by 1 April. Certainly steps were taken to speed up the deployment, and to some extent they were effective. But the result was really to deliver a large number of the UNTAG military personnel with little or no equipment. Instead what should have been done was to change the plan and send in a small, effective force. As it was, this lack of foresight robbed the force commander of an adequate force to deal with the situation as it developed.

The Impact of Poor UNTAG Command and Control

Notwithstanding the difficult position in which UNTAG found itself, there were many things that could have been done to prepare for 1 April, and to address the crisis once it had occurred. However, UNTAG was plagued with poor command and control right from the start of the mission. This situation improved somewhat for the civilian component, but never significantly improved for the military force.

The first problem was a structural one. The mission was civilian-led, due in large measure to the fact that once the military forces had withdrawn or been demobilized, the UN military role was a supporting one. However, this view was not shared at the senior levels within UNTAG. The result of this was often two different approaches to the same problem, and a lack of cooperation that pervaded the whole mission.

Second the senior military staff lacked the necessary ability to deal with an uncertain and rapidly changing situation.

Third, there was a lack of staff organization. The military headquarters lacked the firm control necessary to provide good and timely direction. In fact it was all the headquarters could do to stay abreast of what happened.

Finally, there was a lack of common understanding between the military staffs and the civilian staffs at UNTAG Headquarters. The result was a lack of cooperation, animosity and often worse.

None of these problems are alien to the UN. Many missions have had the same problems in some measure. However, with all of them present in the same mission, its inability to respond to the 1 April crisis nearly destroyed it. It was unable to respond to the crisis in anything but a slow and disjointed manner, and the pressures it placed on the Headquarters thwarted its development such that it never achieved an adequate level of operational capability even when the crisis was passed.

The Impact of Poor UNTAG Composition and Organization

The final major factor was one of internal composition and organization. While this is related to the problem with command and control, I prefer to deal with it separately because it raises sensitive issues.

The reality of UN military forces is that they include a wide range of contingents with varying capabilities. This is a situation that most missions have been able to overcome, or at least manage, by depending on the more capable contingents to handle the more demanding tasks. In those areas where small teams are required, such as headquarters staffs or UN Military Observer (UNMO) teams, the trend has been to mix personnel so that the strengths and weaknesses are balanced.

With respect to the UNTAG infantry battalions, only one of the three was really capable of carrying out its tasks. The other two, while perhaps good as pure line infantry battalions, lacked the flexibility and initiative required in peacekeeping. With such a high proportion of his force in this category the Force Commander's flexibility was very limited. However, this flexibility was further eroded by an ill-advised deployment plan that was not changed. The most capable battalion was placed along the northeastern sector into the Caprivi strip. This was the least demanding sector, and could have been assigned to either of the other battalions. One of the other battalions was placed in the northwest of the country where all of the fighting had been, and where the demands would be greatest; the other was placed in the centre, largely in a reserve position.

The same type of problem was encountered with the UN military observers. Given the speed with which the UNMOs had to be deployed, there was not enough time to organize them as well as would have been liked. However, they were kept as homogeneous groups—i.e., in national groupings—and deployed around the country with no thought to capability or experience. Perhaps the extreme example was the deployment of the Irish contingent. Virtually the whole contingent was made up of experienced UN observers. Despite that, they were deployed in the south of the country along the South African border, where there was virtually no job to do.

In summary, while UNTAG was a successful mission, that success was, in large measure, in spite of the UNTAG military force. Had the planning at UN Headquarters responded more rapidly and realistically to the delay, then perhaps many of the problems could have been averted. However, the situation could have been dealt with far more effectively had the force composition and the command and control been better.

Impact if a Rapid Reaction Capability Were Available

In preparing this overview, I was asked to answer the question: "Would this situation have been different if the UN had a rapid reaction capability, and, if so, what type of capability would have been required?"

There is no question in my mind that an effective force deployed quickly into Namibia would have resulted in a significantly different mission. The final outcome might not have been any different, but many of the problems would have been avoided and the military force of UNTAG would have accomplished a lot more. I would like to look at the type of force required before returning to the matter of what that force could have accomplished.

First, given the limited time available to UNTAG, the force needed to be a capable functioning military force ready to operate as soon as it hit the ground. There was no time for in-theatre organization and training. This is particularly important when one thinks of multinational models. My experience within the UN calls me to question the effectiveness of a multinational approach. I believe only two models really would work: either a national force deployed in the service of the UN, or a standing multinational force that has trained and operated together. Here that cooperation has to be sufficiently regular to ensure the level of training and cohesion essential to commence operations immediately on arrival. The level of training, etc., would very much depend on the diversity of the national elements and the state of their national training.

Having said that, the force needs to be appropriately structured. There were a number of specific capabilities required in Namibia. It needed an effective means of command and control—a commander with the flexibility to deploy his force over a large area and conduct a variety of operations. Given the problems we had in UNTAG, I have concerns that even with a capable reaction force, the limits of the military leadership would have curtailed its effectiveness. Although this situation is perhaps an anomaly, some consideration may need to be given to the reaction force deploying under its own command until the main force is ready to take over. This would alleviate the problem of a main force commander having to concentrate on operations while setting up his force, and would avoid the potentially difficult political situation where a commander is not up to the task.

The reaction force also would need a working and effective staff. A cohesive staff with clear standard operating procedures is essential. Equally important is good long range communications. While the UK contingent performed exceptionally well in Namibia under difficult conditions, they were not up to the task that faced them. This was primarily due to a misunderstanding of the requirement by UN Headquarters in New York. A dedicated communications capability was essential as the civilian telephone system was not up to the task. While the force had long range communications, they were late in being deployed. The main problem, however, was that traditional tactical VHF communications were inappropriate for the mission. HF communications or even satellite communications were needed at least down to company and probably platoon level.

Of primary importance was information. UNTAG was blind from the day it arrived, and had no real capability to improve the situation. In our case we needed a reconnaissance capability with both air and ground elements. Also, given the mine threat in the area, an engineer reconnaissance capability was required. In this case, the threat might have been quite low. However, the fear generated among the few UNTAG troops we had in the north by the presence of mines further reduced their effectiveness. The ability just to confirm the mine state would have significantly reduced the problem.

The bulk of the force must itself be an operational rapid reaction force. The role of such a force in Namibia would have been two-fold. First, it should have provided a rapid capability, preferably heliborne, to deploy to any trouble spots. Second, a light but highly mobile force could have moved quickly throughout the country to establish the UN's presence and credibility. This would have required vehicles, preferably wheeled APCs because of their relatively high mobility on roads and tracks, and because in Namibia the ground permits good cross-country mobility. This mounted force would also enable heliborne deployed troops to be backed up relatively quickly.

Finally the force would have to be logistically self-sustained for 60 days. This would not have needed to be a large element, as the country had a well developed infrastructure and virtually all commodities are easy to obtain from the local economy.

The size of the force is also important. Here it is more difficult to be precise. Given the size of Namibia, especially over 1,600 km of northern border, a large military force would be required to provide a reasonable level of security and to retain a flexible reserve to deal with the unexpected. Indeed one of the initial but unaffordable UNTAG plans forecast a requirement for 10 large battalions. My views here are guided by two factors, the first being an inherent belief in the superiority of manoeuvre warfare: a small well-organized and well-led force with superior mobility can defeat a larger force that lacks the requisite mobility. Second, no matter what we would like to have, the size of any force will be very much affected by the ability to deploy it rapidly, and by the cost of doing so. The tendency here, of course, is to keep the force as small as possible.

In short, a relatively small but capable force with a high level of tactical mobility could have established a presence in northern Namibia where the need was greatest, provided an adequate level of tactical intelligence on the movements of all factions, provided a rapid reaction capability to deal with problems and become a force credible to both sides. Such a force would have been able quickly to establish a presence in Namibia, and to start the essential building of credibility. I do not believe that any amount of UN military capability would have been able to stop SWAPO crossing the border on 1 April. The seeds of that fiasco had probably been sown long before UNTAG arrived. However, a military force as identified would have been able to identify early the crossing of the border and should have been able to halt the advance, thereby eliminating the need for South African forces to become engaged.

I acknowledge that this is accepting risk, and that the force would lack depth. Indeed for a surge requirement such as that posed by the SWAPO cross-border incursion, it would be taxed to the limit. Increases from this small core would add depth and flexibility. The optimum force would be brigade size with the same basic elements, requiring a doubling of the reconnaissance and helicopter lift capability, and a tripling of the infantry.

Summary

In summary, while the ultimate success in Namibia was not in jeopardy, the availability of a small but effective military force early in the mission would have overcome many difficulties and allowed UNTAG to accomplish far more with less effort.

Efforts to Establish
UN Stand-By Arrangements:
An Historical Account and Appraisal

Alex Morrison

Introduction

The recent expansion of United Nations peacekeeping operations throughout the world has re-kindled debate on whether and to what degree stand-by agreements can give the international community greater ability to manage conflict. Various models of force packages and deployment/sustainment arrangements have been proposed by critics of existing *ad hoc* approaches to mustering forces for peacekeeping duty, and by advocates of more muscular operations involving combat. Two such models are standing forces and stand-by forces. Although these terms will be elaborated on later, it is worthwhile to distinguish between them thus: standing forces imply the collection of a band of "international civil servant soldiers" trained, paid and commanded by the appropriate UN organ; stand-by forces imply voluntary contributions of human and material resources by Member States which are earmarked for UN duty, but which otherwise remain under national command and are supported and trained by their respective national authorities. Neither of these are the forces referred to in Article 43 of the Charter of the United Nations. The matter of the desirability of establishing a force headquarters to carry out pre-deployment planning, and to handle the command and control aspects of a mission, has long been a topic of discussion and will be explored later.

The notion of a global army is not new. Indeed, in recent times, interest in creating a standing intervention force has surfaced time and again. Praised by some and pilloried by others, a permanent UN army represents perhaps the pinnacle of international co-operation. Following an examination of the roots of this concept, this paper will trace the evolution of the various models with a view to understanding the merits and demerits of each. Attention will be paid to the post-

Mr. Alex Morrison is President of the Lester B. Pearson Canadian International Peacekeeping Training Centre.

1991 period where the hitherto discredited standing force option has seen some-thing of a renaissance, despite formidable and enduring obstacles to its implementation.

From War to Peace

The international political context of the mid-1940s was characterized by an atmosphere of anticipation and optimism. On the threshold of victory in Europe, the Great Powers, led by the United States, collectively tallied the costs of global conflict and resolved to take decisive action to ensure that such conflagrations would never again occur. Recalling the failure of the League of Nations to check German expansion between the World Wars, and the hopelessly ill-conceived Kellogg-Briand Pact which sought to outlaw war entirely, the Great Powers laid the groundwork for new institutional guarantees (or, at least safeguards) against inter-state aggression at Dumbarton Oaks in the summer of 1944.

A year earlier, US Secretary of State Cordell Hull had devised a moral frame-work from which these theoretical guarantees would be derived. He suggested that the most politically and militarily powerful members of the international com-munity should refrain from going to war with each other or against any other member of the international community, lest a third and perhaps final world-wide conflict erupt. In addition, he proposed that the Great Powers co-operate with each other and with the wider global community to maintain the hard-won peace. To ensure that joint action to suppress threats to peace and security would be effec-tive, Hull encouraged states to maintain armed forces of adequate size and configuration.[1]

Although medium and minor powers were excluded from Dumbarton Oaks, and although the discussions were a deliberate move by the Great Powers to estab-lish a collective hegemony over the entire globe, what is important in the context of this paper is that, initially, there existed a positive factor that was key to the success of the proposals put forth at Dumbarton Oaks: political will. A commit-ment by the most powerful to construct mechanisms to ensure the peace and security of all, requiring the participation of all, would be a recurring theme as efforts to establish standing and stand-by arrangements progressed.

In the run-up to the signing of the UN Charter in San Francisco in May of 1945, conflicting views on an international force (no mention was yet made of a standing army with fully-integrated national contingents) were voiced by Canada and France. Canadian concerns centered around command and control: there ex-isted a resistance to the idea that Canadian troops could be ordered to any crisis area at any time by a fiat of the Security Council.[2]

This led to the inclusion of Article 44 in the Charter. This did not constitute resistance to the establishment of stand-by arrangements *per se,* although it did highlight a point of contention which would be taken up by other states in later years—namely the question of national versus international control of what were hitherto considered to be national resources. (US President Woodrow Wilson had rejected this arrangement outright, leading to America's shunning of the League of Nations).[3]

Canadian attitudes contrasted with those of the French, who maintained that, in order to carry out its mandate effectively, the Security Council should have a standing force available for immediate mobilization and deployment. In particular, the Soviet Union was opposed to any significant change. Despite these differences of opinion, there were no calls for a wholesale re-evaluation of the Dumbarton proposals when the delegates convened in San Francisco. The signing of the UN Charter reflected a general consensus that plans to build an international force should be put into effect without delay.

Operationalizing the Concept: Clarity of Purpose, Ambiguity of Execution

In recognition of the fact that a great deal of co-ordination would be necessary to carry out military operations using contingents supplied by various nations, a Military Staff Committee (MSC) was provided for under Chapter VII of the Charter. Composed of the Chiefs of Staff of the five permanent members of the Security Council (P-5), the MSC was tasked with advising and assisting the Security Council in the strategic planning of operations and the employment of the armed forces placed under its control. The latter were to be a formidable deterrent to would-be aggressors. Unlike the League of Nations, the integrated international force would boast two million ground troops (with half being provided by the P-5), thousands of combat aircraft, and hundreds of warships.[4] A proposal to place atomic weapons at the Council's disposal was considered in light of the intent of the founders of the UN—to deter aggression through an awe-inspiring display of military power.

Indications of which of the two models would form the conceptual basis of the force surfaced in October, 1944. US President Franklin D. Roosevelt suggested that US military power could be made available to the Security Council without prior approval by Congress. While this arrangement raised constitutional questions (questions which remain unresolved to this day), it seemed to solve others—at least initially. In declaring that the new world body would have to be able to act immediately if the peace was threatened, Mr. Roosevelt seemed to indicate a clear preference for a stand-by approach. There was no mention made of anyone but the Americans training and equipping their soldiers, and although the "immediate reaction" concept was suggestive of a standing force model, there was no indication that US forces would be permanently placed under international control. In any case, US Congressional opposition (another recurring theme in the history of the UN military operations) soon killed the idea.[5] By opting out of standing arrangements, the most powerful nation on earth had, perhaps unwittingly, set an example for the rest of the international community. While the goal of mustering an international force was still very much alive, America's eschewing of the stand-by option did not bode well for its future.

In what could be interpreted as a further set-back for efforts to create a military force along the lines of one or other of the two models, there were indications that the entire concept had not been adequately defined. While some believed that the still-theoretical force would be a standing one—stationed in one place and under the command of a single authority—others were led to believe that nations would maintain contingents which would be earmarked for deployment but would otherwise remain under national command and control. Many contemporary media accounts of the debate took the latter perspective.

Further stymieing these efforts was the wording of the UN Charter itself. Article 43 seemed to impose compulsory military service on member states, but then Article 44 made contributions to a collective effort to restore international peace and security subject to prior consultation. With no obligation on the part of the member states to serve as members of an international force in the absence of an agreement with the UN, the likelihood of hammering out a standing arrangement was dealt a significant blow. While hope for formal, binding arrangements remained, and do so to this day, there were, and still are, overwhelming indications that rhetoric would not be matched by resources.

Into the Cold War

Even before the East-West ideological conflict took shape, consensus among the P-5 began to come undone. In 1947 the MSC released a report entitled, "General Principles Governing the Organization of the Armed Forces Made Available to the Security Council by Member Nations of the United States." The document spelled out how national contributions could be designated for UN duty: their numbers, equipment, location, and level of readiness were made known, as well as the procedures for pooling them into a large multinational force. In all, the report laid down 41 articles, of which only 25 gained the support of the P-5.

Soon after, co-operation became a rarity in the Security Council. To the dismay of the West, the Soviet Union consolidated its hold on Eastern Europe, while in Asia, the victory of the Chinese communists in 1949 convinced the United States that a monolithic communist threat committed to the political destabilization of its neighbours was at hand. Agreement on any initiative foundered on the rocks of a Security Council veto. The one exception—UN action against North Korea in 1950—was made possible only because the Soviets had boycotted Security Council proceedings to protest America's refusal to recognize Communist China. In any event, the multinational response to aggression on the Korean peninsula saw the US acting as an "agent" of the UN. The Security Council and the General Assembly were barely involved in the organization and direction of the "police action" and orders received by the theatre commander, US General Douglas MacArthur, originated in Washington, not New York. Clearly, impromptu arrangements composed of "coalitions of the willing" were gaining the upper hand on standing agreements.

The desirability of hammering out more formal arrangements—be they standing or stand-by—never completely vanished, however. In 1952, Secretary-General Trygve Lie proposed that a "volunteer reserve" be forged out of national contingents. But it was not until the aftermath of the Suez Crisis in 1956 that the standing force model received serious attention. Recalling the frantic way in which the United Nations Emergency Force (UNEF I) had been cobbled together and sent to the Sinai (in fact, the first units of this first "peacekeeping" force arrived in-theatre within 72 hours!) officials began to talk more openly about a Standing Military Force. Pakistani Foreign Minister Firoz Khan Noon first broached the subject in November 1956 by suggesting that the structure and resources which composed UNEF I be retained following the end of its mandate. The force, he said, would be made the nucleus of a permanent army, with the UN hiring, training, and paying for the salaries and upkeep of the soldiers and their equipment. These would be deployed to a series of "strategic areas" around the world—a euphemism for potential flash-points.

In April 1957, five months after he had been presented with the Nobel Peace Prize for "inventing" peacekeeping at the time of the Suez Crisis, Canadian Secretary of State for External Affairs, Lester B. Pearson, wrote an article in *Foreign Affairs* in which he suggested that peacekeeping should be approached in a more organized fashion. In an attempt to reduce the complex issue of formal arrangements into simple terms, the media took Pearson's suggestion to mean that a permanent force was the preferred option. In truth, Pearson advocated a less ambitious path, saying that national governments should make known their willingness to contribute contingents for peacekeeping missions. No mention was made of extending the duration of those commitments beyond the length of the mission's mandate, nor did Pearson call for the mustering of forces as might be needed to fight a war. Rather, the only permanent aspect of this otherwise stand-by proposal would be the appointment of a permanent Military Advisor to the Secretary-General who, along with a small number of staff officers, would carry out the day-to-day tasks associated with the direction of ceasefire monitoring, border patrol, etc. Indeed, Pearson's vision of this UN "machinery" took on the form of a cross between the standing and stand-by/volunteer models, as witnessed by his suggestion that the non-permanent members of the Security Council should be willing (but not compelled) to contribute troops.[6]

Novel as the idea was, the creation of a standing force was an unlikely prospect in the political context of the Cold War. With mutual suspicions and tensions running high, there was little hope that the UN and its organs —chief among them the MSC—would evolve into something greater than the sum of their parts. The old game of power politics and the primacy of national interest (reminiscent of America's inter-war desire to remain isolated from international affairs) resulted in a decisive lack of collective political will. In this climate, calls for either a standing or a binding stand-by arrangement may have seemed hopelessly utopian. But the sheer emotional appeal of the idea—an effective "fire brigade" responsible to the entire international community—led some to keep the dream alive and to suggest

ways in which it might be put into effect. While the political obstacles were ac-
knowledged to be formidable (to say nothing of the military and financial ones)
the notion that a permanent force could be a cure for all of the world's ills was not
frozen out by the Cold War. All that was needed to see a renaissance in the idea
was fertile political ground.

After the Gulf War: Optimism and Realism

The resurgence in interest in a standing force model was largely attributable to
the success of the UN handling of the Persian Gulf crisis of 1990-91. While some
criticized the alleged co-opting of the UN by the US, the fact that the basis for
international action (in the form of economic sanctions on Iraq, later followed by
forcible ejection from Kuwait) lay in Security Council resolutions rather than uni-
lateral action clearly breathed new life into Article 43. The provision of forces for
UN duty needed to be clarified to determine the feasibility of expanding the "permanent machinery" to include a standing force.[7] One possible reason why this was
not considered feasible lies in the enduring inability or unwillingness of the principal state actors to subordinate their national interests and resources to
supra-national bodies. Indeed, the speed with which the most powerful members
of the coalition acted following the outbreak of the Gulf crisis may be attributable
to the fact that there were key national interests at stake. Ownership of and access
to petroleum resources, plus the political-military balance of power in the region
compelled the US, Britain, France, Canada and others to muster their diplomatic
and military resources. There was no indication that such a level of commitment
could be sustained, let alone duplicated, had the nature and location of the crisis
been different.

Not to be deterred, a number of interested parties have, since 1991, put forth a
barrage of proposals to explore various force models. One US university study
suggested a three-tier model based on a 500,000-strong volunteer reserve force
composed of units under national command, a smaller, more tightly-centralized
rapid-reaction force under UN command, and a standing peacekeeping force whose
units would be centrally based and trained.[8]

In a separate although not altogether unrelated development, the North Atlantic Treaty Organization (NATO) has made offers of troops and infrastructure for
peacekeeping duties in the former Yugoslavia. These offers were quickly accepted,
and the headquarters of NATO's Northern Army Group (NORTHAG) was dispatched to the Balkans. The genesis of this stand-by arrangement can be traced
back to the Rome Declaration of December 1991, when the 16-member alliance
decided to re-configure its force structure to bring it into line with the anticipated
challenges of the post-Cold War era. The new three-tier structure comprises a 10-
division (approximately 250,000 men) Allied Rapid Reaction Corps (ARRC)
backed up by more numerous Main Defence Forces, and followed by Augmentation Forces which are kept at lower levels of readiness. Under normal circumstances,
decisions regarding the employment of NATO forces would be made by the 16-
member North Atlantic Council, but the fact that the UN is the *de facto* lead agency

in the Balkans means that the ARRC, with its powerful air and land forces and logistics capability, would be employed only with the prior approval of the Security Council.

The most significant development in recent years occurred on 31 January 1992 at the first-ever meeting of the heads of state of the UN Security Council. Interestingly, proposals concerning both force models were put forth. A force composed of volunteer contingents was given a boost by the French who committed themselves to providing 1,000 troops for UN peacekeeping. There was nothing new in this initiative. Canada, for its part, had for some time kept an infantry battalion earmarked for UN duty, as had many other committed peacekeepers. Still, the proposal was somewhat mistakenly treated as a new initiative and accorded great—and undeserved—media attention. (Contrary to some media interpretations, there was no indication that this contingent would be permanently placed under UN control). What received markedly less publicity was the fact that the French tied their offer to the condition that the MSC operate as envisaged in the Charter—an unlikely prospect to say the least. In any event, the French proposal was significantly less than what Canada had been doing for decades: maintaining a UN stand-by battalion and skilled individuals ready to be deployed at short notice.

At the January 1992 meeting, the heads of state also asked Secretary-General Boutros Boutros-Ghali to investigate and report on the possibility of making the Security Council more responsive to threats to peace and security. Released six months later under the title, *An Agenda for Peace,* his report drew upon Article 40 of the UN Charter to raise the possibility of establishing units for peace enforcement. The provision of forces for a standing army is mentioned, as is financial and logistical support, as well as some of the other issues which are critical to successful peacekeeping.[9] Additional calls for formal arrangements have been made by the UN Committee of 34 (Peacekeeping Operations) in its 1994 report.[10] The work of the stand-by arrangements team was welcomed, as were the commitments already made.

In February 1993, in what was seen as a major shift in US foreign policy, President Clinton unveiled Presidential Draft Directive 13 (PDD-13), establishing a new set of criteria for US participation in UN peacekeeping operations. Included among these are a clear and present danger to international security, a demonstrable threat to US interests, and sufficient domestic support for the operation. Some analysts maintain that these criteria cannot be easily satisfied, thereby lessening the chance of US involvement in crises where its presence may be key to the operation's success. What was significant was that the US would allow the placing of its troops under foreign command so long as the size of the formation did not exceed battalion strength and the possibility of combat was negligible. However, no mention was made of keeping any US forces available on stand-by. Indeed, the directive permitted US troops to question the orders of their non-American superiors on the grounds of military competence. This was hardly a vote of confidence in the UN.

In any event, PDD-13 was never signed, ostensibly because "apart from a small intellectual/practitioner community, there was little support for peacekeeping in the US."[11]

It was superseded in 1994 by Presidential Decision Directive 25 (PDD-25) which set down even more conditions for American participation. Most notable among these was that the UN mandate be extremely clear, that the disputants agree in advance to a cessation of hostilities, and that the duration of the mission would be known in advance. A tall order to be sure. Regrettably, it is doubtful whether these criteria can be met either in whole or in part, and the loss to the international community (which is still struggling to address the types of conflict that the US has pledged to avoid) has yet to be measured. However, there is still room for the US to play a pivotal role in peace and security operations, even if it is not on the front lines. By lending its vast logistical and strategic transport resources to the UN, some of the troubles which have plagued past and present multinational operations—namely the timely deployment and medium- and long-term sustainment of forces—can be overcome. Whether the new Republican-controlled Congress will carry through on its statement that the US should not be a major player in peacekeeping remains to be seen.[12]

Enduring Issues and Challenges

At present there is little chance that the P-5 will move any closer to the conclusion of any formal arrangements for a standing force. Rather, UN operations will for the foreseeable future be characterized by *ad hocery*. The reasons for this are political and operational. In the first place, the reluctance to relinquish control of one's human and material resources—resources which have been acquired and maintained at enormous expense—is understandable where freedom of action is considered key to the realization of foreign policy goals. If a crisis affects the core interests of a given state but does not, in the opinion of the UN, present a threat to international peace and security, the state in question may find itself powerless to respond if its forces are not under national command. Suggestions that the United States, either unilaterally or with its closest allies, could well have gone ahead and ejected Iraqi forces from Kuwait without the consent of the UN is a case in point.[13] The matter is further highlighted by the (overly) stringent conditions for US involvement in peacekeeping operations. Recent declarations by senior members of the Republican Party that US troops will neither take part in initiatives which are tangential to US interests, nor serve under foreign command suggest that any formal arrangements will be made without US support. In that case, efforts to establish standing/stand-by arrangements are bound to fail.

Another dimension of political will involves faith (or lack thereof) in the ability of international organizations to devise and implement effective mandates. If the mission objectives and rules of engagement are unclear (as is the case in Somalia where there was disagreement over whether the warring factions could or should be disarmed), or if disputants are permitted to defy the terms of the mandate (as was the case in the former Yugoslavia where Bosnian Muslim and Serb armies have been permitted to attack and launch attacks from UN-designated "safe havens") conflict management will surely fail. What results in such cases is a mandate which is no longer enforceable, and an organization which is neither credible in the eyes of the combatants, nor worthy of support in the eyes of its members. Moreover, the intractability of a conflict can act as a strong disincentive to multinational intervention, thereby undermining one of the principal justifications for maintaining standing or stand-by forces.

The desirability of a standing UN force has its roots in the belief that such a force would be more professional, responsive, and efficient, and financially supportable than those available under current arrangements.[14] This argument is plausible as soldiers will be trained to similar standards, with an emphasis on UN methods of operation (likely including a mix of diplomatic, policing, and traditional military skills), and will have the means to project and sustain military power over long distances and for long periods of time. There is, however, no reason to believe that the quality of training offered by experienced peacekeeping countries such as Canada, Norway, and Australia is inadequate for one's own needs nor that it could not be passed on to the less experienced through bilateral contacts.

Reaction time may indeed be shortened if troops are already organized into well-trained, formed units stationed in various theatres around the globe with the requisite air and sea transport capabilities. But responsiveness may not be dependent on organization and material resources if the deployment is delayed by political wrangling over the substance of the mandate. Indeed, international criticism levelled at the relief mission to Rwanda did not focus on any lack of air transport capability, but rather at the reluctance of the international community to employ it in a timely fashion.

Efficiency in the planning and preparation stage may heighten the chances of mission success, particularly if the size of the planning staff is enlarged to facilitate co-ordination between the relevant departments and organs of the UN, as well as between the force commander and UN headquarters. A permanent, 24-hour, staff in New York may have deflected criticism by senior members of the United Nations Protection Forces (UNPROFOR) that their concerns regarding the progress of the mission went unheard after-hours and on weekends. On the other hand, it remains to be seen whether efficiency has suffered decisively under the current *ad hoc* system. What may well be needed is a military headquarters outside of New York. The notion that a standing peacekeeping/enforcement force would be more financially stable assumes that a secure source of funding will be available throughout the duration of the mission. It is undoubtedly true that a mission would not be irrevocably set back by refusals to support it, since money would have been collected in advance and held in a peacekeeping fund. However, such arrangements may be inadequate if the level of peacekeeping activity rises sharply and missions go on for long periods of time. In the 1990s, an unforeseen increase in the number and scope of UN missions has led financially-strapped governments to avoid open-ended commitments, and to withdraw political and financial support for missions that, in their estimation, are not proceeding well. The departure of Canadians from Cyprus after almost three decades and the withdrawal of the Italian contingent from the Somalia operation following a disagreement with the force commander are good examples. In any event, the fact that the sizeable debt accumulated over decades of peacekeeping has not demonstrably crippled UN operations suggests that the reputed financial advantages of the standing force model may be illusory.

Doubts surrounding the comparative advantages offered by permanent arrangements over impromptu ones may be overcome if states with common interests share a clarity of purpose which will help forge a consensus on what is at stake and what action must be taken. Operationally, planning and execution may go considerably smoother, and command and control may be more solid if the partners have previously taken part in joint command and field exercises. Increasingly, states are coming to recognize the benefits of the New Peacekeeping Partnership (NPP): the military, government and non-government agencies dealing with humanitarian assistance, refugees, and displaced persons; election monitors and media; and civilian police personnel as they work together to improve the effectiveness of peacekeeping operations.[15]

If efforts to fine-tune (not replace) the *ad hoc* approach to fit different mission contexts can be made, there may be even less of a requirement for alternate arrangements. Given the complexity of conflict in the 1990s, where a multitude of security threats acting alone or in combination may threaten international peace and security, the peacekeeping force which responds must possess diverse capabilities. As events in Bosnia and Namibia have shown, traditional peacekeeping methods must be buttressed by peacebuilding if a war-torn society is to be re-built and restored to long-term self-sufficiency.

Clearly, this inclusive approach to peacekeeping is not only responsive, but flexible. The partnership can be configured to suit the unique requirements of each mission, and various non-military actors may, if they wish, be able to pool their efforts with the Blue Helmets, thereby creating a truly integrated peacekeeping/ building "force". Although co-ordination of effort between the partners may not necessarily imply integration under a single authority, the NPP concept allows the constituents of the force to draw upon one another's experience and strengths. With this concept under constant development at the Pearson Peacekeeping Centre (PPC) in Cornwallis, Nova Scotia, an important new dimension has been added to the debate over how best to meet the security challenges of the 1990s and beyond.

Conclusion

It is questionable whether the idea of a permanent army for UN operations has ever been seriously regarded as a viable tool for conflict management. It has certainly generated a significant amount of interest among scholars, statesmen, and the media, and its emotional appeal is still strong. But the barriers to its adoption have historically been, and arguably still are, quite insurmountable. The spirit of co-operation which, it was hoped, would characterize the post-Cold War international system has not materialized. But neither is it non-existent. While national interest and a fear of costly entanglements has dampened enthusiasm, there is broad agreement that existing measures can and should be improved. In the near-term, it is unlikely that these improvements (if they are made) will take the form of a greater willingness to allocate resources to a UN volunteer reserve, since national interest and national control are, for many states, synonymous. But if the ultimate objective is to improve the chances of mission success, other alternatives (including an operational HQ with regional branches) and improvements to existing arrangements (through the New Peacekeeping Partnership) may have much to offer.

Notes

1. For a survey of Hull's remarks, see B.. Ferenez, *Enforcing International Law—A Way to World Peace: A Documentary History and Analysis* (London: Ocean, 1983) p.425.

2. *The Bulletin of International News,* Vol 22, No. 9.

3. It will be recalled that the issue of command and control has surfaced on at least two occasions in recent years: once with the Italians in Somalia, and repeatedly with the Americans everywhere the UN is involved. Of course, it is one of the myths of UN peacekeeping that forces are at all times commanded by the UN. In fact they are only when so permitted by national authorities.

4. "Big 5 to Provide 1/2 of Force," *The New York Times,* 24 March 1946, p.1.

5. Arthur H.l Vandenberg, Jr., ed., *The Private Papers of Senator Vandenberg,* (Boston: Houghton Mifflin, 1952) p.112.

6. Lester B. Pearson, "Force for UN," *Foreign Affairs,* No. 35, April 1957, pp.395-404.

7. Brian Urquhart, "For a UN Volunteer Military Force," *The New York Times Review of Books,* 10 June 1993, p.3.

8. Alan K. Henderson, "Defining a New World Order," (discussion paper delivered at The Fletcher School of Law and Diplomacy, Medford, Mass. Tufts University, 1991) pp. 42-46. See also J. Dennehy et.al., *A Blue Helmet Combat Force,* (Cambridge, Mass.: John F. Kennedy School of Government, Harvard University, 1993).

9. *An Agenda for Peace: Preventive Diplomacy, Peacemaking, and Peacekeeping,* Report of the Secretary-General pursuant to the statement adopted by the Summit Meeting of the Security Council on 31 January 1992, 17 June 1992.

10. United Nations, *1994 Report of the Special Committee on Peacekeeping Operations,* A/49/136, 2 May, 1994.

11. Christopher Brady and Sam Daws, "UN Operations: The Political-Military Interface," *International Peacekeeping,* Vol 1, No. 1, Spring 1994, p.63.

12. Already, many Republicans have advocated the reduction of "non-defense expenditures"—of which peacekeeping is one—in order to fund higher-priority programmes. See P. Finnegan, "Republicans Eye Conversion, Peacekeeping Cuts," *Defense News.* Vol 9, No. 5, November 14-20, 1994, p.1.

13. Brady and Daws, 64. According to the authors, experience in Korea and Kuwait has persuaded high-ranking US officials that a separation of policy-making (UN responsibility) and implementation (US responsibility) is efficient, and that stand-by arrangements are unnecessary.

14. For an in-depth analysis of these "advantages", see Paul F. Diehl, *International Peacekeeping,* (Baltimore: Johns Hopkins University Press, 1993).

15. See Alex Morrison, "The Fiction of a UN Standing Army," (discussion paper delivered at the Fletcher School of Law and Diplomacy, Medford, Mass: Tufts University, 1993).

Étude sur les capacités de réaction rapide de l'ONU

Roméo A. Dallaire

En tant que soldat entraîné au combat pendant plus de trente ans dans la force militaire de l'OTAN, j'étais de ceux que la fin de la guerre froide rendait optimiste et enthousiaste. L'émergence d'un « nouvel ordre mondial » et les dividendes auxquels on l'associe souvent, notamment la paix, le désarmement et la prospérité économique, étaient autant de facteurs qui contribuaient à mon optimisme. Cependant, le nombre constant et croissant de catastrophes et de conflits humains qui ont frappé notre monde est venu rapidement atténuer une grande part de cette exaltation et de cet optimisme. Et cela ne m'est jamais apparu aussi évident que lorsque j'ai été envoyé au Rwanda pour participer à une opération de soutien de la paix, obligé de regarder se dérouler sous mes yeux un holocauste des temps modernes, les mains politiquement et militairement liées pendant plusieurs mois.

La communauté internationale

Que la communauté internationale ait été incapable de désamorcer la catastrophe qui commençait au Rwanda à la fin de 1993 et au début 1994, a été, en mon sens, scandaleux et immoral. À tel point, en fait, que même aujourd'hui je me demande si celle-ci n'aurait pas réagi plus rapidement, voire plus énergiquement, si les victimes des massacres avaient été les gorilles des grandes montagnes du Rwanda—une espèce en danger—plutôt que des êtres humains.

Après coup, je trouve tout de même ironique que Diane Fossey, qui a consacré sa vie à s'occuper des gorilles du Rwanda, ait réussi à attirer l'attention de la communauté internationale sur la cause de ses protégés et que les Nations Unies, organe institutionnel de la communauté internationale, ait été incapable de rallier ses membres à celle de centaines de milliers de personnes massacrées systématiquement dans ce même pays. D'après ce que j'ai pu observer personnellement au Rwanda, dans le cadre de la MONUOR, puis de la MINUAR, je dirais que la communauté internationale a autant le devoir que l'obligation morale

---

Le major général Dallaire a été l'Observateur militaire en chef pour la Mission d'observation des Nations Unies au Rwanda et par la suite le Commandant de la MINUAR (Mission d'assistance des Nations Unies au Rwanda). Il est aujourd'hui le Commandant adjoint des Forces de l'armée de terre canadienne.

de réformer l'ONU. Par les réformes envisagées, l'ONU deviendrait une organisation proactive plutôt que réactive. Si la situation l'exigeait, elle serait en mesure de
gérer les conflits et de réagir au nombre croissant de catastrophes humanitaires de
façon beaucoup plus efficace.

Je signale que c'est à la communauté internationale qu'il incombe de réformer
l'ONU. L'ONU a été créée au lendemain de la Deuxième Guerre mondiale dans le
but d'établir un monde plus pacifique et plus humain. Cependant, elle est vite
devenue un lieu d'affrontement pour les superpuissances engagées dans un virage
idéologique, rendant ainsi vaine toute possibilité de réagir rapidement aux crises
inter et intraétatiques, même si la sécurité d'une région s'en trouvait menacée.

La guerre froide étant terminée, nous constatons désormais un niveau de consensus sans précédent parmi les cinq membres permanents. Et pourtant, les
Nations unies n'ont pas encore été capables de créer une force de réaction rapide.
Ce qui m'amène à dire que les problèmes que traverse l'ONU nécessitent une
réforme institutionnelle de l'ONU elle-même. Or, toute réforme de l'ONU commence d'abord par celle de ses membres, à savoir la communauté internationale
qui la compose.

Après tout, l'ONU n'est pas un pays souverain; elle n'a ni le statut ni les pouvoirs
d'une superpuissance. L'ONU est une institution qui traduit la volonté collective
et qui agit sur celle-ci et sur les moyens qui lui sont conférés par la communauté
internationale. Très franchement, comme dans le cas du Rwanda, l'ONU sert trop
souvent de bouc émissaire pour l'apathie, l'opportunisme et l'impuissance de la
communauté internationale. Ce n'est pas l'ONU qu'il faut pointer du doigt, mais
plutôt chacun de nous. Les Nations unies sont le reflet de chacun de nous et
vice versa. À mon avis, la communauté internationale a tort de refuser à l'ONU les
moyens de réagir efficacement aux crises qui surviennent dans le monde entier,
dans ce que nous appelons cette ère nouvelle.

L'ONU, et surtout, la communauté internationale, a échoué au Rwanda. La
communauté internationale a subi un échec parce qu'elle a refusé aux Nations unies
son appui ainsi que les moyens dont celle-ci avait besoin pour gérer cette terrible
crise. Au moment d'écrire ces lignes, le conflit se poursuit et est en train même de
resurgir. Jusqu'à présent un million de personnes ont été tuées, un demi-million
blessées, un million déplacées, et quelque deux millions se sont réfugiées dans les
pays voisins, semant sur leur parcours les germes du prochain conflit et de la
prochaine catastrophe humanitaire dans la région. Tout cela est très chèrement
payer en vies humaines pour l'inaction et l'apathie de la communauté internationale.

Je suis conscient que personne ne souhaite la répétition de cet horrible massacre. Cependant, s'il y a quelque chose que la communauté internationale devrait
faire, c'est de tirer une leçon du génocide rwandais, et de prendre les mesures
nécessaires pour mandater l'ONU et lui donner les moyens de gérer les crises,
dans un monde où les conflits et les catastrophes humanitaires semblent resurgir
encore et encore.

Opération de soutien de la paix de l'ONU : la MINUAR

La MINUAR, dont j'ai assumé le commandement dès sa création en 1993, devait être l'exemple même de la réussite du maintien de la paix pour l'ONU. Or, en moins d'un an, nous avons vu un accord de paix, porteur d'espoir et d'optimisme, dégénérer à un point tel qu'on en est arrivé à une reprise de la guerre, à un génocide politique et humanitaire, à l'exode des populations, à la maladie et à la mort. Pour à nouveau donner lieu à l'insécurité et à la stagnation.

Ce cercle vicieux a commencé avec la signature de l'accord de paix d'ARUSHA le 4 août 1993, accord qui prévoyait le déploiement d'une force internationale neutre en cinq semaines. Le Rwanda ne représentant pas d'intérêt stratégique, il fallait réduire la mission au « minimum », m'avait-on informé. En fait, le Secrétaire général de l'ONU était tenu d'essayer de limiter l'effectif et les dépenses qu'il allait engager. Étant donné l'état d'esprit dans lequel était la communauté internationale, plusieurs problèmes sont survenus presque immédiatement après la mise sur pied de l'opération, causant plusieurs retards. Ce n'est donc pas avant le 5 octobre 1993, soit deux mois plus tard, que nous avons connu notre mandat. Puis, il a fallu cinq autres mois avant de constituer une force suffisamment équipée pour le remplir.

On invoque souvent pour expliquer ces retards que les États qui disposaient de l'équipement nécessaire pour les opérations de la MINUAR refusaient de donner une partie de cet équipement aux États qui n'en avaient pas mais qui étaient en mesure de fournir des contingents. Si la MINUAR n'a pas pu remplir son mandat, c'est entre autres, parce qu'elle ne disposait pas du personnel politique capable de mettre en oeuvre une stratégie propre à la mission. L'opération de la MINUAR a tout simplement débouché sur une impasse politique. De la même manière, le représentant sur place du PNUD a travaillé dur, mais il était évident que les organismes de secours avaient des mandats distincts, avant et même pendant la guerre. La mission n'avait pas non plus de coordonnateur humanitaire pour mettre en contact les dizaines d'organismes humanitaires et d'ONG et pour coordonner leurs activités avec celles des forces militaires de l'ONU.

La quatrième et dernière raison invoquée pour expliquer l'incapacité de l'ONU à remplir son mandat, a été que cette celle-ci ne disposait pas d'un système administratif ou logistique pouvant rapidement déployer une force de maintien de la paix et la soutenir. Il lui était, par conséquent, impossible de réagir à une situation de crise dans un délai acceptable. C'est comme si chaque fois, les opérations de soutien de la paix de l'ONU recommençaient à zéro. En somme, l'opération MINUAR manquait de personnel militaire bien équipé, n'avait pas de contrats et n'avait pratiquement pas de budget six mois après sa création.

Même après le 17 mai, date de l'adoption de la résolution 918 de l'ONU, tout était encore au ralenti. En effet, le 17 mai, la MINUAR avait 471 soldats sur le terrain, deux mois plus tard, elle en avait 550, et enfin le 10 août, il n'y avait encore au total que 1 257 soldats au sol. Ce n'est pas avant septembre, soit quelque quatre mois après l'adoption de la résolution du Conseil de sécurité de l'ONU, que le contingent de la MINUAR a été pleinement déployé.

Réaction de la communauté internationale

Le 6 avril, la guerre civile éclate de nouveau au Rwanda. Il faudra près de trois mois à la communauté internationale pour réagir. Cette procrastination se poursuit malgré les appels répétés du Secrétaire général de passer à l'action et de fournir les moyens matériels nécessaires à l'opération. Plutôt que de répondre à ces appels, la communauté internationale se contente, impuissante, d'assister à la télévision à l'un des plus grands génocides depuis la Deuxième Guerre mondiale.

Enfin, en juillet 1994, à Goma, au Zaïre, la culpabilité provoquée par la couverture de CNN, pousse la communauté internationale à agir. Peu de temps après, celle-ci entreprend de stabiliser la crise provoquée par près d'un million de réfugiés, et fournit ainsi l'occasion aux médias internationaux de couvrir l'événement. Cette situation se confirme d'autant plus que, pendant que les secours sont acheminés à Goma, à seulement 100 km au sud de Goma, une plus grande tragédie humanitaire impliquant un million et demi de déplacés prend naissance : un second Goma. À la différence que cette fois-ci comme les médias n'y sont pas, aucune mesure n'est prise.

La nécessité de réformer l'ONU

Shakespeare nous dit dans Hamlet que nous savons ce que nous sommes, mais nous ne savons pas ce que nous pourrions être. Je crois en effet qu'il est possible de remédier aux lacunes que je viens de décrire, dans la mesure où l'on demeure ouvert et aussi selon le genre de réponses que l'on veut bien donner aux questions suivantes. En premier lieu, voulons-nous que l'ONU gère les crises mondiales en réagissant rapidement et efficacement à des conflits et des catastrophes humanitaires? Ou plutôt, que des coalitions de puissances, ou même des pseudocoalitions d'une puissance et de « suiveurs », gèrent les crises mondiales en répondant aux conflits ou aux catastrophes humanitaires? Ou encore, préférons-nous ne rien faire?

Laissez-moi aborder la troisième question d'abord en vous disant qu'il ne sert à rien de se laver les mains de ces situations perçues comme lointaines, car nous pourrions tôt ou tard nous retrouver aux prises avec elles, qu'il s'agisse des réfugiés, des problèmes économiques, des pressions environnementales, ou des troubles sociaux et politiques. Du reste, si nous ne voyons pas à ces situations, elles deviendront un jour une menace à notre sécurité nationale.

En outre, en raison des progrès technologiques récents conjugués à une présence accrue des médias à ces événements, il est devenu très difficile pour la communauté internationale de demeurer indifférente à ces événements, peu importe le continent sur lequel ils peuvent survenir. Le Canada, par exemple, se sent obligé d'intervenir dans des conflits, même lorsqu'il n'y a pas de menace apparente à sa sécurité. Les questions de sécurité ne sont plus strictement d'ordre national, ce qui renvoie à ce que certaines personnes, dont le commodore (retraité) Basil Moore, appellent l'internationalisme pearsonien, par lequel les Canadiens non seulement endossent un multilatéralisme canadien significatif, mais veulent également faire leur part lorsqu'il est question d'action collective dans le domaine de la sécurité internationale. Bref, tôt ou tard, nous devrons réagir.

Dans cet esprit, je crois que nous y gagnerions tous si l'ONU était capable d'intervenir à court terme plutôt qu'à long terme. Outre la justification morale de sauver des vies, ce qui s'est d'ailleurs révélé être un critère peu fiable pour évaluer l'intervention de l'ONU, il est plus économique d'agir ainsi. Par exemple, nous avions évalué en août 1993, que la mission de vingt-deux mois au Rwanda coûterait quelque 200 millions de dollars US. Or, nous n'avons reçu qu'une fraction de cette somme. Comparez ces sommes aux milliards qui ont été, et qui continuent d'être consacrés aux actions militaires et humanitaires pour venir en aide aux millions de personnes déplacées et de réfugiés du Rwanda, et pour aider à reconstruire le pays. On peut dire sans ambages qu'une opération de soutien de la paix, mandatée, équipée, soutenue et armée rapidement est en fait beaucoup plus rentable à moyen et à long terme. J'ajouterais également que je considère l'idée de s'abstenir d'intervenir comme moralement inacceptable pour nous tous.

Quant à la deuxième question, il y eu récemment plusieurs exemples récents de coalitions, dont une pendant la guerre du Golfe contre l'Iraq, suivie par l'*Opération turquoise* menée par la France au Rwanda, pour n'en nommer que quelques-unes. Je crois cependant qu'on ne devrait faire appel aux forces des cinq membres permanents du Conseil de sécurité qu'en dernier recours. Au Canada, par exemple, lorsqu'il y a des troubles publics ou des émeutes, nous déployons d'abord notre force policière pour contrôler une situation et rétablir l'ordre et la loi. Si cette force échoue et que les troubles persistent, le gouvernement du Canada peut choisir de déployer un contingent des forces canadiennes (FC). De la même manière, je vois les forces armées des cinq membres du Conseil de sécurité comme des forces armées de «réserve stratégique», et je considère les forces d'autres membres de la communauté internationale, opérant sous les auspices de l'ONU, comme une force de police.

Souvent, en raison de leur passé colonial et néo-colonial et même du rôle qu'ils ont joué dans la guerre froide, les cinq membres permanents n'ont pas la transparence voulue pour affronter une situation de conflit et les belligérants n'ont pas le niveau d'acceptation nécessaire à leur égard. En effet, ils sont souvent perçus avec méfiance, voire avec hostilité. Néanmoins, si une coalition de l'ONU n'incluant pas les membres permanents ne parvient pas à maîtriser la situation, les capacités des cinq deviennent alors essentielles, et doivent être employées avec force, comme ce fut le cas lors de la guerre du Golfe. C'est donc dire que, selon moi, une force de police ou une coalition excluant les membres permanents du conseil de sécurité devrait être la première force de réaction rapide à une crise. Les cinq formeraient cependant une force de «réserve stratégique», prête à intervenir advenant l'échec de la coalition initiale. L'ONU conserverait ainsi sa légitimité morale dans le sens où la communauté internationale reconnaîtrait que l'ONU donne la priorité à la gestion des crises et au maintien de la paix inter et intraétatique fondés sur le droit international et la collaboration des grandes puissances. Avec le temps, les belligérants deviendraient sensibles à cette surveillance et en tiendraient compte en modifiant leur comportement.

Dans ce contexte, nous devons nous poser la question suivante : l'ONU est-elle, dans sa forme actuelle, capable de gérer tous les conflits grâce à des opérations de soutien de la paix, et de coordonner les efforts d'aide humanitaire? En un mot, non. J'avancerais que, dans sa présente forme, l'ONU ne peut remplir ce mandat car elle n'a ni le personnel, ni le matériel ni le mécanisme de prise de décision qui lui permettraient de réagir rapidement.

Pour ce faire, la communauté internationale doit donner à l'ONU les compétences qu'exige la gestion des crises. Cependant, d'importantes réformes devront d'abord être instaurées. Certaines d'entre elles sont déjà à l'étude par le gouvernement canadien, entre autres, dans le but d'accroître la capacité de l'ONU de réagir rapidement au moyen d'une opération de soutien de la paix. Cet examen coïncide avec la décision du gouvernement de créer et d'appuyer le Centre canadien d'entraînement du maintien de la paix Lester B. Pearson, situé à Cornwallis, en Nouvelle-Écosse. Le centre effectue des analyses et émet des recommandations concernant l'effet des politiques de maintien de la paix sur différents gouvernements et organismes.

Compte tenu des observations susmentionnées qui découlent de mon expérience personnelle au Rwanda en tant que commandant de la Force de MINUAR, je crois que les options suivantes doivent être étudiées de façon plus approfondie avant que l'ONU ne puisse devenir un organisme de gestion de crises et un fournisseur d'aide humanitaire accompli.

Possibilités de réforme de l'ONU :

A) CRÉATION D'UNE UNITÉ MULTIDISCIPLINAIRE DE GESTION DES CRISES

L'ONU doit mettre sur pied une équipe multidisciplinaire de gestion des crises. À mon avis, la résolution des conflits et des catastrophes humaines exigerait qu'une telle équipe conçoive et mette à exécution un plan d'action intégré et dont les composantes seraient interdépendantes. Depuis trop longtemps, ces composantes de l'ONU fonctionnent indépendamment les unes des autres. On a ainsi créé un milieu où la théorie ne mène pas à l'action, où les opérations militaires ne servent aucune fin politique, où l'aide humanitaire ne bénéficie pas des ressources nécessaires, tandis que les systèmes logistiques ne peuvent répondre adéquatement aux besoins des commandants sur le terrain. Ils ignorent ainsi qui dirige les opérations et ne peuvent trouver les ressources nécessaires pour les organiser et les soutenir.

Il faudrait peut-être créer un Secteur des plans et des politiques chargé de la planification préalable, de la collecte de renseignements et de l'alerte rapide, et ayant la responsabilité de fournir le personnel pour la planification d'urgence et de définir les normes de formation et les consignes permanentes. À l'heure actuelle, il existe une unité embryonnaire au sein du Département des opérations de maintien de la paix ayant de telles caractéristiques. Elle pourrait convenir à condition d'être élargie, munie d'un mandat et dotée des ressources nécessaires. En outre, je recommanderais que la personne placée à la tête de cette unité ait un accès direct au Secrétaire général.

De plus, pour que l'approche multidisciplinaire réussisse, je crois qu'elle doit être mise en pratique par un personnel qui est, lui aussi, multidisciplinaire, c'est-à-dire dont les membres appartiennent à différents domaines d'expertise (politique, militaire, humanitaire et logistique) tout en ayant une connaissance des autres disciplines. Pour ce faire, l'ONU doit élaborer des cours de gestion des crises pour les cadres supérieurs et les candidats (École supérieure des cadres et du commandement) et former le personnel qui gérera les crises au siège de l'ONU à New York et sur le terrain. Ce programme de cours, offert à New York sous les auspices du Secrétaire général, regrouperait le personnel politique, militaire, humanitaire et logistique et comporterait les éléments suivants: enseignement de nouvelles spécialités, exercices de gestion de crise, rédaction de mémoires de recherche et de plans d'action, et définition d'une réponse multidisciplinaire aux crises. Ces recommandations contribueraient à réduire le caractère *ud hoc* des opérations de paix courantes de l'ONU et à créer une solidarité reposant sur la loyauté et le dévouement, qui tendrait vers le même but dans un climat de confiance.

B) RÉFORME DU SYSTÈME ADMINISTRATIF/LOGISTIQUE DE L'ONU

À l'heure actuelle, l'ONU possède une garnison compétente, ainsi que des systèmes d'administration et de logistique convenables pour gérer ses missions et ses opérations ordinaires un peu partout au monde. Cependant, elle ne dispose pas d'un système de soutien d'urgence rapidement mobilisable pour les nouvelles opérations ou les situations de crise. Le système de garnison actuel prend environ de 6 à 8 mois pour préparer une mission. Ce délai est évidemment trop long pour permettre à l'ONU d'empêcher l'éclatement d'une crise, mais reste convenable si la crise est passée ou que la mission a été déployée et fonctionne normalement. L'ONU doit donc se doter d'un système administratif et logistique d'urgence qui soit rapidement mobilisable, avec un minimum d'obstacles bureaucratiques et un certain degré de responsabilité pour lui permettre de réagir à une crise, en l'espace de quelques semaines, et pour soutenir une opération n'importe où au monde.

C) L'ONU DEVRAIT AVOIR UN FONDS DE RÉSERVE

Ce fonds serait employé à la discrétion du Secrétaire général pour financer des activités d'urgence comme les missions de reconnaissance ou les missions techniques, les dépenses préétablies pour l'entretien, la préinstallation du matériel, et les frais de déploiement avancé qui ne font pas partie du processus budgétaire régulier. Une fois le budget approuvé, ces fonds pourraient être affectés au soutien d'une opération. Le fonds de réserve donnerait au Secrétaire général les moyens nécessaires pour mobiliser une réaction rapide et opportune après l'éclatement d'un conflit ou d'une crise humanitaire.

D) *L'ONU* DOIT AVOIR DES FORCES ET DU MATÉRIEL MILITAIRES EN ATTENTE

Pour réagir rapidement à l'éclatement d'un conflit ou d'une crise humanitaire, l'ONU doit avoir à son immédiate disposition des forces militaires entièrement équipées, autonomes et indépendantes pouvant être déployées en quelques semaines dans n'importe quelle région du monde. L'ONU ne peut plus se permettre d'agir de façon ponctuelle à la manière des détachements de cavalerie des vieux *westerns*. Il serait possible d'établir, avec l'appui de la communauté internationale, une force faisant appel à des contingents nationaux, formés et équipés sur leur propre sol et attachés à une force de réaction rapide ayant un quartier général minimal sur le terrain. Les cinq membres permanents du conseil de sécurité de l'ONU pourraient aider à transporter et à maintenir ces troupes sur le terrain jusqu'à l'arrivée des contingents de relève. Le ministère de la Défense nationale étudie plus en détail la question du transport stratégique. La marine se penche, par exemple, sur la possibilité de déployer des troupes outre-mer par transport maritime—un concept reposant sur le navire polyvalent. Les forces de relève seraient formées de troupes appartenant aux nations qui fournissent des contingents pour des temps de service réguliers ou prolongés.

Souvent, ces contingents arrivent mal équipés sur le théâtre des hostilités. Ne pouvant accomplir leurs tâches, ils deviennent un fardeau pour la Force et mettent la mission en péril. Les contingents devraient être équipés et formés par les pays donateurs, puis déployés uniquement lorsqu'ils possèdent les capacités opérationnelles et logistiques pour diriger des opérations. À ce moment-là, la force en attente se retirerait et attendrait sa prochaine mission. Cette procédure de déploiement permettrait d'établir des consignes permanentes pour le personnel et les opérations. De plus, elle doit être capable de réagir rapidement pour empêcher l'éclatement ou l'extension d'un conflit. L'ONU aurait pour rôle de fournir sécurité et assistance en situation de crise humanitaire d'urgence.

Si une telle force avait été à ma disposition à la mi-avril 1994, à l'époque où j'étais le commandant de la MINUAR, la mission de l'ONU aurait pu sauver la vie à des centaines de milliers de personnes. À preuve, avec 450 soldats placés sous mon commandement durant l'intérim, nous avons sauvé et protégé plus de 25 000 personnes et déplacé des dizaines de milliers de personnes entre les lignes de contact. Qu'aurait pu prévenir une force de 5 000 membres? D'abord, manifestement, les massacres dans les régions sud et ouest du pays parce qu'ils n'ont commencé qu'au début du mois de mai, soit environ un mois après le recommencement de la guerre.

E) L'ONU DOIT CRÉER UNE AGENCE D'AIDE HUMANITAIRE QUI ENCADRE TOUTES LES AUTRES

Au Rwanda, plus particulièrement durant la catastrophe de Goma, une multitude d'ONG à vocation humanitaire ont envahi la région sous l'influence du facteur CNN (ce que Jeff Sallot du Globe and Mail a appelé le phénomène CNN). Certaines d'entre elles, comme les petits groupes de particuliers, ont fait preuve de beaucoup de compassion, mais de peu de compétence. D'autres avaient beaucoup de compétence, mais peu de compassion. Néanmoins, règle générale, je peux affirmer que la majorité des organisations humanitaires avaient beaucoup de compassion, certaines compétences et la volonté de se rendre utiles. Une agence cadre de l'ONU pourrait jouer un rôle central pour planifier, organiser, diriger, coordonner et gérer la mise en application du plan d'assistance humanitaire. Elle pourrait alors intégrer ce plan à celui de la force militaire là où ce serait possible. Goma est l'exemple parfait d'un excès de bonne volonté, surtout lorsqu'on le compare à la situation dans le reste du pays qui n'a pas été approvisionné pendant des mois après l'éclatement de la crise de Goma. Cette situation était en partie le résultat de l'absence d'une agence cadre de l'ONU. Une meilleure intégration des deux groupes aurait été beaucoup plus efficace et aurait facilité la maîtrise de la crise au Rwanda.

F) L'ONU DOIT JOUER UN RÔLE DANS LA DIFFUSION DE L'INFORMATION DANS LE MONDE

En réalité, l'ONU devrait avoir ses propres moyens de diffusion de l'information (télédiffusion, radiodiffusion, presse). L'ONU doit avoir un accès direct aux médias internationaux et être en mesure de présenter la situation réelle plutôt que de réagir à des reportages faussés, à de la propagande ou à de la désinformation --qu'elle soit voulue ou le produit du sensationnalisme. Puisque la plupart des activités de la communauté internationale portent sur des questions politiques, militaires et humanitaires qui font l'objet d'une couverture médiatique, l'ONU doit être elle-même une source d'information exacte, factuelle et opportune. De plus, comme ce fut le cas au Rwanda, une station de radio et des journaux appartenant à l'ONU auraient pu être utilisés pour lutter contre la propagande diffusée par les médias rwandais, qui a créé et nourri l'hystérie directement liée au génocide et, à quelques reprises, pris pour cible des membres de la Force de MINUAR elle-même.

G) L'ONU DOIT SE DOTER D'UN SERVICE DE RENSEIGNEMENTS

Durant mon temps de service auprès de la MINUAR, j'ai constaté que de nombreuses pertes ont été infligées, tant à la mission qu'à la population en difficulté, par l'insuffisance des communications sur le terrain. Le nombre de pertes subies par le personnel militaire de l'ONU pourrait être réduit à l'avenir si celui-ci avait accès à de l'information en temps réel qui pourrait l'aider à prendre des décisions correctes et informées. Les cinq membres permanents du Conseil de sécurité de l'ONU possèdent une technologie avancée de l'information. Pourtant, on s'attend à ce que l'ONU réussisse à fonctionner dans un vide d'information. Comment des décisions opportunes, informées et exactes peuvent-elles être prises dans ce contexte? C'est tout simplement impossible. L'ONU doit se doter d'un centre d'information à New York, secondé par quelques agences d'information importantes dans le monde, et dont le personnel inclurait des agents d'information prêts à être envoyés sur le terrain pour fournir l'information.

H) L'ONU DOIT POUVOIR INTERVENIR POUR DES RAISONS HUMANITAIRES UNE FOIS UNE MISSION DE SOUTIEN DE LA PAIX AMORCÉE

Fondamentalement, l'ONU a l'obligation humaine, légale et morale d'empêcher les meurtres, les crimes contre l'humanité et les génocides une fois une opération de soutien de la paix amorcée. À cette fin, la force militaire de l'ONU sur le terrain doit pouvoir compter sur de meilleures règles d'engagement, non seulement dans les cas de légitime défense, mais aussi pour des fins de dissuasion ou lorsque la situation locale le commande. Ce débat dépasse nettement les questions du chapitre six, du chapitre 7 élargi et du chapitre 8. Il porte sur la volonté, le courage et la force d'intervention nécessaires pour être proactifs.

Pour conclure, je tiens à dire que j'ai vu trop de cadavres, de souffrance humaine et de destruction au Rwanda. J'ai également renvoyé au pays un trop grand nombre de jeunes Casques bleus courageux dans des sacs à dépouilles ou sur des civières pour accepter que nous, c'est-à- dire la communauté internationale, continuions de fonctionner comme par le passé. Pour cette raison, j'espère sincèrement que l'ONU obtiendra un jour le mandat et l'appui de la communauté internationale pour prévenir et gérer les crises efficacement.

Troop Contributors and the UN's Capability for Rapid Reaction

Cathy Downes

Introduction

The UN has struggled to cope effectively with the demands of the post-Cold War international security environment. While not to detract from its achievements, in recent notable crises affecting international peace and security, the UN's efforts have proven to be, in varying degrees, flawed, tardy, and inadequate. In response, the UN Secretary-General has called for initiatives to improve the organization's rapid response capability.

The UN's capacity to react effectively to crises involves a physical ability to act and the political will to take action. Deficiencies in both have significant time burdens which handicap the UN's ability to respond rapidly to crises. If the UN lacks the capability for response, this will influence the political will to act. Yet, if there is limited political will in the first place, then having the technical capability to act may not materially improve the UN's performance in responding rapidly. The time needed to garner political consensus depends on the particular crisis and the extent of evident and predicted effect upon the international community. However, regardless of the nature of any crisis, the UN requires the technical capability to respond effectively. Therefore, leaving to one side the issue of better management of political consensus for action, there remains a ubiquitous imperative to improve the UN's technical capabilities to prepare, employ and sustain appropriately-sized and -shaped UN forces in a timely manner.

It is not entirely possible to leave all aspects of political will to one side. Behind any reform to improve the UN's rapid reaction capability lies the political will to carry it through. It is clear that there is no dearth of obvious improvements to rapid reaction that should be made. It is also clear that the lack of progress, the inability to move significantly forward, demonstrates a lack of commitment on the part of Member States, the Security Council and the UN Secretariat to paying the price to implement them.

Dr. Cathy Downes is a Senior Research Officer, New Zealand Defence Force. The observations in this paper are those of the author. They do not necessarily reflect New Zealand Defence Force, Ministry of Defence, Ministry of Foreign Affairs and Trade, or New Zealand Government policy.

No reform is without cost. Therefore, no reform will meet with the approval of all. However, despite the enormous human, social, economic, environmental and moral costs of the international community's shortcomings in responding to crises, most Member States continue to function only within frameworks of narrow, short-term national and personal self-interest—the WIFUS ("what's-in-it-for-us") syndrome. Until there is a preparedness on the part of the majority of Member States to set aside at least some of this self-interest, the prospects for significant reforms to the UN's rapid reaction capability can only be viewed as restricted.

Rapid Reaction Capability Improvements

Two approaches have been adopted by those responding to the UN Secretary-General's call for action. The first concerns mechanisms for creating a military force available at high states of readiness for use by the UN, either through the Security Council or the Secretary-General. A second approach, being pursued by Canada, recognizes that Member States have been, and are becoming more, reluctant to commit forces and personnel expeditiously to the UN because of concerns over the organization's capability to use them in a professional and effective manner. If practical and realisable improvements can be made to the UN's structures, processes, and personnel, it is hoped that Member States will promptly make available the troop contributions which, in the absence of a standing force, are the other crucial component of a UN rapid response capability.

As a general notion these assumptions appear sound. However, the professionalism or otherwise of the UN to use contributed forces and personnel effectively, is not the only factor influencing Member States' decisions to contribute. The contribution risk-benefit calculation has changed with the new generation of UN peace support operations. Traditional peacekeeping has involved relatively low risk of casualties, positive publicity, and little financial expenditure—indeed for some troop contributors, a financial boon. By contrast, the current conflicts to which the UN is seeking to respond involve:

- significantly higher risks of casualties;

- greater demands upon national military capability;

- greater risk that contributed troops may perform poorly causing national embarrassment;

- increased requirement to upgrade national military capabilities for use in UN operations that may not be totally covered by UN reimbursements; and

- greater risks of mission failure, bad publicity, and public rejection.

Measures to reform the UN's crisis response processes will go only so far to improve parts of the UN's ability for rapid response. In so doing, it may shift the balance for some troop contributing nations' risk calculations. However, many of the unpopular risks will remain and continue to influence the willingness of nations to contribute forces and personnel.

The Canadian initiative is a holistic treatment of the capacities which make up the UN's capability to respond rapidly to crises. This discussion paper focuses on one of the possible sets of relationships (civil, military, political, humanitarian agencies etc.) that make up this capability: that of the roles for troop contributing nations in supporting the military component of a UN rapid response capability. In this context, there are issues that should be addressed by the UN and those that are more properly the concern of troop contributing nations. It is unfortunate that the performance of various UN agencies in recent crises has been such that it is easy to blame them solely for poor results and failure. It is evident that in the preparation, contribution and involvement in the employment of their contributions, some Member States have also acted in ways that have handicapped the UN's ability to react rapidly to crises.

Therefore, it is crucial that issues relating to the contribution performance of troop contributing nations, as well as how the UN calls for and employs troop contributions as part of a rapid reaction capability, are canvassed. We need a clear, frank and common understanding of what the UN should expect of troop contributors, and conversely, what troop contributors need, and have the right to expect, from the UN.

A UN Rapid Reaction "Vanguard" Concept

Had an early and rapid response been achieved in recent UN missions, it is evident that some crises might have been directed towards less violent if not peaceful resolutions. Indeed, it can be argued that had early and prompt responses been made, the need for significantly larger and in every sense more expensive responses could have been avoided or reduced. Leaving aside diplomacy, there is a growing consensus that a major component of the UN's capability for rapid response involves the availability of a force or group of personnel that can be rapidly activated and inserted into a crisis or conflict circumstance to carry out a range of taskings such as those identified by Sir Brian Urquhart[1] and presented in Figure 1 below.

Figure 1: Tasks for a Rapid Response Taskforce

- establish a stabilizing UN presence in a crisis area;
- prevent violent escalation of conflicts;
- facilitate conditions which encourage cessation of violence;
- protect UN and other international Special Representatives;
- secure airheads for subsequent UN force insertion;
- protect designated zones of safety for civilians;
- secure essential humanitarian relief supplies; and
- assess situation and provide a reliable and informed assessment of the feasibility of future UN involvement.

Sir Brian posits these tasks being carried out in the future by a UN standing force. The premise here, drawn from the Canadian initiative, is that, at least in the near-term, it is more politically feasible that mission-specific taskforces could be brought together from personnel contributed at the time by troop contributing nations to perform such tasks. At the same time, the Canadian initiative also recognizes that if such mission-specific taskforces are to be activated and deployed in a timely manner, significant planning and preparatory activity must be undertaken ahead of time by troop contributing nations and the UN.

Reviews of the UN's recent performance highlight the delays and inefficiencies of launching each UN mission almost totally from scratch.[2] The current UN Secretariat practices have proven sufficient in most cases where the uncontested insertion of a peacekeeping force has not been time-critical and where the consent of all protagonists has been secured and is likely to hold. However, such practices are inadequate where the need is to activate and deploy the type of rapid reaction or "Vanguard" taskforce that can give effect to a UN rapid response to a crisis.

Meeting these time frames requires more than simply improving the existing practices of the UN Secretariat. An entirely different way of planning and organization to that currently in place is needed. This has been recognised in the Canadian initiative's call for a standing, operational-level, deployable integrated, multinational, military/civilian headquarters. Such a UN Operational Headquarters (UN OPHQ) would stand at the heart of a broader Vanguard rapid response concept.

The parts of this Vanguard concept could include:

- troop contributing nations providing qualified personnel to staff a standing UN OPHQ;

- a UN OPHQ responsible for directing and supporting Vanguard taskforces, and contingency planning for future taskforces and follow-on peacekeeping forces;

- detachable, deployable Vanguard HQs held, prior to deployment, as a component of the UN OPHQ, including the ear-marking of designated force commanders and alternates, which can then be married up with Vanguard units and personnel activated by Member States when a Vanguard mission is declared; and

- troop contributing nations maintaining and supplying ear-marked national military units and civilian personnel held at specified degrees of readiness.

These components are arranged in Figure 2.

Figure 2

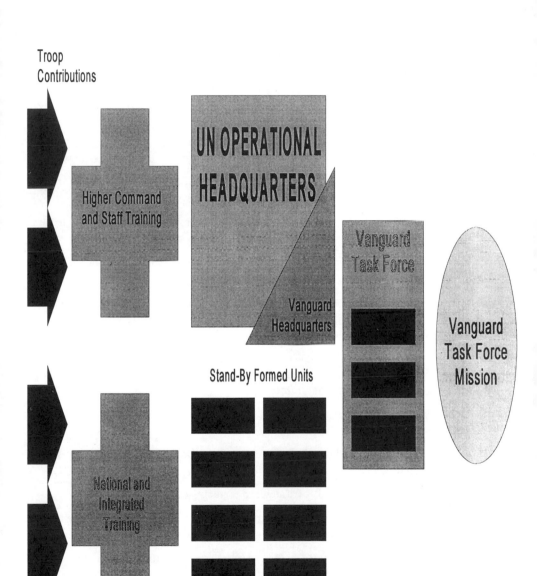

UN OPHQ and Vanguard Taskforces

There is a need to clarify the functioning of a UN OPHQ relative to Vanguard taskforce operations. In the Canadian working papers, it is not clear whether a UN OPHQ would be responsible for the operational command and control of *all* UN peace missions, or only Vanguard missions. If an OPHQ were tasked with command and control of Vanguard operations, it could be of a different size, location and staffing. It would also have different implications for the sorts of participation that troop contributing nations may wish to or should make.

For the purposes of this paper, a UN OPHQ is proposed with three sub-organizations. One sub-organization (perhaps a modified Department of Peacekeeping Operations) would be responsible for planning and control of traditional peacekeeping missions, and follow-on-forces with mandates to replace Vanguard taskforces.

A separate Operational Planning Cell would be responsible for:

- preparing operational-level advice and support to the Secretary-General and Security Council;

- developing standard operating procedures and standardised rules of engagement for all UN peace missions;

- collating and analyzing UN and other experiences to derive "lessons learned" for promulgation to troop contributing nations and non-governmental organizations (NGOs); and

- developing UN follow-on-forces and Vanguard taskforce training standards and training packages for inclusion in national military and civil personnel training programmes.[3]

The third sub-organization of a possible UN OPHQ would be the OPHQ (Vanguard taskforces), with responsibility for:

- preparation of Vanguard contingency plans and force packaging of Vanguard taskforces;

- simulation and analysis of Vanguard concepts of operations;

- co-ordinating inputs from national military intelligence and NGO sources relative to potential conflict areas;

- maintenance of records of status of forces that are earmarked by nations for UN Vanguard assignment;[4]

- preparation of Vanguard HQs; and

- provision of operations staff support to deployed Vanguard HQs and Vanguard taskforces.

This possible arrangement is presented in Figure 3.

Figure 3

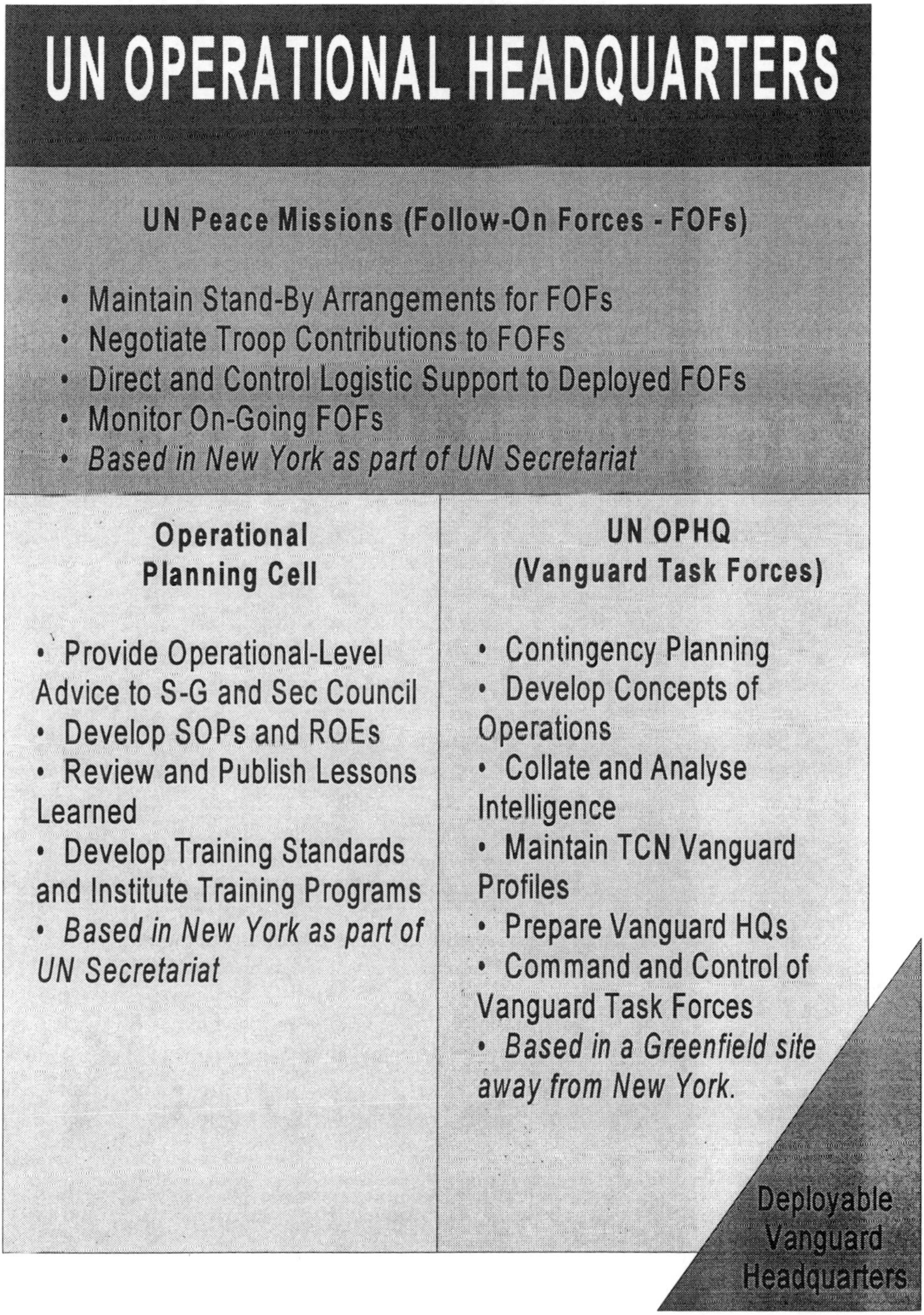

UN OPERATIONAL HEADQUARTERS

UN Peace Missions (Follow-On Forces - FOFs)

- Maintain Stand-By Arrangements for FOFs
- Negotiate Troop Contributions to FOFs
- Direct and Control Logistic Support to Deployed FOFs
- Monitor On-Going FOFs
- *Based in New York as part of UN Secretariat*

Operational Planning Cell	UN OPHQ (Vanguard Task Forces)
• Provide Operational-Level Advice to S-G and Sec Council • Develop SOPs and ROEs • Review and Publish Lessons Learned • Develop Training Standards and Institute Training Programs • *Based in New York as part of UN Secretariat*	• Contingency Planning • Develop Concepts of Operations • Collate and Analyse Intelligence • Maintain TCN Vanguard Profiles • Prepare Vanguard HQs • Command and Control of Vanguard Task Forces • *Based in a Greenfield site away from New York.*

Deployable Vanguard Headquarters

Troop Contributing Nations and a UN OPHQ

If a UN OPHQ is to contribute to the UN's capability for rapid response in violent crises, it must be organized, sized, and staffed in a manner consistent with the conduct of large-scale military operations. There is debate as to whether this principle should have primacy over how the UN Secretariat has historically been organized to conduct peacekeeping operations. However, it is evident that these organizing practices have proven inadequate to the task of activating, deploying, employing and supporting peace missions in circumstances other than traditional peacekeeping.

If a UN OPHQ were to be organized and staffed using a military operational staff headquarters model, three matters—among many—are worthy of stressing as issues for troop contributing nations. First, it has been the practice of the UN Secretariat to balance merit against geographical inclusiveness in its staff recruitment and selection policy. As Berdal has observed, this has resulted in "...an exceptionally uneven quality of UN staff."[5] The deleterious effects of this staffing principle are exacerbated by an insufficiency of funding. This means in some cases, the UN has no choice but to accept the offers of staff it receives, rather than being able to select those most qualified and suited for the service in a UN position.[6]

Clearly, any UN OPHQ should have a multinational character given the multinational nature of the forces (both Vanguard and Follow-On Forces) to be planned for, commanded and supported. Moreover, it is likely that many Member States will see the attachment of staff to a UN OPHQ as an indispensable condition of their willingness to contribute troops and personnel, particularly to Vanguard taskforces. However, if a UN OPHQ is not professionally competent, regardless of whether nations have personnel on its staff, they will be reluctant to contribute troops promptly to any Vanguard or Follow-on Force. Therefore, the principles of inclusiveness and multinationality must be managed so as not to compromise the evolution of a professionally competent and responsive OPHQ staff. This calls for the setting of professional qualifications and performance standards for OPHQ staff which are firmly adhered to even when this may run counter to the principle of inclusiveness.

A second and related issue concerns the preparatory training and qualification of staff personnel contributed to a UN OPHQ. To give effect to an improved UN rapid response capability, personnel contributed by Member States need to be able to slot quickly into a function and perform it to a high standard soon after arrival. Therefore, personnel, ear-marked for contribution to a UN OPHQ, should have received prior training and experience in performing staff functions in an operational-level military headquarters, either in the armed forces of their own nations, or in that of an alliance formation.

In the case of many small nations, providing this sort of preparatory experience is difficult; the size of their armed forces is insufficient to provide realistic training and experiences. If such nations are to be able to contribute staffs to a UN

OPHQ, it will be necessary for access to be negotiated to selected national training establishments that can provide higher command and staff training. These training establishments should be selected on a "best practices" basis (see below for more on this subject).

Many lessons can however only be learned through experience. In this regard, larger nations need to be encouraged to permit, and if possible financially facilitate, secondments of staff officers from smaller nations to the operational headquarters of existing, ongoing operations, or large formation peacetime headquarters. Some larger nations and military alliances, particularly the United States, and NATO, have the capability to provide multinational setting simulation training and command post exercise opportunities for smaller nations. Both of these training vehicles can be used to train potential commanders and headquarters staffs in operational-level staff procedures. Multinational participation in these training events provides opportunities for US/NATO and smaller nation staff officers to interact with each other and develop the understandings which are a crucial component of any effective OPHQ. The contribution that these training opportunities can make should not be underestimated or under-valued.

As a UN OPHQ established itself, it could be expected to customize its own staff procedures. Simulation training and command post exercises would need to be developed to train potential OPHQ staffs in these procedures. Over time, these procedures will either need to be integrated into national military higher command and staff training programmes, or imparted through UN dedicated training courses.

A third area worthy of consideration concerns the scope of staff activity in a UN OPHQ. If a UN OPHQ should have a multinational and multi-functional character, then the nature of effective modern military operations mandates that a future UN OPHQ must also be joint, not only in terms of military and civilian staffs, but in terms of environment: land, sea and air. It can be argued that the current military capacity of the UN is preoccupied by land peacekeeping. This focus may have been proper for traditional peacekeeping.

This approach is no longer sufficient. Although still predominantly land-based in nature, the size and scale of peace support missions underway, and which look likely in the future, have significant ongoing maritime and air dimensions. Maritime and air activities are not simply restricted to the provision of uncontested logistic support. Battlefield air interdiction, close air support of troops and maritime sanctions monitoring and enforcement are examples of naval and air involvement in the prosecution of peace support missions.[7]

Recent experience would suggest that there is a considerable dearth of expertise in the UN as to how these forces can be most effectively used in such missions. Insufficient advice has led to much misunderstanding as to maritime and air capabilities and restrictions on their effectiveness. With the concentration on land-based operations, little attention has been focused on developing maritime or air employment concepts which could maximize the advantages of these operational mediums in supporting and prosecuting peace support missions. A joint-oriented UN OPHQ could provide a focus for the development of such employment concepts.

An important function of a UN OPHQ is to look to the future in terms of operational demands and to be ready to meet them. Currently, land-dominated ethnic conflict has a very high profile and much attention is focused on how to improve the UN's ability to cope with such conflicts. However, it cannot be presumed that such conflicts will remain the chief source of violent conflict in the world. There are dormant and emerging security concerns with significant maritime dimensions that may provide other challenges to international security in the future.[8] Concepts for maritime peace support operations, and maritime peace support forces, need to be developed by a joint UN OPHQ ahead of time, if the UN is to develop a robust rapid response capability across the spectrum of crises and conflicts.

Vanguard Taskforces

Another significant component of the Vanguard concept concerns the provision of trained, fully-equipped, capable personnel, available at relatively short notice, who can be integrated into taskforces and deployed into crisis situations to carry out the taskings described in Figure 1. The Canadian initiative proposes that such personnel should be contributed by member-states through "stand-by" arrangements rather than through the maintenance of permanently-assigned UN standing forces. This recognizes the reality that no troop contributing nation has yet signed an agreement with the UN which puts national forces unconditionally at the disposition of the UN.[9] The Canadian Vanguard concept is designed to offer a viable alternative to the more difficult task of developing a UN standing "first-to-arrive" force. At the same time, its implementation would have significant implications for troop contributing nations, and for what troop contributors would expect in performance terms from the UN.

Vanguard Taskforces—General Conditions

The Vanguard concept aims to provide the UN with a mechanism for responding rapidly and effectively to crises. The presumption is that, while natural disasters may be coincident, these crises involve ongoing violent conflict, or conditions of such instability and anarchy that there is a very real threat of violent escalation. The Vanguard concept is designed to get appropriately-sized and capable taskforces in the air, at sea and on the ground, in time to make an effective difference; that difference being to deter further escalation, and to start creating the conditions supportive of cessation of violence.

In this context, a crucial condition must underpin any concept of operations for a Vanguard taskforce: that is, as a general rule, it must expect to function in a non-permissive or semi-permissive environment; i.e., the consent of protagonists is likely to be at best conditional, unevenly applied and liable to retraction without warning.

In too many recent cases, after diplomatic initiatives (which were either a qualified success or even still ongoing) the international community's next response has been to call for a peacekeeping force with a peacekeeping mandate. The result has been the creation of UN forces, sized and equipped for traditional peacekeeping, but inadequate for functioning in a semi- or non-permissive environment. The feedback response from the UN has been to incrementally expand the mandate to cover situations which it never foresaw on the ground as protagonists continue their war around, through and over peacekeepers.[10] Unable to stop it, because of their limited arms and mandate, peacekeepers become pawns in the protagonists' war-waging strategies;[11] the Serbian use of UN peacekeepers as human shields to protect their munitions storage facilities in late May 1995 is only the most recent example of this behaviour.

There needs to be a clear understanding and agreement, particularly among members of the Security Council, the Secretary-General, any military advice committee that is established, and the UN Secretariat, that, as a *sine qua non,* Vanguard taskforces must be sized and equipped to cope with the possibility of hostile engagement with some or all protagonists in an ongoing conflict. There are various viewpoints on this issue.

Some argue that equipping, preparing and deploying taskforces that can cope with the worst-case could be viewed negatively by protagonists as having the potential to upset the balance of power in a conflict. Therefore, the insertion of such taskforces will be resisted by all or some protagonists, ending any prospect that the UN may act as a mediator. However, as recent experiences demonstrate, small numbers of lightly armed or unarmed peacekeepers with restricted mandates have little prospect of deterring hardened warring factions from escalating or continuing a conflict. Moreover, the vulnerability of such peacekeepers increases their value as targets, hostages and instruments to be manipulated by warring factions in conducting their own campaigns and controlling the international community's options for action.

Fewer nations are prepared to commit their military forces when such risks occur and they may be expected to caveat their contributions when crises erupt. We need to return constantly to the purposes of a rapid reaction capability, and the underlying conditions which are needed to make it a reality. The principle of disinterested neutrality must be weighed against the need to be able to act rapidly to forestall further loss of life and environmental destruction which, after all, only entrenches the determination of protagonists to continue fighting.

Other general conditions and assumptions which underpin the concept of Vanguard taskforces include:

- Vanguard taskforces would be treated as first-to-arrive forces in an overall planned UN response encompassing follow-on forces configured for peace-keeping mandates;

- Vanguard units would be held under national command until requested by the UN and authorised by their respective governments; and

- Vanguard taskforces could reasonably expect to be replaced by follow-on peacekeeping forces as a general rule no later than six months after activation.

Vanguard Taskforce Issues

Using the conditions described above as a starting point, the aim here is to outline a selection of issues that affect troop contributing nations and their ability to effectively contribute the forces needed to give effect to the Vanguard taskforce concept.

PREPAREDNESS STATES

In any decision to participate in UN Vanguard taskforce pool arrangements, a critical factor for troop contributing nations is the preparedness state at which ear-marked units and personnel would need to be kept. During the Cold War, many nations held their military forces at high states of preparedness for conventional war-fighting missions. The demands of traditional peacekeeping were sufficiently limited that they could usually be met from within these forces. In the post-Cold War period, many key troop contributing nations have down-sized their military forces and reduced the levels of preparedness of those they have retained. Also, with the increase in demand for peace support forces, the UN has spread its requests to more countries and asked more of regular troop contributors. Together, these conditions have led to mounting pressures for responses to UN requests to become at least one determinant of the preparedness states at which national military forces are held.

Given that the Vanguard taskforce concept is based upon case-by-case activation, ear-marked Vanguard national force components will need to be held at quite high states of preparedness if the goal of rapid response is to be achieved. There will need to be a resolution between what constitutes a rapid response, and the time required to make ready forces, and integrate and deploy them into theatre. Thus for example, at a minimum, ear-marked units may need to be held at seven days notice to complete final preparations, with seven days for deployment to a form-up location, and seven days for integration before insertion. This means that the availability state for a Vanguard taskforce could be no less than 21 days from the decision to commit a force.

There are significant funding implications of holding forces at these states of preparedness. Given that most troop contributing nations insist that forces remain under national command and on national territory prior to any decision to contribute, these costs would be incurred by those nations. Without information on the likely availability state required of Vanguard pool units, troop contributing nations cannot make assessments as to whether they can afford to contribute.

The value and feasibility of UN "readiness subsidies" to troop contributing nations to assist in meeting the costs of holding forces at such states of preparedness should be considered. Such subsidies might be less expensive than the costs of maintaining a full-time UN standing force which in itself would need to be sized to handle at least two crisis response circumstances in near-simultaneous fashion (i.e., one force deployed on mission, and one working up or down). Alternatively, assessed UN contributions for those nations agreeing to contribute Vanguard force units could be commensurately reduced to take account of the indirect financial contribution of holding forces routinely at high states of preparedness. Acceptance of such subsidies or reduced financial contributions would not commit a nation to contribute ear-marked units in response to every request for their activation. It would however place a stronger obligation on nations that have taken the payments to respond more frequently.

TRAINING AND DOCTRINE

The employment conditions for Vanguard taskforces have implications for the standard, type, and quantity of preparatory training required of national ear-marked units. The two significant components of those conditions are: the requirement to function effectively in a semi- or non-permissive environment immediately from the moment of insertion, and the requirement to respond rapidly. Meeting both these requirements depends upon minimizing post-activation taskforce integrative training and work-up. To achieve this goal the following activities need to be undertaken regularly by ear-marked units and personnel:

- advanced, standard, collective-level training as part of annual in-country unit training programmes;
- collective-level, multinational training exercises which bring ear-marked Vanguard units together;
- collective-level, multinational contingency activation exercises which test the readiness of ear-marked units;
- Vanguard taskforce command post exercises (CPXs) to test command and control arrangements, concepts of operations, and provide learning experiences for potential staffs and commanders.

If these training activities are to be effective, they must be supported by:

- concepts of operation, including rules of engagement and mechanisms for changing ROEs;
- common or compatible operational-level doctrine;
- common standard operating procedures;
- realistic training scenarios; and
- common training performance standards.

If these documents and policies can be developed, then they must be promulgated and distributed widely among those troop contributing nations that have committed units to a Vanguard pool. Follow-on action is needed to routinely update publications and make them available. While these actions seem obvious, there is an issue of country access to doctrine and training publications that needs to be addressed. In the Gulf War for example, there were time-consuming integrative incompatibilities between those forces that had not been able to keep up with NATO-led doctrine and procedures and NATO forces.[12]

There are significant impediments to the development of standardised military training and doctrine support foundations for Vanguard taskforces. Some troop contributing nations have already voiced scepticism about the feasibility of finding sufficient common ground among the pool of troop contributors to warrant the effort involved in such an exercise. Moreover, the search for agreement on common standards risks degenerating into a search for lowest-common-denominators. The result would stand at odds with the requirement for a high common performance level required for effective functioning in semi- or non-permissive environments.

If such standards can be set in place, there is a follow-on requirement for national and UN discipline in adhering to the agreed standards. This means a determination on the part of the UN to reject, if necessary, national ear-marked units that are assessed as not meeting the standard and to replace them with units that do. To support such decision-making, the UN Secretariat, perhaps as part of a UN OPHQ, needs to develop and set in place a standardised training assessment system based on objective performance measurement techniques. All national ear-marked units would be routinely tested. It would be a national responsibility—particularly if readiness subsidies were instituted and accepted—to insure that ear-marked units performed within assessment parameters on Vanguard readiness evaluations.

There are examples where large multinational groupings have achieved consensus on military procedures, functional levels of interoperability and common training standards. NATO is the most obvious case in point. A fundamental requirement is to establish a UN organization that is responsible for taking a lead in putting forward doctrine and standards that can form the basis for negotiation among troop contributing nations. This is one of the roles envisioned for the Operational Planning Cell of a possible UN OPHQ outlined earlier in this paper.

The issue of multinational collective-level training raises the possibility of different types of contributions that nations can make to Vanguard taskforces. Overwhelmingly this paper has focused on *troop* contributions. However, some countries, such as the United States of America, United Kingdom, France and Germany, are uniquely placed to make other meaningful contributions. This includes the provision of subsidised or marginal cost training assistance, such as access to instrumented test training areas, training simulators, and the provision of transportation assistance to deploy ear-marked units to and from training areas.

Previously, during the Cold War, such assistance was limited by country affiliation and simple national and alliance demand issues. However, it may be timely for such nations to review the retention of surplus training area capacity for contribution to the preparation of Vanguard taskforces. To offset the costs of retaining training facility capacity that is surplus to national requirements, a similar arrangement to that being proposed in respect of readiness subsidies could be examined, or a trade-off reduction in assessed national financial contributions to the UN.

A JOINT OPERATIONS PERSPECTIVE

A joint operations perspective is needed to guide the effective sizing and required capability of Vanguard taskforces. By identifying and integrating the advantages of land, air, sea and space capabilities, this perspective can focus on optimal combinations of forces necessary to give effect to Vanguard concepts of operations. For example, the addition of an aircraft carrier to Vanguard pool arrangements can provide a Vanguard taskforce with a combat air support, heliborne logistic support, and operational C3I capability; all of which can be based in international waters without incurring operating restrictions or making demands upon a host nation, the crisis nation or territory. However, if attention is focused unduly upon brigade-sized ground formations as the military mainstay of Vanguard taskforces, then these other effective ways of putting together forces and conducting operations will not be effectively harnessed and applied.

Joint planning and concepts of operations for Vanguard taskforces could effect the size and diversity of the pool of troop contributing nations. For example, some smaller nations use relatively high levels of technology to compensate for small manpower bases. For these nations, there are significant limitations on their ability to contribute manpower-intensive ground units. However, such nations can contribute "at or above their weight" if an effective joint planning perspective integrates naval and air contributions into Vanguard concepts of operation.

FORCE STRUCTURE ISSUES

For most troop contributing nations, traditional peacekeeping has had a purposely restricted influence upon force structures. The aim has been to maintain forces organized for national defence missions that can be reconfigured as necessary to meet peacekeeping requests. However, because of its stress on high availability states, and expected insertion of its taskforces into conflict situations, the Vanguard concept is likely to raise a number of force structure issues. These issues include: levels of self-defence, unit sizing, and sustainment.

The possibility of operating in non- or semi-permissive environments calls for Vanguard self-defence capabilities well above the accepted norm for traditional peacekeeping. Self-defence features could involve:

- armoured rather than non-armoured vehicle transport;

- weaponry, targeting systems and intelligence warning systems not seen as acceptable in traditional peacekeeping;

- significant levels of transport helicopter support to "over-step" man-made and natural obstacles;

- close air support of ground troops;

- electronic jamming equipment;

- secure communication systems; and

- ground-force units sized to provide self-defence coverage for UN special envoys, civil affairs and humanitarian relief agency components of a Vanguard taskforce.

Effective provision of self-defence in semi- or non-permissive environments also imposes capability standards upon the shape and internal capability of ear-marked units. For some troop contributing nations, these standards will be higher than those applied to units ear-marked for traditional peacekeeping. It will be necessary to do more than re-assign such units to a Vanguard role. Some nations will need to upgrade the self-defence capability of units if they are to be offered to a Vanguard pool. Here again, the UN must be prepared to inspect all proposed contributions against Vanguard tables of organization and establishment. If proposed units do not meet required standards and troop contributing nations indicate a disinclination to bring units up to standard, then resolve must be exercised to decline such units, at least for inclusion in a Vanguard pool.

Unless this discipline is applied, both in this respect and in regard to training standards, then unacceptable risks must be carried by units contributed by other nations. Over time, understandably, these latter nations will be less willing to contribute. Without this discipline, the risk is increased that Vanguard forces will be no more competent in rapid and effective response in semi- or non-permissive environments than traditional peacekeepers. Such ineffectiveness would challenge the basic credibility and value of the Vanguard concept.

Another notable feature of peace support operations (over traditional peace-keeping) is the increased size of ground units for such operations. In peace support operations in semi- or non-permissive conditions, the norm is increasingly war-strength battalion-sized units operating within brigade-level or equivalent size formations. Most proposals currently under development for rapid reaction forces focus on brigade-sized formations. It is beyond the capacity of many smaller nations to contribute forces at this level. To overcome this, such nations, at the sub-regional level, may need to investigate and negotiate agreements that provide for the peacetime or post-activation integration of bi- or multinational formations that can be ear-marked for contribution to a Vanguard pool. There are risks inherent in this approach. Failure to secure agreement among all nations party to such arrangements, if activation was requested by the UN, would result in the non-availability of the combined unit.

A third issue concerns sustainment of contributions to UN Vanguard taskforces. For many nations, contributing to UN operations can significantly distort national force structures as whole sections are tasked to sustain the commitment. This effect is noticeable in rotation or roulement terms, where the commitment involves the deployed unit, a similar-sized and capable unit working up to replace it at the end of its tour, and another working down and re-roling having returned from its tour of duty. If it is a reasonable assumption that Vanguard taskforces would be extracted after a maximum of six months, then Vanguard arrangements may well suit many nations. Vanguard participation would not commit them to circumstances where significant proportions of their national forces would have to be diverted into sustaining long-term commitments.

FORCE PACKAGING

Further influences can affect the package of military capabilities most suited for Vanguard missions. For example, Vanguard taskforce units need to include sufficient language-qualified officers and senior Non-Commissioned Officers (NCOs) to provide liaison teams responsible for establishing and maintaining good communications with warring factions, and with non-governmental organizations. Such liaison teams have proven critical in recent anarchic and conflict situations.[13]

Competing transport priorities, poor weather conditions, interdiction actions of warring factions, main supply route conditions and long lines of communication are all operational impediments that can lead to significant delays in setting up support echelons and pushing support forward to dispersed units. These factors call for Vanguard military capabilities that are as self-reliant in as many respects as possible. To achieve this, it may be preferable to design taskforce packages of smaller-sized units than might be conventionally recommended, but which are more comprehensively capable. These units would include in their make-up the self-support capabilities that would more usually be provided by specialised units deployed separately in a supporting echelon.[14] In sizing these self-support capabilities, a UN OPHQ would also need to identify minimum periods of operations in which Vanguard units would need to be self-sustaining, and estimates of operating tempos.

Some nations have traditionally relied upon their contributions being "rounded-out" or supported by other units in a multinational force. A requirement for more self-reliant units would challenge this practice. A concept of self-supporting units also implies a greater need for units to be manned by multi-skilled and qualified personnel capable of undertaking general maintenance of equipments as well as operating them. Here again, there is a need for personnel qualification standards to be set that provide sufficient guidance to troop contributing nations in the development of national armed forces training and personnel management programmes.

A further influence on Vanguard force packaging is the need for manpower efficiency. As a general rule, the equipment tables of Vanguard units should include, wherever possible, equipments that save on labour and the time taken by available manpower to achieve results.[15] The application of this concept would need to be balanced against the principle of sizing units with sufficient manpower to sustain operations at anticipated operating tempos and the extension of self-defence coverage to other components of a Vanguard taskforce.

Another force packaging issue concerns transportation for bringing together activated Vanguard units and their operational deployment into theatre, and for taskforce support once in theatre. The usual practice for raising peacekeeping forces involves negotiation, at the time, of commercial or national arrangements for transportation assets. There are risks that these *ad hoc* arrangements may not be able to meet the deployment schedules anticipated for Vanguard taskforces. As part of operational planning, a Vanguard component of a UN OPHQ would need to prepare contingency plans for rapidly activating means of collecting national contributions and deploying them to form-up areas. Different types of transport assets (with higher levels of self-defence against ground fire for example) are likely to be required for inserting formed-up taskforces into crisis areas.

Vanguard force packaging also needs to include sufficient organic transportation support if standards of self-defence and self-reliance are to be achieved. These standards heighten the need for air assets that are functional in anticipated conditions, for example, short take-off and landing cargo planes that can land on rough strips and helicopters, to get over poor and fractured infrastructure, mines, and road-blocks. Again, these transport assets need to be equipped with self-defence measures.

In both deployment and operational transport functions, there are roles for troop contributing nations; particularly for those nations that may, in specific circumstances, be reluctant to provide larger-sized or combatant contributions. Such nations need to assess the implications of maintaining transport assets at high availability states for contribution to a Vanguard pool. This is particularly relevant given the utility of such assets across a range of tasking, and the probability of unrelated civil tasks and the deployment of other national ear-marked contributions that could occur coincidentally when these assets were planned for contribution to a UN Vanguard transportation force.

If effective force packaging is to be achieved, it needs to be looked at from a broader perspective than simply issues of structure and capability. Regional conditions, historical experience and cultural sensitivities have led particular nations to develop "best practices" in specific military capability areas. In packaging Vanguard taskforces, use needs to be made of "best practice" units or approaches. "Best practice" approaches should be identified by a UN OPHQ, and selected nations invited to develop "best practice" training packages, staff manuals, etc for incorporation in Vanguard contingency and staff planning.[16] Over the long-term, this will improve the overall level of capability among Vanguard units and have flow-on benefits to other military units of troop contributing nations.

FORCE INTEGRATION

Traditional peacekeeping involves an iterative process of building a force as requests, offers, counter-requests and counter-offers are exchanged between the

UN Secretariat and troop contributors. National decision-making timeframes, and military preparation and deployment schedules all lengthen the time needed to integrate a force. Clearly, rapid reaction is not possible if such an approach is applied to Vanguard taskforces. The whole aim of pre-activation UN and national planning, development of agreed standard operating procedures, holding of forces at agreed preparedness states, and undertaking collective peacetime training is that the time required to integrate a Vanguard taskforce will be significantly shorter than the norm for traditional peacekeeping forces.

In addition to the issues already discussed above, other actions can be taken both by troop contributors and a UN OPHQ to facilitate the smooth integration of joining units into a Vanguard taskforce. These concern the setting of minimum size and capability specifications for earmarked units, and the achievement of high levels of interoperability among force contributors. Both conditions are also essential to the effective in-theatre functioning of a Vanguard taskforce.

Force integration time can be reduced if ear-marked units conform to common sizing and capability specifications, as the need for post-activation integration of smaller-sized and capable units is avoided. Troop contributing nations need to be involved, possibly through military staff representatives on a UN OPHQ, in setting the minimum size and capability of units planned for Vanguard taskforces. These specifications are essential if nations are to plan their own contributions and where necessary look to establishing bi- or multinational integrative arrangements that can be exercised and integrated in peacetime circumstances.

The setting and disciplined achievement of high standards of interoperability is also essential for reducing force integration times and for the effective functioning of Vanguard taskforces. If high standards of interoperability are not inherent in ear-marked units prior to their activation, this level of interoperability must be achieved during force integration and prior to insertion into theatre. Experience in the 1991 Gulf War with the formation of a multinational coalition highlighted communications and logistic support as critical areas of interoperability that would need to be addressed in the design of Vanguard taskforces.

VANGUARD TASKFORCE DISENGAGEMENT

Much attention has been focused on the rapid deployment of taskforces into crisis or conflict area. Somewhat less attention has been paid to the employment of the taskforce once inserted. Even less attention has been devoted to the withdrawal of such taskforces. The broad military objectives for Vanguard taskforces see such taskforces being employed to hold, and where possible de-escalate or contain a crisis until such time as a follow-on UN peacekeeping force can be activated, integrated and deployed or a decision is made to abandon efforts, other than diplomatic, to contain or resolve the conflict. It is estimated that the job of Vanguard taskforces can be accomplished within a maximum time frame of approximately six months. At this time, the Vanguard concept calls for the withdrawal of taskforces.

However, these withdrawal assumptions need testing. Disengagement might not be simple after-thought that it currently is dealt with as. If it is decided that it is not feasible to replace the Vanguard taskforce by a UN follow-on peacekeeping force, and the conflict is ongoing, then Vanguard taskforce withdrawals may be contested, or simply made very difficult by reason of ongoing hostilities. This issue becomes another influence of operating in a semi- or non-permissive environment that needs to take into account when the size and capability of Vanguard taskforces are set. It is also an issue for good contingency planning: i.e., the setting of a desired end-state for participation, and the selection of appropriate methods for withdrawal under contested or peaceful circumstances.

Another issue concerns the success of Vanguard taskforces in achieving their goals of stabilization and creating conditions for the cessation of violence. It is often the very circumstance of violence and its graphic portrayal by the international media that holds pressure on national leaders to act in contributing forces to UN initiatives. However, if a Vanguard force is effective in stabilizing a situation, then these pressures may be eased. This could lead to delays in constituting a more substantive follow-on force. The possibility of such circumstances where the maximum desirable commitment time of six months for Vanguard units could be exceeded increases the importance that should be attached in Vanguard planning to sizing and equipping taskforces with high levels of self-reliance logistic support.

Rights, Responsibilities and Reality

This discussion paper has addressed only one set of the relationships which go into a UN capability for rapid reaction to crises affecting international peace and security. The Canadian initiative to improve the UN's rapid reaction capability is premised upon a series of partnerships of shared and separate responsibilities and obligations between Member States, the institutions of the UN, regional organizations and private volunteer organizations.

In the case of the partnership between troop contributing nations and the UN, the former have the right to expect a UN organization capable and competent in its ability to plan, support and command and control contributed forces which may be required to operate in semi- or non-permissive environments. These nations have the right to expect professionally developed operational level guidance on matters such as preparedness states, Vanguard force structures and required capabilities. They need to have a role in setting performance and capability standards for Vanguard taskforces and a functional UN OPHQ.

For its part, the UN needs the support, (material, personnel and financial) of Member States and particularly troop contributing nations. Rapid reaction to crises is not a responsibility that can be carried by the UN with only the passive and qualified involvement of Member States. If improvements are to be achieved in the UN's rapid reaction capability, this partnership must be put on a significantly more selfless and disciplined footing.

At the same time, the partnerships underpinning a UN rapid reaction capability must be based upon recognizing the reality of the circumstances that call for rapid response on the part of the UN. As Henry Cabot Lodge observed, the UN was not set up to take us to Heaven, but to stop us from going to Hell. The requirement for *rapid* response is that a particular nation, region or territory *is* going to hell in a hand-basket and fast. In almost all cases, these circumstances do not fit the conditions for Chapter VI peacekeeping mandates. The success of the Vanguard concept rests not only on troop contributing nations participating or not, but also on adequate recognition being made of the semi or non-permissive nature of the environment in which Vanguard taskforces are most likely to operate. If there is a powerful lesson to be taken from recent UN operations it is that the international community has successfully convinced itself that it was embarking upon a traditional peacekeeping operation. Impotence and ineffectualness have followed when this assumption has proven unfounded. If Vanguard responses are launched under the guise of traditional peacekeeping then we risk repeating history, having seemingly learnt nothing from it.

Notes

1. See Chapter 3 for the views of Sir Brian Urquhart.

2. See for example, Mats R. Berdal, *Whither UN Peacekeeping?* (London, International Institute of Strategic Studies, Adelphi Paper No. 281, 1993).

3. Commander I.M. Bartholomew, RN, "Command and Control--A Strategic View" (Symposium on US Options for Participation in UN Sponsored Military Operations, US Naval War College, Rhode Island, 30 March 1993), pp. 11-12.

4. Drawn in part from Sir James Eberle, "Agenda for Peace—Military Issues" *Naval Review* (Vol. 81, No. 1), January 1993, p. 6.

5. *Op. cit.* Mats Berdal, 1993, p. 48.

6. Uncritical inclusiveness is evidenced even in the ongoing reforms to the Department of Peace-keeping Operations; for example, while the number of military personnel in the DPKO has increased to 122, they are drawn from 37 countries.

7. See Jeremy Ginifer, "The UN at Sea? The New Relevance of Maritime Operations" *International Peacekeeping* (Vol. 1, No. 3), Autumn 1994, pp. 320-335; Commander D.L.W. Sim, RN, *Men of War for Missions of Peace: Naval Forces in Support of United Nations Resolutions* (US Naval War College Strategic Research Department Report 8-94); Michael C. Pugh, *Multinational Maritime Forces: A Breakout from Traditional Peacekeeping?* (Mountbatten Centre for International Studies, Southampton Papers in International Policy, No. 1, 1992); Eric Grove, "Navies in Peacekeeping and Enforcement: The British Experience in the Adriatic Sea" *International Peacekeeping* (Vol. 1 No. 4), Winter 1994, pp. 462-470; and Director of Defence Studies (RAF, "Crisis Management: The Application of Air Power in the Former Yugoslavia" *Air Clues* July 1993, pp. 244-247.

8. See *ibid.*, Jeremy Ginifer, 1994, p. 323.

9. Canadian initiative on Improving the UN's Rapid-Reaction Capability Discussion Paper (Ottawa, 28 April 1995), p. 8.

10. For example, Berdal notes that up to the time of writing, (1993), in respect of the former Yugoslavia, 42 resolutions and no less than 15 mandate enhancements had been adopted since the February 1992 approval of the Vance Plan. *op. cit.* M. Berdal, 1993, p. 31.

11. See for example, Lieutenant General Sir Michael Rose, "A Year in Bosnia: What has been Achieved" Address to the Royal United Services Institute for Defence Studies, London, 30 March 1995; and Major General L. Mackenzie, "Military Realities of UN Peacekeeping Operations" *Journal of the Royal United Services Institute* (Vol. 138, No. 1), February 1993.

12. See for example, Commander J.C. Neves, "Interoperability in Multinational Operations: Lessons from the Persian Gulf War" *Naval War College Review* (Vol. 48, No. 1), Winter 1995, pp. 53-55.

13. Colonel P.G. Williams, "Liaison—The Key to Success in Central Bosnia" *Army Quarterly and Defence Journal* (Vol. xx, No. x), 1995, pp. 389-392. At the same time, the necessity of these communications needs to be weighed against the physical safety and vulnerability of personnel operating in such teams.

14. See for example, comments in Captain T.A. Weber, "Operation Grapple 1: Some Lessons Learned" Royal Engineer Journal (Vol. 108, No. 1, April 1994, p. 92; and Lieutenant General D. Schroeder, "Lessons of Rwanda" *Armed Forces Journal International* December 1994, p. 32.

15. See for example, *ibid.*, Captain T.A. Weber, 1994, p. 94.

16. For example, the New Zealand Defence Force has developed an expertise in teaching de-mining techniques to local communities. New Zealand should be tasked with developing a de-mining package available for use by UN Vanguard Forces.

A Preliminary Blueprint of Long-Term Options for Enhancing a UN Rapid Reaction Capability

Peter Langille, Maxime Faille,
Carlton Hughes and James Hammond

Overview

The development of an effective UN rapid reaction capability will take time, vision and a coherent goal-oriented plan. It has become all too evident that the UN suffers from a serious capability gap—that it continues to lack the necessary resources and infrastructure for rapid reaction. To fill this gap, there will be a need for a comprehensive and cumulative development process; one that is guided by a long-term sense of purpose and the prospect of contributing to an urgently needed mechanism for war-prevention and humanitarian assistance.

Recent discussion on enhancing UN rapid reaction capabilities have focused on the relative merits of three options: either coordinate better arrangement for the prompt provision of contingents earmarked through the 1993 UN Stand-by Arrangement System; organize stand-by vanguard groups from a coalition of committed Member States; or, initiate a standing brigade of professional UN volunteers. To date, there has been a tendency to regard these proposals as distinct, if not mutually exclusive. Yet in a stage by stage cumulative development process, there is the prospect of a coherent evolution; one that integrates the strengths of potentially compatible and reinforcing options.

At the forefront of the proposed evolution is the establishment of a UN rapid reaction base that can serve as an operational and tactical headquarters and as a dedicated centre for planning, training, equipment stockpiling and staging. As the organization proceeds, nationally-based, stand-by, contingents can be supplemented with standing elements assigned to this base for a period of approximately two years. Ultimately, these efforts should evolve into a UN Standing Emergency Capability comprised of dedicated UN volunteers, national contingents and civilian

---

Messrs. Peter Langille, Maxime Faille, Carlton Hughes and Major James Hammond were members of the Core Group established to analyze the various dimensions of a UN rapid response capability.

personnel that are stationed and trained together. New doctrine and advance preparation, including comprehensive training programmes, will be essential. It is also an appropriate time to begin planning for multiple UN rapid reaction bases. This evolution is seen to offer the best chance of assuring reliability and readiness.

Committed Member States can take a leading role in initiating such a process. Regional representation can be encouraged by the demonstration of organizational competence and by the development of Partnerships between initial contributors and supportive Member States.

There is a need for a variety of blueprints that outline not only the foundation of a rapid reaction capability but also a more durable structure and capacity for expansion. This chapter departs from conventional thinking and assumes the UN requires a rapid reaction capability on a scale commensurate with the tasks it is likely to be assigned. It cannot be asked to improvise and make do with less on an ongoing basis. Consideration of long-term options is, however, inherently speculative. The following proposals offer some guidance to stimulate further discussion, analysis and planning.

A Comprehensive Approach

UN Secretary-General Boutros Boutros-Ghali's *Agenda for Peace* underscores the need for a comprehensive approach to peace and security issues. A new rapid reaction capability cannot succeed in isolation. It must be designed as an integral component of UN crisis management—as a complement to the Organization's ongoing efforts in preventive diplomacy, peacekeeping and peacebuilding. Such a mechanism can only be justified, moreover, if it has the ability to provide a more cost-effective and timely response to a wide array of complex potential challenges.

To address such challenges adequately, it is evident that this new instrument will need to have a multidimensional composition and character. This will entail a comprehensive approach utilizing both military and civilian elements.

Recent UN operations have demonstrated the importance of providing for the diverse needs of people in desperate circumstances. Frequently there is a requirement to provide food and shelter, re-establish communications, restore a sense of order with civilian police services, open schools, rebuild bridges and develop the necessary infrastructure for good governance. Faith and confidence in the future diminish rapidly in the absence of such efforts. While UN forces play an essential role in dissuading violent options, immediate rehabilitation projects play an equally important role in demonstrating an enduring commitment to a sustainable peace process. Together, they facilitate the work of those engaged in peacemaking.

The added complexity of second generation UN multinational operations will demand new cooperative practices and combined efforts. The commensurate expansion of operational and tactical responsibilities is likely to continue. Far-sighted, multi-disciplinary planning and advance preparations will be imperative. Military and civilian elements will have to be well coordinated and sufficiently flexible to respond to a range of future emergencies. An effective UN rapid reaction capability will depend upon combining the skills and expertise within participating Member States, the UN and the community of related non-governmental organizations. An integrated unity of effort and a complementary division of labour can be encouraged through team building, inclusive doctrine and participation in common training.

A Cumulative Development Process

To move beyond the *ad hoc* organizational practices that have been characterized as a last-minute sheriff's posse, sound "building blocks" will need to be firmly established and built up over the next decade. The chance of immediately initiating a UN standing capability is now seen to be quite remote. A cumulative development process appears to be the most feasible.

Such a process would open up a wider range of future options while gradually inspiring greater confidence in the UN's ability to manage new capabilities. Practical experience will be necessary to allay longstanding anxieties.

We envisage several stages in this cumulative development. Each stage will determine the scope and the scale of potential activities. Additional responsibilities and assistance will have to be earned through the demonstration of organizational competence, operational readiness and success in the field.

Overall, however, it is essential that planning begins to build on, and expand beyond, the limited foundation provided by the UN Stand-by Arrangements System and proposals for a relatively small operational headquarters within the Directorate of Peacekeeping. In short, the UN's capability gap can only be bridged by institutionalizing and consolidating an effective rapid reaction capability. Its potential viability will be dependent upon the establishment of a more durable and permanent structure.

While this chapter recommends a cumulative development process, it is a preliminary review of related options and by no means a fixed trajectory nor a definitive or final blueprint. Any process will be open to revision, redirection or expansion at every stage. Member states would not be tied to an agreed process; it would remain entirely up to their discretion whether or not to participate.

Stage 1: Establish a Dedicated UN Rapid Reaction Base

Among the future options meriting consideration is the establishment of a UN rapid reaction base. If UN responses are to be rapid, there will be a need for a dedicated facility from which to prepare, mount and manage future operations. A UN base would enhance multinational cooperation and confidence through joint planning, training and exercises.

In the near term, this base would be expected to assist in the organization and preparation of national stand-by contingents and the necessary civilian elements. Within a relatively short period, it could begin to serve as a central training, logistics, staging and equipment stockpiling centre. Over time, a UN base would offer the optimum prospect of concentrating the personnel, equipment, and combined effort necessary for rapid reaction.

The selection of a rapid reaction base should account for its potential capacity for expansion on the assumption that it will be assigned additional responsibilities. Consideration at the political and strategic level will have to be accorded to a base that can assume responsibility for hosting an expanded standing operational head-quarters and two tactical field or mission headquarters with a range of various deployable elements. At the political level, host nation support from a committed Member State and regular troop contributor will be necessary for a facility that has sufficient terrain and infrastructure to accommodate and train approximately 10,000 personnel.

As early as 1957, William R. Frye wrote that, "as a practical matter, the UN almost certainly would have to rent or buy, on advantageous terms, a base already in existence, and this would mean finding a Member State which was willing to dispose of one of its own".[1] There are new opportunities in this respect. With widespread force build-down occurring in numerous Member States, there are ample opportunities to convert a surplus national defence facility to this task. While a UN base would clearly demand new resources, it need not entail a major capital acquisition and development project.

The operational and tactical requirements of a UN rapid reaction base are straightforward. Site selection can be determined by the need for a secure, sup-portive, cost-effective, easily-accessible, strategic location. For prompt air-lift, this base should be within an hour of an air base that can assist in staging operations. For concurrent sea-lift of necessary equipment and supplies, it would be helpful if it was located within several hours of a sea port that had a roll-on roll-off capabil-ity. Such a location would facilitate stockpiling as well as staging and logistics efforts. Relative proximity to land, air force and naval establishments of the host nation might also offer the potential for joint exercises in a realistic environment as well as valuable assistance in various related areas.

Among the assets required are: officer and other rank quarters, administrative offices, drill and training areas, class rooms, a language training centre, firing ranges, storage depots, hangers, self-contained medical and dental services, rec-reational facilities and approximately 20,000 acres of varied terrain. While not essential, an urban conflict training site would be a useful complement. The sur-rounding area should also have the potential to house and provide for the needs of families and dependents. Community support for a large multinational presence will be essential.

Co-locate Standing Operational and Tactical-Level Headquarters at the UN Base

A priority should be an expanded headquarters at the designated UN base. Experienced officers and qualified planners would be seconded to the base and co-assigned responsibility to expand the operational and tactical foundation for future operations. Together, this headquarters and base could serve as a focal point for contingency planning, training rapid reaction elements and supporting doctrinal development.

Among the priority tasks of this operational-level headquarters would be: forecasting detailed requirements; coordinating civilian and military aspects of operational planning; confirming standing operating procedures; and recommending rules of engagement for mission commanders. It would continue to work on arrangements for equipment procurement and stockpiling, establishing readiness and training standards, promoting interoperability, and the refinement of training curricula and courses for both military and civilian elements. It would also assume responsibility for deployment of all rapid reaction mission elements thereby easing the burden on the mission headquarters, troop-contributors and UN headquarters.

Only an expanded, static operational headquarters at a designated base would provide the capability necessary. To effectively manage a variety of complex tasks, it is in the common interest of all related parties to shift from a skeletal operational headquarters stationed within UNHQ, New York to an operational headquarters at the rapid reaction base. As in numerous other areas within the larger UN system, some tasks can be better managed when unencumbered by the day to day institutional responsibilities of UNHQ. (See Figure 1).

A headquarters of this nature would, by necessity, be quite large. The example provided estimates a military requirement for approximately 203 personnel not including the base infrastructure and support staff. This number is partly accounted for given the need for a 24/7 operations cell to initiate a rapid response and immediate planning in the event of a pending crisis. As this headquarters assumes responsibility for the details of reconnaissance, force composition and deployment, a 24/7 operations cell will be critical.

The civilian component within this headquarters is projected at 83 personnel (not including base infrastructure). These civilians will be required to ensure a comprehensive approach in the planning of multidimensional operations and to develop the integrated unity of effort which must typify UN peace support operations of the future.

Overall coordination of the headquarters and base might best be assigned to a Special Representative of the Secretary-General (SRSG) who would serve as the direct link to the Secretariat. This SRSG should have experience in previous operations and be advised by a senior military officer of a general rank. To ensure the appropriate direction and command of future field operations, it may be wise to designate two to three individuals with military and diplomatic experience as Deputy Special Representatives of the Secretary-General for UN Rapid Reaction.

The operational headquarters and base would be organized to include: the office of the Special Representative of the Secretary-General; a national liaison cell; an operations group consisting of military and civilian staff that would conduct

Figure 1

OPERATIONAL
LEVEL

UN RAPID REACTION CAPABILITY
PERMANENT OPERATIONAL LEVEL HQ AND BASE

(INTEGRATED PLANNING FOR MAXIMUM UNITY OF EFFORT)

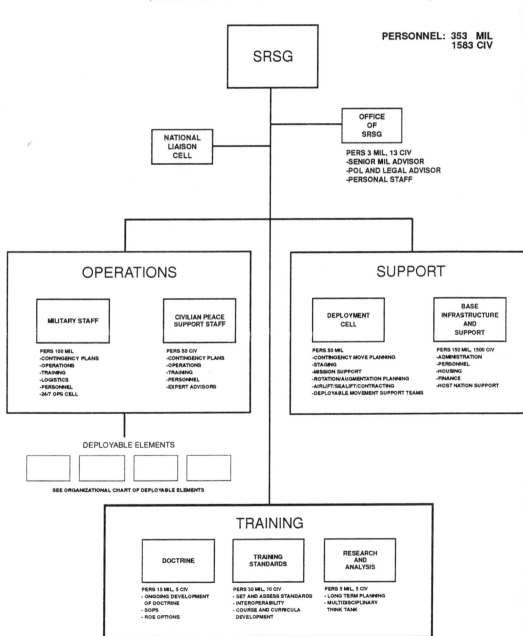

PERSONNEL: 353 MIL
1583 CIV

SRSG

NATIONAL LIAISON CELL

OFFICE OF SRSG

PERS 3 MIL, 13 CIV
-SENIOR MIL ADVISOR
-POL AND LEGAL ADVISOR
-PERSONAL STAFF

OPERATIONS

MILITARY STAFF

PERS 100 MIL
-CONTINGENCY PLANS
-OPERATIONS
-TRAINING
-LOGISTICS
-PERSONNEL
-24/7 OPS CELL

CIVILIAN PEACE SUPPORT STAFF

PERS 50 CIV
-CONTINGENCY PLANS
-OPERATIONS
-TRAINING
-PERSONNEL
-EXPERT ADVISORS

SUPPORT

DEPLOYMENT CELL

PERS 50 MIL
-CONTINGENCY MOVE PLANNING
-STAGING
-MISSION SUPPORT
-ROTATION/AUGMENTATION PLANNING
-AIRLIFT/SEALIFT/CONTRACTING
-DEPLOYABLE MOVEMENT SUPPORT TEAMS

BASE INFRASTRUCTURE AND SUPPORT

PERS 150 MIL, 1500 CIV
-ADMINISTRATION
-PERSONNEL
-HOUSING
-FINANCE
-HOST NATION SUPPORT

DEPLOYABLE ELEMENTS

SEE ORGANIZATIONAL CHART OF DEPLOYABLE ELEMENTS

TRAINING

DOCTRINE

PERS 15 MIL, 5 CIV
- ONGOING DEVELOPMENT
  OF DOCTRINE
- SOPS
- ROE OPTIONS

TRAINING STANDARDS

PERS 30 MIL, 10 CIV
- SET AND ASSESS STANDARDS
- INTEROPERABILITY
- COURSE AND CURRICULA
  DEVELOPMENT

RESEARCH AND ANALYSIS

PERS 5 MIL, 5 CIV
- LONG TERM PLANNING
- MULTIDISCIPLINARY
  THINK TANK

the planning and management of deployable elements; a support group comprised of a deployment cell as well as base infrastructure and support components; and a training group with specific offices for doctrine, training standards and research and analysis. It is clear that a headquarters of this size would require the support of a base infrastructure.

It would also be prudent for cost-effectiveness, as well as for the obvious benefits from a military, doctrinal and administrative perspective, to co-locate two field deployable tactical (mission) headquarters at the UN base. As the number of civilian and military elements on the base increases, so too does the requirement to staff the base. The model illustrated suggests the need for approximately 150 military and 1,500 civilians to provide support and administration at a rapid reaction base capable of hosting a total of 10,000 personnel.

INITIATE AN ONGOING PROCESS OF DOCTRINE DEVELOPMENT

The added complexity and risks of "second generation" UN multinational operations will demand new organizational practices, new methods and new skills. Doctrine is the key to synchronizing multiple elements of a UN rapid reaction capability into effective peace support operations. It establishes the fundamental principles by which the various elements plan and conduct their activities in support of UN objectives.

Among the related doctrinal priorities will be competence, flexibility, mobility, discipline and confidence-building. Detailed consideration will have to be accorded to appropriate rules of engagement, new standing operating procedures, strict control over the use of force, modern command and control procedures as well as common standards for training and readiness.

There is much to be learned and adopted from UN experience as well as established national and multinational doctrine for rapid reaction, particularly in specific areas such as command and control, logistics and staging. However, in other areas, the principles of war and strategy are simply incompatible given the different priorities and objectives of UN operations.

Appropriate doctrine will have to be developed for military and civilian elements participating in multidimensional UN operations. Credible doctrine can be viewed as a pre-requisite to inspiring both the confidence and the financial support of Member States.[2] There are, however, justifiable concerns that the UN is currently "wandering in the void" in charting a new strategic direction.[3] More urgently needs to be done. Further multidisciplinary research and analysis focusing specifically on UN rapid reaction, peace support operations will be necessary. This process must be ongoing.

Operational and tactical doctrine will have to be modified to ensure a more sophisticated response to a wide array of potential tasks. Doctrine must focus on widening the range of available options that minimize the need for force. For example, at the tactical level, doctrine can help to specify a menu of options for the deployable elements that will assist the opposing parties in pursuing appropriate solutions.[4] In this respect, confidence building has to be considered an essential element of doctrine as "success" frequently depends on the extent to which a mission establishes the trust of the belligerent as well as that of the local population. Confidence building measures help to ensure consent and to establish the moral authority of related UN efforts.

Another key to widening the range of options is to resolve problems at the lowest practical level, or what is frequently referred to as the "sharp end" between local forces and UN personnel in the field. Low-level problem solving helps to contain minor conflicts and stem the potential for escalation. It nevertheless demands a greater degree of tactical flexibility in doctrine as well as an assurance that all ranks have sufficient understanding and sophistication to handle the various problems that arise in the field.

Doctrine will also be necessary to guide contingency planning and the development of various generic mission models which outline specific requirements, particularly rules of engagement. Consent and impartiality will depend heavily upon discipline and restraint with respect to the use of force. As Charles Dobbie writes:

> Doctrine should specify a philosophy towards the use of force that takes account of its long-term effects. Commanders will need principles to guide their use of force and also be made aware of the alternatives to its use. A helpful rule of thumb has been defined as minimum necessary force...[5]

A UN rapid reaction capability will require new rules of engagement, particularly those governing the use of force; rules that are different from either those of peacekeeping or enforcement operations. In the words of former UN Under Secretary-General, Sir Brian Urquhart:

> The rapid reaction group will never initiate the use of force, but will be highly trained so that it can take care of its own security and mobility and have the ability and equipment to maintain its operations in the face of harassment and even opposition. It will in no circumstances have military objectives or be required to take sides in a civil war. It will be trained in peace-keeping and problem-solving techniques but will also have the training, military expertise and esprit de corps to pursue those tasks in difficult, and even violent situations.[6]

Contingency planning and appropriate doctrine must be prepared for a new multinational structure and mission. As a UN rapid reaction capability will be a new mechanism for war prevention and humanitarian assistance, one can anticipate the emphasis in doctrinal planning will shift toward dissuasion, de-escalation, non-provocative intervention and the provision of useful services.

The larger task will be one of neutral, and wherever possible, peaceful, third-party intervention. Yet success in future operations will be increasingly dependent upon carefully conceived pro-active and preventive measures. Developing new doctrine and specific skills for areas as diverse as technical reconnaissance deployments, conflict resolution, and well-controlled escalation and de-escalation will be a demanding yet essential task.

PROMOTE COMMON PRIOR TRAINING

Advance planning must be accompanied by prior training for various rapid reaction contingencies. Training provides a crucial link in the process of understanding doctrine and its implications for individual and common efforts in conducting day to day activities as well as field operations.

Even with the provision of UN standards and training guidelines, the quality and capability of units assigned by Member States varies considerably. In the midst of an emergency, there are serious risks in assigning contingents that have little common experience, inadequate training and insufficient equipment. These problems are unlikely to be quickly or easily resolved without extensive cooperation in the advance preparation of rapid reaction elements.

A dedicated training system that provides a comprehensive approach to the various tasks will be necessary to ensure competence, high standards and interoperability. Cooperation may be extended through the active involvement and support of national military and academic establishments, particularly those engaged in the regional studies, conflict resolution, mediation, negotiation, cultural sensitivity training and basic language training. There will also be a need for the ongoing assistance of national peacekeeping training centres and the participation of UN officials working in related fields.

Military credibility and proficiency will be essential for operations in high risk environments. All ranks should also be provided with training in contact skills such as mediation and dispute resolution as these help to ensure that minor conflicts are quickly contained before risking early escalation.[7] Many Member States can assume the responsibility to ensure that their participants are well prepared and of the highest quality available.

Supplementary training efforts should, however, be consolidated at the UN base under the dedicated training group. All participants would be provided with a common understanding of various UN operations and objectives as well as with intensive preparation for their specific roles and responsibilities. There will be a need for comprehensive general, specialized, and mission-specific training programmes. Modern training courses and a wide range of curricula will be required. Participating personnel will need general training in how to manage and diffuse crises, courses in how to conduct themselves with new partners in UN multidimensional missions, as well as specialized training in their assigned tasks. The list of the new skills, methods and tactics required will be rather extensive. At this stage, moreover, it will be important to plan for and secure arrangements to begin hosting stand-by vanguard groups and civilian elements for a four-month period of general and specialized joint training and exercises at the designated base.

ENCOURAGE REGIONAL REPRESENTATION THROUGH PARTNERSHIPS

Widespread legitimacy and support will be important in determining the further development and success of UN efforts in this field. While the development of a sophisticated capability is to be encouraged, any indication of this being an elite "club" of contributors would be counter-productive. The UN must avoid a two-tiered, Northern-dominated rapid reaction effort.

Regional representation can only be assured by developing the confidence and capabilities of members who might otherwise be unable to participate in such operations. Regular troop contributors can facilitate this process by initiating partnerships with new participants to share expertise, training and, where possible, equipment. Partnership programmes could either be initiated on a multilateral basis within a region or on a bilateral basis between two Member States.

It is widely recognized that a relatively small number of nations have developed niche expertise and special skills in areas such as communications, logistics, engineering and training. Similarly, a number of the larger powers retain a surplus of equipment for transportation, defence and surveillance. Yet UN operations continue to be jeopardized by the absence of appropriate understanding, training and equipment among new troop contributors.

The twin objectives of initiating a partnership programme would be first, to expand the pool of available expertise and equipment, and second, to foster mutually-beneficial cooperation and the ability to work together toward high UN standards. Participants would simply agree to a programme of sharing (or combining) their respective resources to assist in the ongoing development of UN rapid reaction capabilities.

Options that promote further cooperation and ensure this remains an "inclusive" process warrant serious consideration. In this respect, there may also be significant potential in the gradual consolidation of multiple regionally-dispersed UN bases. These would facilitate broader representation and expand the prospects for cooperation with regional organizations. Aside from demonstrating a tangible world-wide commitment, the UN would have the benefit of wider access as well as a broad range of facilities for regional equipment stockpiling, training and staging. In time, one would expect regional UN bases to help develop a broader pool of participants and qualified personnel.

Stage 2: Consolidate National Contingents and Civilian Elements at the Designated Base as a UN Standing Emergency Vanguard Group

To institutionalize a more effective rapid reaction capability, military contingents and civilian elements from committed Member States should be assigned to the designated UN base for a period of two years. Common basing would offer the best prospect of enhancing standardization, interoperability and cohesiveness among various national military and civilian elements. Consolidating these elements at the base would provide the UN with a core capability and help to overcome much of the last-minute *ad hocery* that has plagued pre-deployment planning of UN missions and constrained field operations. This cooperative endeavor would maximize readiness and help to ensure a relatively reliable and sophisticated response within five to eight days of warning from the Security Council.

Supplementary arrangements could be negotiated at the political level to identify dedicated participants and units for secondment to UN service for this two year period. Common basing need not be an exorbitantly expensive endeavor for either the UN or participating Member States. Committed members would simply re-locate national elements that already exist and assign them to a UN base. In the event of a national crisis, they would be subject to recall. As they would remain under national command, co-assigned to national and UN service, their governments would retain primary responsibility for their administration, pay and benefits.

For the UN, cost-sharing might be arranged on a basis slightly less taxing than that of field operations wherein the Organization frequently assumes responsibility for incremental costs, transportation of national elements to and from the site, operation and maintenance costs, as well as the provision of accommodation and pay equity allowances.

As in the provision of any new service, one can readily anticipate that there will be new expenses. The nature of a UN standing emergency capability will inevitably demand a high level of professionalism and commitment. Aside from assigning additional personnel to one location, there will be a requirement for high quality equipment, prompt air and sea lift, support and appropriate base infrastructure. Yet this initiative can be designed in a manner that appeals to the common interest of all related parties.

Participation would entail considerable recognition and prestige for both the contributing nation and the various services involved. Moreover, a number of Member States might be encouraged to assign units to a standing capability if it held out the prospect of advancing their unit's training and professional development. Contributors would also retain the option to withhold or veto the deployment of their national contingents. As in current operations, national representatives would be expected to command national elements, with operational control remaining under UN authority.

The general reluctance to move quickly can be partially overcome by stationing multinational elements within a sound operational and tactical structure. Member states will want to be assured of command arrangements and well represented within them.[8] Naturally, they will want checks in the system as national safeguards. Yet several governments would likely set aside their former reservations over a UN standing capability if they were confident that it was professionally organized and well managed. Competent leadership would be widely regarded as a pre-requisite of participation. At this stage, the UN Security Council would only have the authority to establish and deploy rapid reaction capabilities pending national approval.

At the operational and tactical level, the UN would be increasingly assured of a broad range of well-trained military and civilian elements to draw from for future operations. Common basing offers the potential to conduct joint staging, field and command post exercises in a multinational and multidimensional training environment. Controlled simulations in a realistic milieu are among the better tests of various operational conditions and tactical innovations. Doctrine, strategy, tactics, standard operating procedures, and rules of engagement could be developed and refined in both contingency planning and on-site training. In turn, one could also foster a higher degree of confidence, group cohesiveness and the necessary unity of effort.

Comprehensive, prior training is an essential foundation for rapid reaction, particularly in demanding roles such as preventive deployment. If it is achieved to a high degree, a shorter programme of mission-specific training and briefings could commence on site immediately, with all required elements at the first alert provided by the Security Council. Concurrent staging efforts could proceed. The net result would be a faster and more effective response.

COMPOSITION OF DEPLOYABLE ELEMENTS

To ensure the prompt provision of sufficient personnel at the operational and tactical levels, there will be a need to build in, and maintain, a considerable redundancy of personnel and units from various troop contributors. This redundancy would also provide the UN with the option of selecting those national contingents deemed suitable for operations in regions having particular political, ethnic, cultural or religious sensitivities. As in other UN peace support operations, impartiality and neutrality must be maintained to ensure legitimacy.

The military elements stationed at the designated UN base are, therefore, projected at approximately 6,250 personnel. Whereas the majority of battalions will be kept on a relatively high state of readiness, contingency planning should account for deployments that are limited to roughly 3,000 military personnel. This 2 to 1 ratio could facilitate deployment of tasked elements as those that remain on site might assist with logistics and support functions while continuing preparation for future missions

At this stage, the operational headquarters would be expected to ensure the two tactical field headquarters (mission headquarters) were fully functional and capable of assuming operational control over the deployable elements. When deployed, these mission headquarters could be placed under the direction of a Deputy Representative of the Secretary-General supported by a military commander. Each of the two headquarters would include military and civilian staff, political and legal advisors, a translation cell, an NGO liaison team, a communications and signals unit and, a defence and security platoon. This would be a multinational, multidimensional headquarters of approximately 275 personnel with the capacity to act as a vanguard HQ, a sector HQ, or a mission HQ for a limited period of time.

The deployable military elements assigned to each mission headquarters are projected to include: high readiness, technical reconnaissance units; a light armored reconnaissance squadron; light infantry battalions; light-armored (wheeled) infantry battalions; a helicopter squadron; an engineer unit; a logistics battalion; as well as a medical unit.

Among the deployable civilian peace support elements recommended are: a disaster relief and humanitarian response team; civilian police; a conflict resolution team; a peacebuilding advisory team; medical teams; an environmental crisis response team; a transport team; and a public affairs team. The combined strength of the civilian peace support elements that might be assigned to the two mission headquarters is estimated at approximately 550 personnel.

An example of the deployable elements, including the mission headquarters is outlined in Figure 2. Overall, a standing UN rapid reaction capability is projected to require a total of approximately 10,000 personnel.

The posting of dedicated personnel to the UN base might be initiated bi-annually with rotation of personnel staged at six-month intervals. Provision can be made to ensure the necessary overlap of new and experienced contributors. Similarly, periods of leave can be arranged four times throughout the year at staged intervals to assure an adequate strength remains on site for rapid deployment. Those individuals and units that have served for two years in UN stand-by or standing elements and participated in the general and specialized training programmes and operations in either stage 1 or stage 2 could be encouraged by the UN and supportive Member States to serve as reserve or augmentation groups.

EQUIPMENT, SUPPORT AND LIFT

Three generic components of rapid reaction will require a sustained effort. First, is the need for high readiness—all deployable elements, equipment and supplies must be ready for prompt staging. Second, they require a unique degree of self-sufficiency—a capacity to operate on their own for a period of 60 to 90 days. Third, they must have prompt transportation to the mission area and within the specific theatre of operations.

To react rapidly, equipment must be ready to go, pre-packed and prepared for immediate deployment. Similar equipment must also be available at the UN base for training. Current arrangements stipulate that the troop contributors provide nearly all that is necessary. While this results in minimal cost to the UN, it would undermine readiness if a wide array of disparate equipment and parts from various participants had to be loaded, supplied for, and designated to distinct national elements at the last minute. Partnerships may provide an initial foundation for equipment sharing between several participants, but they cannot be expected to provide a standard source of supply for all.

Figure 2
UN RAPID REACTION CAPABILITY
DEPLOYABLE ELEMENTS

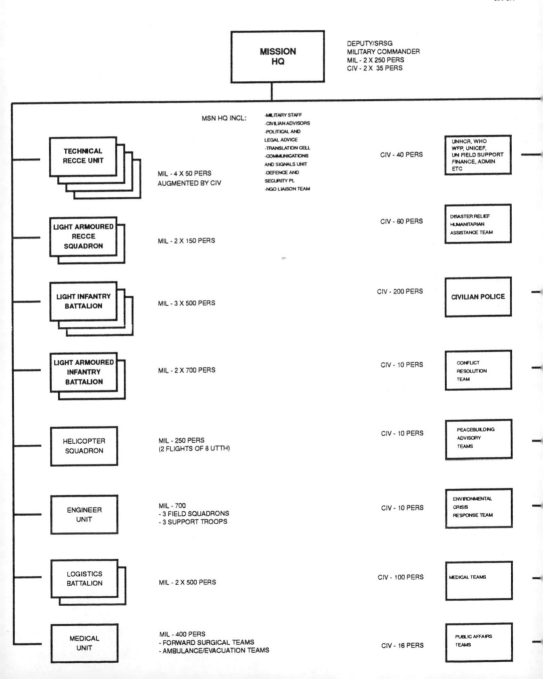

PERMANENT OPERATIONAL LEVEL HQ WILL TASK
EITHER ONE OF TWO MULTIFACETED, FIELD
HEADQUARTERS AND AS REQUIRED, TASK
ANY OF THE ELEMENTS BELOW TO THAT HQ

PERSONNEL: 6,250 MIL
506 CIV

MISSION HQ

DEPUTY/SRSG
MILITARY COMMANDER
MIL - 2 X 250 PERS
CIV - 2 X 35 PERS

MSN HQ INCL:
- MILITARY STAFF
- CIVILIAN ADVISORS
- POLITICAL AND LEGAL ADVICE
- TRANSLATION CELL
- COMMUNICATIONS AND SIGNALS UNIT
- DEFENCE AND SECURITY PL
- NGO LIAISON TEAM

TECHNICAL RECCE UNIT
MIL - 4 X 50 PERS
AUGMENTED BY CIV

CIV - 40 PERS

UNHCR, WHO
WFP, UNICEF,
UN FIELD SUPPORT
FINANCE, ADMIN
ETC

LIGHT ARMOURED RECCE SQUADRON
MIL - 2 X 150 PERS

CIV - 60 PERS

DISASTER RELIEF
HUMANITARIAN
ASSISTANCE TEAM

LIGHT INFANTRY BATTALION
MIL - 3 X 500 PERS

CIV - 200 PERS

CIVILIAN POLICE

LIGHT ARMOURED INFANTRY BATTALION
MIL - 2 X 700 PERS

CIV - 10 PERS

CONFLICT
RESOLUTION
TEAM

HELICOPTER SQUADRON
MIL - 250 PERS
(2 FLIGHTS OF 8 UTTH)

CIV - 10 PERS

PEACEBUILDING
ADVISORY
TEAMS

ENGINEER UNIT
MIL - 700
- 3 FIELD SQUADRONS
- 3 SUPPORT TROOPS

CIV - 10 PERS

ENVIRONMENTAL
CRISIS
RESPONSE TEAM

LOGISTICS BATTALION
MIL - 2 X 500 PERS

CIV - 100 PERS

MEDICAL TEAMS

MEDICAL UNIT
MIL - 400 PERS
- FORWARD SURGICAL TEAMS
- AMBULANCE/EVACUATION TEAMS

CIV - 16 PERS

PUBLIC AFFAIRS
TEAMS

Ultimately, the UN will require its own modern equipment if the deployable elements of a standing rapid reaction capability are to be interoperable and standardized. Standardization of equipment (particularly with respect to vehicle fleets) across a multinational UN capability would greatly reduce overall costs, manpower, overhead and efficiency.

Although each of the two mission headquarters will have responsibility for deployments of up to 3,250 personnel, one set of the more costly standard equipment such as vehicles might be shared in training while a second similar set was either being used in a mission or pre-packaged ready for immediate deployment. Overall, this will entail roughly thirty percent more equipment than might be required for a high-readiness, brigade-size formation.

At the political level, one can readily anticipate initial reservations over the cost of providing the UN with its own new equipment. In the long-term, however, there might be considerable savings for those participants that provide personnel but would no longer have to supply, maintain and replace similar equipment from their own stocks.

At the operational level, the complex job of coordinating and maintaining appropriate equipment for training and missions might be considerably less taxing. At the tactical level, the benefits of standard and interoperable equipment would provide an added measure of safety and reliability. Personnel would be familiar with the tools of their trade and assured of support and immediate re-supply out of reserve or training stocks at the UN base.

Logistics efforts would be considerably streamlined.[9] One deployment cell could oversee mission requirements with a view to ensuring self-contained, smaller logistics elements and self-sufficiency for 60 to 90 days. Planning would be simplified with the development of fully-integrated, task-organized mission support teams capable of managing operations from deployment to the field and early withdrawal.

Similarly, one might anticipate fewer problems in arranging immediate transportation and lift requirements. The ability to move personnel and equipment quickly into and out of any mission will be critical. Coordinating lift out of one airhead near the UN rapid reaction base would be considerably less expensive, quicker, and easier to plan than picking up nationally-based vanguard groups located world-wide. Units on high readiness would have all necessary material pre-packed and ready at the airhead.

Rapid deployment (and the potential need for rapid extraction) inevitably points to a requirement for immediate strategic and tactical air-lift as well as sea-lift that are unencumbered by delays and conditional arrangements.

Large powers such as the United States and Russia are uniquely positioned to provide air and sea lift. These lift capabilities as well as their crews and maintenance personnel might be assigned priority responsibility to the UN operational headquarters for an extended period. Strategic lift might be negotiated through a detailed stand-by arrangement or memorandum of understanding that ensured prompt availability on 12-hour notice.

Options for acquiring UN lift capabilities warrant further detailed exploration. To offset some of the potential acquisition, operation and maintenance costs, aircraft might be contracted out when not required or on a high state of readiness.

Stage 3: Integrate Professional Volunteers into a United Nations Standing Emergency Capability

While the previous proposed stage of standing national elements would represent a vast enhancement of the UN's capacity to react rapidly, it will continue to be restrained by one critical limitation: the requirement for prompt prior Member State approval for deployment of their contingents. Members should not be asked to relinquish national control.

Therefore, to ultimately guarantee that the UN is able to respond rapidly and reliably to a crisis, consideration must be accorded to standing UN volunteer elements that would be under the exclusive command and control of the UN Security Council.

Approximately 5,000 personnel volunteering for professional UN service could be integrated into a composite capability including national contingents, civilians and dedicated UN elements. The overall ratio of national contingents to professional UN volunteers should be roughly equivalent. The size and general structure of the rapid reaction capability would remain largely intact. It would continue to entail a standing operational-level headquarters and two mission headquarters at the designated UN base.

At this stage, however, the UN would assume sole control and responsibility for one of the two mission headquarters and its deployable elements. Volunteers would be developed into cohesive UN units under this headquarters. Planners would have to ensure that the UN volunteers were also equitably represented in the operational-level headquarters as well as in base infrastructure support, administration, training and deployment cells.

UN personnel might be selected from an established registrar within the operational headquarters of volunteers demonstrating competence in the preliminary stages or in previous national commitments to UN service. The gradual integration of experienced individuals would overcome numerous problems that would otherwise impede start-up and the generation of a dedicated UN capability. By initially drawing on qualified personnel from participating national contingents, the UN would have a highly competent nucleus for the training and development of new recruits. These individuals would be required to meet high qualifying standards and display unequivocal dedication to the principles and objectives of the Charter. As this will be an elite UN capability, there should be few problems in acquiring outstanding officers, other ranks and civilians from a wider pool of

Member States in the years ahead. The long-term objective would be to ensure dedicated UN elements were of a heterogeneous composition with no overbearing, distinct national representation.

Any arrangement of this nature would also entail the development of new command and control procedures, comprehensive insurance programmes, specific codes of discipline, as well as status-of-forces and act-of-service agreements. The UN has sufficient experience and expertise to direct the recruitment, administration and management of new personnel.

Constituting approximately fifty percent of the capability's normal strength, UN elements would have a credible stand-alone strength for emergency deployments of approximately 3,250 personnel. By conventional military standards, however, it would represent a discreet capability; one that could effectively manage many of the potential peace support roles assigned, but insufficient in size and composition for peace enforcement.

Moreover, as this would be a composite UN rapid reaction capability, including national contingents, UN volunteers and civilian elements, one might allay fears of a significant, new supranational force. Contributing Member States would retain decision-making authority over the deployment of their national contingents. The Security Council would, however, have sole authority over decisions to deploy UN volunteer personnel. Responsibility for operational command and control as well as day-to-day preparation of the UN volunteers would be vested in the Secretary-General.

A dedicated UN capability would serve many of the long-term interests of Member States. Such an arrangement would help to offset the public and political pressure many contributing governments now confront when faced with difficult decisions over participation in new, potentially high-risk operations. The 1993 report of the US Commission on Improving the Effectiveness of the United Nations highlighted this problem in the following recommendation:

> To strengthen the U.N.'s peacekeeping and peace enforcement capabilities the Commission proposes the creation of a 5,000 to 10,000-(man) blue helmet rapid deployment force of volunteers...The Commission believes that a UN rapid-reaction force is necessary because no nation likes to send its soldiers into potential combat zones when its own interests may not be directly affected by the outcome...On its own (a small international) force has limited value if a large scale conflict breaks out, but a U.N. legion would... be a useful arm of the Security Council for deterring conflict or providing early on-site reconnaissance. It could also be used to give the U.N. an immediate presence in a troubled region while a larger force is formed using units contributed by member nations.[10]

As professional volunteers were developed into a cohesive UN capability, the burden of responsibility for managing peace and security would be more equitably shared and gradually shifted toward the one Organization initially designed for this purpose.

A composite rapid reaction capability may also be viewed as a cost-effective development—one that would partially offset the need for, and expense, of major peace support and enforcement actions, as well as the heavy financial burden now frequently shouldered in rebuilding war-torn societies. In the words of Sir Brian Urquhart:

> A rapid response group, whatever its basis and nature, should be seen as a vital investment for the future, and one which by its nature, is designed to act at the point where action can be most effective, thus eliminating or reducing the necessity for later, larger, less effective, more costly options.[11]

Although there would be approximately 5,000 new personnel on the UN payroll as well as new equipment, managerial and administrative requirements, the overall costs incurred would likely be reduced with the ongoing participation of national elements. This would continue to be a cost-sharing arrangement whereby committed Member States assumed all but the incremental costs of their assigned contingents, and the UN covered the expense of its own volunteer personnel as well as the various costs associated with accommodation, equipment, transport, operations and maintenance.

The financing requirements for a standing UN capability will be qualitatively different than those related to peacekeeping, as costs will be recurring, rather than episodic. While it is difficult to project even a notional estimate of total costs, Dr. Jean Krasno estimates the start-up costs for a UN base facility capable of sustaining a rapid reaction unit of 10,000 personnel (operations and support) at approximately US $400 million.[12] On the basis of Krasno's figures for recurring costs, this composite capability proposal can be roughly estimated at US $253 million per annum. Overall, it is apparent that this new UN capability would not entail a significant financial burden if shared proportionately among over 180 Member States. For example, the initial start up cost to Canada under the present scale of assessments, would be roughly US$12.3 million with annual recurring costs of approximately US$7.8 million. By way of comparison, the Canadian government spent $35 million in emergency assistance in Rwanda from April to September 1994; an expenditure than many have argued could have been largely avoided if the UN had the capability to respond quickly to the crisis.

Enlisting 5,000 personnel into UN service would constitute little, if any, drain on the existing defence resources of a particular nation. There are, however, those who dismiss the gradual integration of UN volunteers into a composite group on the grounds that it would be fundamentally incompatible with national elements. Some have claimed it simply will not work. Clearly, there are few, if any, equivalent precedents. The former experience of the French Foreign Legion and the British experience with the Gurkhas is noteworthy. Through ongoing participation, these forces were able to prove, largely on the basis of competence and loyalty, that they were capable of being successfully integrated into various missions over an extended period. Although of a different nature, there was similar resistance towards the integration of civilian personnel into UN multidimensional operations. They have since proven to be a net benefit and an essential contribution to numerous successful missions.

The integration of UN volunteers into this composite group can be viewed as a complementary and mutually reinforcing stage in the development of an increasingly effective UN rapid reaction capability. This option may yet offer the UN the best prospect of a dependable and sophisticated rapid reaction capability. With dedicated UN personnel, the response to a pending crisis would be shortened considerably. Initial deployments could occur within 18 hours after a decision of the Security Council.

Aside from the potential to fill an apparent gap in the UN's mechanisms for preventive deployment as well as prompt assistance for disaster and humanitarian relief, considerable advances could be anticipated in peacekeeping and in the new grey area of "second generation" multinational operations. By expanding the operational and tactical structure of this rapid reaction capability to include dedicated UN personnel, one would also expand the range of options at the political and strategic level. As the 1995 Commission on Global Governance reported:

The very existence of an immediately available and effective UN Volunteer Force could be a deterrent in itself. It could also give important support for negotiation and peaceful settlement of disputes. It is high time that this idea—a United Nations Volunteer Force—was made a reality.[13]

Conclusion

The primary focus of this paper has been the further development of a multinational and multidimensional UN rapid reaction capability; the requirement for a designated UN base; the organization of a static operational headquarters and two mobile mission headquarters; the composition of deployable military and civilian elements; and the modernization of appropriate doctrine and training.

As proposed, this will entail an evolution from an initial reliance on home-based, stand-by contingents to standing national elements assigned to service at the UN base for a period of two years and, ultimately, to the integration of dedicated UN volunteers into a composite United Nations Standing Emergency Capability. This would offer the optimum prospect of assuring reliability and readiness for a wide range of UN peace support operations.

After 50 years of growth and development, there can be little doubt that the international community has the ability to develop an effective UN rapid reaction capability. When previously confronted by urgent requirements, numerous UN Member States have demonstrated their ability to respond promptly. It is evident that there are now few, if any, insurmountable operational or tactical impediments.

Once again, the international community is confronted by a unique opportunity at a critical juncture. Once more, there is a need for vision, new thinking, and bold initiatives. The further development of a multidimensional UN rapid reaction capability will not be a cure-all; there will be situations where it is neither appropriate nor likely to succeed. In this respect, Nobel Laureate, Dr. John Polanyi presents a fitting analogy:

> Fire departments and police forces do not always prevent fires or crime, yet they are now widely recognized as providing an essential service. Similarly, a rapid reaction capability may confront conditions beyond its capacity to control. This should not call into question its potential value to the international community. It is a civilized response to an urgent problem.[14]

At the very least, the UN would have an effective new mechanism for war-prevention and humanitarian assistance—a civilized response to the emerging challenges of a very uncertain future.

Summary Recommendations

- Pursue a comprehensive and cumulative development process;

- Institutionalize and consolidate UN rapid reaction efforts to bridge the capability gap;

Stage 1: Establish a Dedicated UN Rapid Reaction Base;

- Co-locate standing operational and tactical headquarters at the UN base;

- Initiate an ongoing process of doctrine development including the refinement of standing operating procedures, rules of engagement, command and control procedures as well as common standards for training and readiness;

- Solicit the support of peacekeeping training centres and encourage stand-by vanguard and civilian elements to commence general and specialized training as well as joint exercises at the designated UN base;

- Encourage partnership programmes to ensure a wide range of Member States participate in the development of UN rapid reaction capabilities;

- Initiate preliminary planning and site identification for the potential establishment of five additional UN rapid reaction bases in various regions.

Stage 2: Assign national vanguard groups and civilian elements to the designated base for a two-year period of service in a UN Standing Emergency Vanguard;

- Accord a priority in the development of doctrine and on-site training to fostering an integrated unity of effort and purpose between all elements of the UN capability;

- Provide all participating personnel with advance preparation and comprehensive general, specialized and mission-specific training programmes;
- Initiate further research into the acquisition of appropriate standard and interoperable equipment for a UN standing capability;
- Secure arrangements for immediate air and sea lift.

Stage 3: To guarantee a reliable and rapid response, integrate professional UN volunteers into a composite United Nations Standing Emergency Capability;

- Commence further detailed study of the United Nations' options for enhancing a rapid reaction capability.

Notes

1. See William R. Frye, *A United Nations Peace Force,* (New York: Oceana Publications, 1957), p.77.

2. See the case presented by Augustus Richard Norton in "Peacekeeping, Civil Society and Conflict Regulation", *Canadian Defence Quarterly,* vol.23, no.1, special issue no.2, September 1993, p.33.

3. The lack of appropriate UN doctrine for current operations is highlighted by John Gerald Ruggie in "Wandering in the Void: Charting the UN's New Strategic Role", *Foreign Affairs,* Nov./ Dec. 1993, pp. 26-31.

4. For an earlier review of doctrinal considerations pertaining to UN operations see Major James C. Wise, "Putting Together a US Army Force for a UN Peacekeeping Mission: How to Not Fight" *Military Review,* vol. 62, no. 12, December 1977, pp. 21-31.

5. Charles Dobbie, "A Concept for Post-Cold War Peacekeeping", *Survival,* vol.36, no. 3, Autumn 1994, p.137. Dobbie draws from "Wider Peacekeeping", (Fourth Draft) Army Field Manual, to elaborate on minimum necessary force as "the measured application of violence or coercion, sufficient only to achieve a specific end, demonstrably reasonable, proportionate and appropriate; and confined in effect to the specific and legitimate target intended."

6. See Sir Brian Urquhart, "Prospects for a UN Rapid Response Capability", Chapter 3.

7. For an overview of the various contact skills required see: A. B. Featherston, "Toward A Theory Of United Nations Peacekeeping", *Peace Research Report* no.31, Department of Peace Studies, University of Bradford, February 1993, pp.70-85.

8. Several options warrant consideration as a means to speed up and enhance the process of consultation and decision-making at the political and strategic levels. Among the various related proposals are the development of an alert system, the establishment of a strategic consultative mechanism, a liaison office for troop contributors and a rapid reaction planning cell and crisis management team within the UN Secretariat. For further elaboration, see the expanded text of this chapter.

9. In current stand-by arrangements, those nations that have the resources to deploy well-equipped personnel often find themselves faced with the prospect of providing national logistics units to provide support. The logistics tail is often quite large and invariably unforeseen. National support elements are required to provide spare parts for their own vehicle fleets, maintain and resupply specific items including ammunition. Each large contingent deploys its own logistics support, thus increasing the manpower requirement in the mission area and the cost.

10. See James A. Leach and Charles M. Lichenstein (co-chairs), *Final Report,* ("Defining Purpose: The UN and the Health of Nations"), US Commission on Improving the Effectiveness of the

United Nations, (Washington: US Government Printing Office, September 1993), p. 6 and 20. Cited in John G. Heidenrich, "Why US Conservatives Should Support a UN Legion", unpublished paper, John F. Kennedy School of Government, 1994, p.21.

11. Urquhart, "Prospects for a UN Rapid Response Capability", Chapter 3.

12. Jean Krasno, "A United Nation's Rapid-Deployment Permanent Force: Cost Analysis", (paper prepared for the Yale University United Nations Study Program, 1994) .

13. Report of the Commission on Global Governance, *Our Global Neighbourhood,* (New York: Oxford University Press, 1985), p. 112.

14. Dr. John Polanyi, Co-Chair, International Conference on a United Nations Rapid Reaction Capability, Montebello, Quebec, April 8, 1995.

The Lester B. Pearson
Canadian International Peacekeeping
Training Centre

Le centre canadien international
Lester B. Pearson pour la formation
en maintien de la paix

THE PEARSON PEACEKEEPING CENTRE
AND THE NEW PEACEKEEPING PARTNERSHIP

The mission of the Lester B. Pearson Canadian International Peacekeeping Training Centre is to provide national and international participants with the opportunity to examine specific peacekeeping issues, and to update their knowledge of the latest peacekeeping practices. To guide its activities, the PPC has developed the concept of the **New Peacekeeping Partnership**, the term applied to those organizations and individuals that work together to improve the effectiveness of modern peacekeeping operations. It includes the military; civil police; government, and non-government agencies dealing with human rights and humanitarian assistance; diplomats; the media; and organizations sponsoring development and democratization programmes.

The Pearson Peacekeeping Centre offers a multifaceted curriculum of special interest to all the stakeholders associated with peacekeeping operations, through an extensive schedule of conferences, seminars, workshops, training, and educational courses. Off-campus activities are conducted by mobile training teams or through electronic distant-learning technology.

The Centre also sponsors field research with deployed peacekeeping missions, and a Visiting Scholar Programme. Researchers in any peacekeeping-related discipline can arrange for access to the Centre's archives. The Canadian Peacekeeping Press publishes proceedings, journals, newsletters, bibliographies, and books derived from the Centre's activities. In addition to its scheduled functions, the Centre has the ability to respond quickly to requests for specialized research or customized training packages. It also functions as an information clearing house and research centre and its multi-disciplinary approach reflects the changes in the international environment and "The Changing Face of Peacekeeping." The Centre also conducts a sizeable and active internship programme, which allows students to gain valuable working experience while learning more about peacekeeping.

For more information on the Pearson Peacekeeping Centre's programmes, activities and publications, please contact:

Alex Morrison, President, The Pearson Peacekeeping Centre
Cornwallis Park, PO Box 100, Clementsport, NS B0S 1E0
Tel: (902) 638-8041 Fax: (902) 638-3344
Email: amorriso@ppc.cdnpeacekeeping.ns.ca

The Pearson Peacekeeping Centre is named in honour of Lester B. Pearson, former Prime Minister of Canada. In 1956, at the time of the Suez Crisis, he invented peacekeeping for which he was awarded the 1957 Nobel Peace Prize.

The Centre (a division of the Canadian Institute of Strategic Studies), established by the Government of Canada in 1994, is funded, in part, by the Department of Foreign Affairs and International Trade and the Department of National Defence of Canada.
Le Centre (une division de l'Institut canadien d'études stratégiques) a été établi par le Gouvernement du Canada en 1994. Le soutien financier du Centre provient, en partie, des ministères des Affaires étrangères et du commerce international et de la défense nationale.

The Lester B. Pearson
Canadian International Peacekeeping
Training Centre

Le centre canadien international
Lester B. Pearson pour la formation
en maintien de la paix

THE CANADIAN PEACEKEEPING PRESS

The Canadian Peacekeeping Press, the publishing arm of the Pearson Peacekeeping Centre, has a number of new publications of interest. These include: *The Persian Excursion: The Canadian Navy in the Gulf War,* (Commodore Duncan "Dusty" Miller and Sharon Hobson, hardcover, 239 pp., $35 + GST and shipping); *The New Peacekeeping Partnership,* (the proceedings of Peacekeeping '94, edited by Alex Morrison, softcover, 229 pp., $20 + GST and shipping); and *Canada and Peacekeeping: Dedication and Service* , (a good introduction to Canada's contribution to international peace and stability, written by Alex Morrison and Stephanie A. Blair, softcover, 32 pp., $5 + GST and shipping).

Publications slated for release in the upcoming months are: *The Centre-Periphery Debate in International Security* (copublished with Queen's University's Centre for International Relations, edited by David Haglund, softcover, 230 pp., $20 + GST and shipping); *UN Peace Operations and the Role of Japan*, (edited by Alex Morrison, softcover, $20 + GST and shipping); and *Peacekeeping and the Coming Anarchy,* (the first title in the Pearson Paper series, the content of which was derived from a roundtable held at the Pearson Peacekeeping Centre in March 1995, edited by Dale Anderson, softcover, price to be determined).

To obtain a Publications Catalogue or for more information on the Canadian Peacekeeping Press, please contact:

James Kiras
Publications Manager
Pearson Peacekeeping Centre
Cornwallis Park, PO Box 100
Clementsport, NS B0S 1E0
Tel: (902) 638-8611 x 161
Fax: (902) 638-8576
Email: jkiras@ppc.cdnpeacekeeping.ns.ca

The Centre (a division of the Canadian Institute of Strategic Studies), established by the Government of Canada in 1994, is funded, in part, by the Department of Foreign Affairs and International Trade and the Department of National Defence of Canada.
Le Centre (une division de l'Institut canadien d'études stratégiques) a été établi par le Gouvernement du Canada en 1994. Le soutien financier du Centre provient, en partie, des ministères des Affaires étrangères et du commerce international et de la défense nationale.